# MASTERS
# OF THE GAME

# MASTERS OF THE GAME

A Conversational History of the
NBA in 75 Legendary Players

**SAM SMITH** AND **PHIL JACKSON**

PENGUIN PRESS | NEW YORK | 2025

PENGUIN PRESS

An imprint of Penguin Random House LLC
1745 Broadway, New York, NY 10019
penguinrandomhouse.com

Image credits appear on pages 357–58.

Designed by Cassandra Garruzzo Mueller

LIBRARY OF CONGRESS CONTROL NUMBER: 2025012533
ISBN 9798217060702 (hardcover)
ISBN 9798217060719 (ebook)

Printed in the United States of America
1st Printing

The authorized representative in the EU for product safety and compliance
is Penguin Random House Ireland, Morrison Chambers, 32 Nassau Street,
Dublin D02 YH68, Ireland, https://eu-contact.penguin.ie.

# Contents

# Preface

BY SAM SMITH

John Havlicek was talking about his brief stint in the NFL. He was blocking from his receiver position on a sweep and laid out a linebacker, enabling Jim Brown to go forty-eight yards to the two. The Boston Celtics legend had also been an all-state quarterback and had been drafted by his home-state Cleveland Browns. On the next play, from the two, John was lined up as the tight end against "Big Daddy" Lipscomb, then the NFL's only three-hundred-pounder. "Big Daddy grabbed people and sorted them out and then grabbed the runner," Havlicek recalled. "I ended up on the bottom of the pile, my helmet knocked half off." The Browns passed for a touchdown on the next play in that preseason game, which also pretty much ended John's football career. He was cut—the Browns decided to keep his buddy Gary Collins instead. Collins would go on to be a three-time all-pro multiple years, but he always said Havlicek had better hands. It all worked out OK, Havlicek told me with a laugh.

Averaging more than forty-five minutes per game in one five-year stretch during his Hall of Fame career didn't seem too rough in comparison to Big Daddy Lipscomb. Havlicek once said that you're only tired when you think you are, and how could anyone really be tired playing basketball? Like Forrest Gump, John Havlicek kept running from his small-town Ohio upbringing into a life of celebrity as part of the greatest team in the game's history, alongside Russell and Cousy and the Jones guys and against Oscar and Wilt and even Kareem. The rugged, square-jawed "country boy," as teammate Bill Russell occasionally called him, was the man who took the baton from the greatest dynasty ever, the first leg of the Celtics' great sprint through NBA history, raised two more banners, and handed it off to Larry and Kevin and Chief.

Havlicek once came into Red Auerbach's office when he was making $20,000. He was scoring 20 points off the bench in the great Celtics sixth-man tradition, and he asked for a raise to $25,000. The coach / general manager said he'd jump out the window first before giving Havlicek a $5,000 raise. "I settled for $21,000," John said to me during a stretch of conversations not long before he died, talks that were the inspiration for this book.

The NBA's history needs to be told and remembered and told again. These days it's often papered over and forgotten, like one of those old houses from the fixer-upper TV shows.

I was writing a book a few years back about the players, led by Bob Cousy, Tom Heinsohn, and Oscar Robertson, who sued the NBA and finally established the right to free agency and eventually the level financial playing field that has carried the NBA to the colossal global success it now enjoys. I couldn't get through to Havlicek while preparing the interviews for the book. It seemed strange, many Celtics friends and organization members told me. That wasn't John. Finally, I arranged to meet him at his place in Florida. That day as I arrived, he said sorry, it couldn't be that day. We never did connect in person, but we eventually had multiple phone calls to talk about the case and the old times. It was a similar story with the only other player among the thirteen of the suit's fourteen original plaintiffs still living whom I didn't meet face-to-face, Wes Unseld. We set a time and I drove to his farm in far northwest Maryland, but as I drove up he was heading back to the hospital after having recently spent nine weeks there for heart problems he never mentioned to anyone. We also had several phone conversations; he died not long after Havlicek. I wondered if those were the last interviews either man did.

What I didn't understand during my courtship of Havlicek was that he was suffering from Parkinson's, and there were good days and bad ones. On the bad ones he just didn't want to be seen that way. He was once perhaps the fittest man in the league, the marathon runner turned wing mismatch. It can be difficult to find oneself hitting the wall in life's marathon, especially for the men who spent their lives being first and fittest.

I was thinking about my conversations with John and Wes and how all the stories were going to be lost to history. I know, it's just sports, as we're often told. But it's also often the passion play of our times, and the rare inspiration that can transcend generations. Like Martin Luther King Jr. said, we are made by our history.

When the NBA continued its tradition of adding, every quarter century, twenty-five more names to its roster of all-time greatest players, this time bringing the tally up to seventy-five for the league's seventy-fifth birthday—I was one of the voters among many—I read through the list and realized that, between seeing games live starting as a kid in Madison Square Garden in the late 1950s and reporting on the NBA for the *Chicago Tribune* and the website of the Chicago Bulls from the early 1980s into the 2020s, I'd seen in person every one of the players on that list except George Mikan. And I did have a few interviews with Mikan in his final years. Through my reporting and the books I'd written, I'd gotten to know and interview most of the players on the list.

I thought I should write down my experiences with those players and the stories I know and make one more contribution to the bookshelf of NBA history. Then I asked Phil, who basically played or coached against every one of those all-timers—also except Mikan—if he wanted to join me for a basketball history version of *My Dinner with Andre*. I didn't think he would be interested. He was.

I've never enjoyed writing the books as much as I loved researching them, sitting with the players and coaches and everyone else around basketball and listening to their stories, and now I could do so with Phil. Phil spends the winters in Los Angeles at his home in Playa del Rey, facing the setting sun. Every sundown brings out people hoping for a sight of that famous kaleidoscope of light, a mystical blue or purplish glow that Phil told me his kids said they'd seen. He said he hadn't yet but was still looking. Life is about never looking away. He delights in the Pacific of it all, the lady in the pink sweatsuit jogging by every day, the gulls chasing the fishing boats for a snack. Phil's a cook; it's a hobby. He makes a lot of soups. We went down to the store one day and he examined the ham hocks. He makes a sweet paella.

Summers for Phil are spent south of Kalispell, Montana, on the massive Flathead Lake, where he and his brother built an A-frame decades ago and have since had a partner home built. His former wife June also has a place in the cozy lake compound where they welcome their dozen or so grandkids in a summerlong baton exchange of weeks of swimming and boating and Phil's lessons on life for the little ones. Oh, Gramps!

After the kids depart back to school following Labor Day, I stop by for a few days. We sit down to reminisce. I've also dropped by his LA place a few times to fill in the blanks. It's been the best part of the project for me, including wading through digressions about esoteric books and ancillary events. It reminded me of when I was writing my first book, *The Jordan Rules*. The big-shot New York publishing house editor kept sending the first-time author notes that the book wasn't linear enough. Be more linear! Sorry, life, and basketball, are just not that way.

I first got to know Phil Jackson, in person anyway, in the early 1980s. I'd watched him as a Knicks fan for many years, the wild stork of basketball, the guy we all noted from the balcony in the old Madison Square Garden with the clothes-hanger physique, all flapping arms and legs off the Knicks bench during that magical early-seventies run of two championships. Our gold ticket as kids was the GO card, the bonus ID that New York City public school kids got, at least in my view, as recompense because we were subjected to triple sessions in the overcrowded schools—some years you started at seven and were done by eleven, and sometimes it was noon till five. In classes with fifty kids the teachers never bothered to learn your name if you weren't raising your hand all the time. I can't recall ever having done so, though an English teacher once told me before giving me a D on a paper that I shouldn't worry because in a hundred years we'd all be dead and who would really care? It might have been the most vital lesson I learned in Brooklyn public schools.

Anyway—see a digression here?—that GO card was our entry to the magic world of the NBA. It enabled you for seventy-five cents to get a ticket on Tuesday nights, NBA doubleheader nights established to try to draw fans for the pathetic Knicks. And so, remarkably, it was Oscar and Elgin and West and Russell and Chamberlain and, OK, they were kicking the crap out of our home team just about every game, but what a basketball education. So fifteen cents for the subway and for a slice of pizza—the subway and pizza costs were always the same and, no, I don't know why but they were—and ten cents for a drink and seventy-five cents to get in. It wasn't always easy to see through the haze of cigarette smoke wafting upward by the second game from behind the basket where the sharpies were wagering on point spreads, but for about $1.50 it was dinner and four hours of NBA basketball.

My family never understood.

My mother, Betty Pritzker, was from five generations of mostly Orthodox rabbis in Ukraine, south of Kyiv. She should have been Yentl, the woman in Isaac Bashevis Singer's short story living in a Polish shtetl who dresses like a man so she can secretly receive a rabbinical education, the way she always read and told us to get our own supper. We were strict Orthodox, which I abandoned pretty quickly when they never gave me a good reason why I couldn't use electricity on Saturday, the Sabbath, after I explained there was no electricity five thousand years before. The family name was Pritzker, and while I've done well and don't need a Hyatt hotel, I've wondered about being a relative. We were the only Pritzkers in the New York City phone book, nine million people at the time.

When you live in New York, it is depicted as the center of the universe, so I'd never heard of those Pritzkers. We weren't even sure where Chicago was. But in 1979 when I was hired by the *Chicago Tribune*, I began reading about the squabbling billionaire family. And what do you know, their patriarch was an Orthodox rabbi from near Kyiv just like mine. C'mon, that can't be coincidence. So I wrote to Jay Pritzker, then the dean of the family, explaining my curiosity. He wrote me back a brief note that I was probably related to the Pritzkers of Baltimore. No hotel for you!

My family was from a place called Golovanevsk, where the anti-Jewish pogroms were in full swing after World War I when we left. Golovanevsk organized a militia unit after a 1917 incident, like the *Fiddler on the Roof* scene in the marketplace. Without the dancing. That self-defense unit was defeated in 1919. My mother was born there in 1920 and, after more pogroms, the family finally fled in 1925. My father's family was from Lithuania. They fled to England, where my great-grandfather, Pincus Amran, changed his name to Smith.

Phil's roots are on the other side of the American revolution. He comes from Loyalists who received a land grant in Canada when the victorious colonists were kicking out the British. Phil's father, Charles, was a dairy farmer and lumberjack. When his first wife died, he went to Central Bible College and met Elizabeth Funk, from a family of German Mennonites who were farmers. They embraced the evangelical Assemblies of God and faith healing, which actually seemed to work when Phil contracted polio when he was five years old; despite a lack of professional medical care, he recovered. There was no turning back then.

As traveling preachers/evangelists, Phil's family moved around, and Phil was in Great Falls, Montana, in fifth grade when he began to play basketball seriously. He was also always the quarterback in football and the pitcher in baseball. Phil was about six five and a bony 150 in high school, and determined to succeed in baseball, still the national sport. In the summers he was playing semipro baseball and seeing possibilities. He hit a double off a barnstorming team featuring Satchel Paige. Of course, Paige was about sixty at the time. But in the end it had to be basketball.

I never had the growth spurt. In fifth grade, I was third tallest and winning all the medals at Field Day. In seventh grade, I was third shortest. Still, I had my moments on the mound, a pitching win in a city-title semifinal game at the fields next to the old Yankee Stadium. It got me an invite to a tryout with the Yankees when I was a high school sophomore. Not ready, they said. I was five eight and about 120. They said, Gain 30 pounds. That winter I ate spaghetti and bread for every meal, and the next spring I weighed . . . 120.

I still harbored those fantasies of a professional sports contract. Hey, maybe D-ball and I could at least say I was there. My tipping point came during preseason for my Division II team at Pace University. I was the number one starting pitcher as a sophomore, though on a historically bad team. My junior year, Bruce Hildebrandt, six two, 185, shows up with ninety-mile-an-hour splitters and the coach asks me if I'm keeping up with my grades. Yes, time to pay attention in class, son. I finished my business degree. But maybe there was something to this sportswriting I was doing to pick up a few bucks in college.

So after two years with the New York City office of Arthur Young

& Co. as a staff auditor, I was off to graduate school to take journalism classes for the first time. And if you were keeping score in journalism in the 1970s, it was Watergate and DC. So I got myself there, covering Congress and the White House, and it really was cool. I was with a regional wire, States News Service, but I went to the same places and covered the same stories as the big guys: the Camp David Accords, the White House press conferences, though with the local angle for New Haven, Connecticut, or Brockton, Massachusetts, or Allentown, Pennsylvania. I even got in a question once for President Carter. I was at the Show. And there's James Reston from the *Times* and Bob Woodward from the *Post* and Sam Donaldson and Dan Rather from the TV networks, and they're asking questions and it's occurring to me, "Hey, I was going to ask that. They don't know more than I do. It's not about going to Harvard; it's opportunity." Which I came to understand is also what sports is often about.

Because being famous doesn't make you smarter or more entitled. The truly great players loved the challenge more than the acclaim. It was always a big part of what separated them. It's why you can see their eyes glazing over with the "How's it feel" postgame questions. Michael Jordan, for example, much preferred when you pointed out a miss or mistake. Because those sorts of things drove him. Similarly with Kobe Bryant and Larry Bird. They loved the trash talk, which effectively was challenges to them and their play. Jordan loved when you bet against him, like that scene I talked about in the *Last Dance* documentary from the 1989 first-round playoff series with the superior Cleveland Cavaliers (6–0 against the Bulls that season) that effectively began the Bulls' rise to immortality. Each of the three traveling Chicago beat writers picked the Cavs to win in our previews, though I had the most faith in the Bulls, predicting the Cavs in five. So there was Jordan after he was the goat (small letters to mean the cause of the loss) in the Game 4 overtime, which was supposed to be the clincher. So it's the Game 5 decider back in Cleveland and, pregame, Jordan goes down the then-cozy media table and points to my colleagues who picked Cleveland in three or four and then comes to me and says, "We take care of you today." C'mon, who does that starting an elimination game as an underdog? That is how you become the GOAT. We all know how it ended. Jordan always delighted in the last word. In the locker room later he grabbed me and said, "See, I told you."

As Michael's father, James, would say, Michael has a competition problem. He needed something on the line. It got me in trouble with him when I was invited one time to join a golf foursome with him. So we get to the first tee. It's maybe 1987 or 1988 and I'm probably making $25,000 at the *Chicago Tribune*. He's agreed to his new deal, which was the then-groundbreaking eight-year, $25 million contract that upended the sports world. Jordan wants to play for $100 a hole, and I know the price is only going up. Being a former accountant, I'm doing the math and I'm wondering how I'm going to explain that I lost a quarter of my annual salary playing golf with Michael Jordan. So I explain I'd do it by a ratio of my $25,000 to his $3 million. The next time he spoke to me was about the eighth hole.

You didn't get anywhere sucking up to them, unless you wanted a place as a sycophant. It often paid well, but it lacked respect. Having grown up in Brooklyn, whose motto is So What Are You Looking At?, turned out to be an advantage.

When I first got my foot in the door at the *Chicago Tribune* in 1979, I ended up with one of those Sunday magazine feature-writing assignments, a story about basketball's bush leagues with a team from Gary, Indiana, following Carl Nicks, Larry Bird's best Indiana State teammate. The road trip was to play the Albany Patroons, coached by that old, wily stork of a Knick, Phil Jackson.

As with the triangle offense, which eschews set and specific plays to react to circumstances and the defense—the basketball tai chi, as Phil has said—life's best choices often are made in reaction to circumstance. Once Phil became so successful, his Knicks teammates were often quoted saying they never expected him, the hippie, to be a coach: the facial hair, the leather jacket and T-shirt wardrobe and all that. But at his core Phil is a coach's coach. He studied under Red Holzman, operating essentially as his lone assistant when Phil sat out the 1970 season after back surgery. Holzman often had Phil lead a film session or do advance scouting. With the Bulls, Phil would have discussions with assistant Johnny Bach about Horst Pinholster's Pinwheel Offense and Tex Winter's role in formulating the rules of basketball as a pioneering college coach.

When his playing career ended, Phil tried some TV with Marv Albert but felt disconnected. Phil went back to Montana to finish that A-frame and invest in a health club business, Second Wind. He thought about maybe a side job coaching Flathead Valley Community College in Kalispell, which was reviving its basketball program. But that never materialized. It looked like basketball was a "what ever happened to" for Phil.

Bulls general manager Jerry Krause had scouted Phil when he was playing in college for Bill Fitch and kept in touch, asking about CBA players. Phil asked if he could do some regional scouting for the Bulls. Krause said nothing was available but got Phil an interview with Stan Albeck for an assistant's job. It famously didn't work out. The Albany CBA job was getting him nowhere and Phil resigned. Driving home to Montana, Phil stopped at the NBA predraft camp in 1987, chatted with Krause, and moved on, still thinking about running the health club, only to get a surprise call a month later: Did Phil want to join Doug Collins's staff as an assistant? Gene Littles was leaving for Charlotte.

So having had introductions, when I had a basketball story assignment at the *Tribune*, I'd call Phil for some perspective and background. And then the Bulls' beat opened. I'd helped out on Bulls coverage and even spent a day writing a feature with this Bulls rookie, Michael Jordan, a few days after he arrived in Chicago. He had an ironing board set up. Nice prop for the story, I said. Nah, he insisted. He had taken home economics courses because he was ashamed of his looks and doubted girls would be interested. Yes, a rare air ball.

So there I was, traveling with the team, and there was Phil, sitting in coach. Back then, all NBA teams traveled commercial. They arranged for planes with twelve first-class seats for the twelve active-roster players. Coaches in the back. My little trick was to book an aisle seat and then trade with Phil, who couldn't get his legs under the middle and window seats. And thus began my basketball education. Sitting with Tex Winter on a few flights, he walked me through all the diagrams in his triple-post offense (triangle) book. There were Johnny Bach's war stories, in the NBA, as bullpen catcher for the Yankees, and in the navy with a landing party headed for Okinawa and eventually Tokyo. Krause had a good eye for young coaching talent, and Doug Collins has gone on to the Hall of Fame. Doug got the Bulls back on the rails, like when you were adjusting an old Lionel set. But the Bulls didn't think Doug was ready to finish the race. Phil had grown up in Red Holzman's passing and movement game with the Knicks. Then he got a crash course in the triangle from Tex and suddenly Phil had found his coaching destiny, the triangle offense. Phil was hired as Doug's replacement in 1989.

So before games we'd often sit in his office talking basketball. John Paxson told me later he always was fuming because everyone was sitting around waiting for the pregame talk and Phil was still in there chatting with me. Not every game, and I wasn't exactly the person he'd go to with problems, hopes, and dreams. But we liked talking basketball. And all these years later, when I told him what I was doing and why, he said sure, "Come on up to Montana and we'll talk."

*November 2024*

# Preface

## BY PHIL JACKSON

I'm intrigued by the NBA's "75 for 75," the choices for the best players in the seventy-five-year history of the National Basketball Association. I was asked to be a part of the group that made the decisions on which players were chosen, but I declined. I remember the fiftieth anniversary and the fifty who made the cut. I remember Red Holzman, my New York Knicks coach, talking about two guards he played with in Rochester with the Royals, Bobby Wanzer and Bobby Davies. If my memory serves me right, Wanzer was left off the list. Red remarked on it: As a backup guard to those two, he really saw their game. The Royals were a championship team after the Minneapolis Lakers' dominance and before the Boston Celtics reeled off their string of championships. He asserted that Davies was better than Bob Cousy.

Anyway, my friend Sam, over lunch on his annual trip to LA, suggested that we join forces and talk/write about the seventy-five chosen players. Sam was on the panel for the "75 for 75." I avoided being among the choosers of the chosen because the decision about who is the "best" is always hard. Every era of the game of basketball has remarkable players who stand out, but I think the last twenty-five years are the most difficult.

The initial group from the 1940s was composed of only a few teams, some of which are gone, like Syracuse, St. Louis, and the Rochester/ Cincinnati Royals. When I broke into the game in 1967, the league had expanded from ten to twelve teams. At our opening game in '67, the original New York Knicks team was introduced before the tip-off. They played the first NBA game in Toronto thirty years prior to my rookie season: The first basket was scored by Ossie Schectman. Since that year the league has expanded to thirty teams, so picking "the greatest" of each new era is really not as simple as it was in the forties and fifties. From under 100 players in the league per year to 450 players on the NBA rosters now, just the increase in volume makes choosing the best difficult. Add to this the fact that the court has changed from having a six-foot lane to a twelve-foot lane to the present sixteen-foot lane, to say nothing of the advent of the three-point shot. Basketball has changed from a game dominated by big men to a game of guards and forwards playing from the outside in. Now they don't necessarily even choose a center for our All-Star games. They have been left off the list of All-Stars, but they're not forgotten.

So Sam and I have labored the past few years to talk about the chosen players over LA visits, emails, and summer visits in Montana. Sam was one of the many guys I got to know in New York who had student tickets or passes that allowed "kids" to see the Knicks games for seventy-five cents. Match that with the Knicks playing three or four doubleheaders each season, and New York kids had a chance to see NBA players from the fifties and sixties in their prime. Sam has had a seat at many arenas, from the old Madison Square Garden on Forty-Ninth Street and Eighth Avenue to the United Center in Chicago. He has seen more games than I have. But I've played or coached players from my era as an NBA player from 1967 to 1980 on through my coaching and GM years. As I said, I found ranking the players from this era the most difficult. A great career in the NBA is a marathon; some players who shined brightly at first faded down the stretch, often through no fault of their own. Dwight Howard was a dominant center in the first decade of the 2000s but became almost irrelevant the last ten years of his career as the game and the rules changed for the big men of the NBA. As the game continues to evolve, we wonder what the "100 for 100" years of the NBA are going to look like a generation from now. I'm hoping the NBA continues to evolve and change with the advent of more athletic players and finds a way to keep the game relevant and not let money be the sole rationale for how the game is played.

*November 2024*

# George Mikan

George Mikan was the first big thing, and though he wasn't athletic like the tall centers and moved deliberately, all elbows and knees, to diminish his impact and effect on the game would be like saying George Washington didn't deserve to be president because no one was voting for a guy with a wig. Mikan was Bill Russell first, winning seven championships in nine seasons, though in three different leagues during the NBA's incubation period prior to the merger of the Midwest's National Basketball League and the Basketball Association of America in the East. When Mikan came to New York, the famous Madison Square Garden marquee read "Geo. Mikan vs Knicks." There was no one bigger in the sport, figuratively and literally. No one in the history of the game is responsible for more rule changes to try to level the playing field and limit his dominance. Goaltending was banned, and the lane was expanded from six to twelve feet. The 19–18 game in 1950 where Fort Wayne stopped Mikan by holding the ball was one of the big selling points for the twenty-four-second shot clock. If modern fans and media don't get it, the big men do. Both Shaquille O'Neal and Bill Russell said Mikan was their inspiration. George Mikan reminds you of the Jimmy Dean country song "Big Bad John": "He stood six foot [10] and weighed 245 . . . / And everybody knew, ya didn't give no lip to Big [George]."

Mikan sort of came from nowhere—Joliet, Illinois—where the penitentiary was the big business. The big kid with the thick glasses wanted to become a priest. His high school wouldn't let him play basketball because of the danger of the glasses. So he went to a seminary preparatory school on Chicago's North Side two hours from home. He finished up at Joliet Catholic High School and was going to pursue law at DePaul when he met the new coach, Ray Meyer, who was a Notre Dame assistant when Irish basketball passed on recruiting Mikan. Meyer became Mikan's Henry Higgins. Meyer had coeds dance with George for balance, had him box and jump rope, all to learn footwork and become quicker, and then there was the famous Mikan Drill of putting up layups with each hand in constant sequence, Mikan doing so for hours. By George, he got it. DePaul with Mikan became a dominant basketball program, NIT champion, and Mikan two-time Player of the Year with a 53-point tournament game.

Mikan turned pro in 1946, intent on remaining near home with the Chicago American Gears. But when the Gears' owner's power play to become commissioner failed, he pulled his team and started a third league. It quickly failed, and with Chicago out of business, the NBL staged a dispersal draft. Mikan was chosen by the new Minnesota Lakers franchise. Mikan was reluctant to leave Chicago but signed with the Lakers, and the first NBA dynasty was born. Between 1949 and 1954, before the introduction of the shot clock, Mikan's Lakers won five NBA titles in six seasons. In his first three years with the Lakers, when teams averaged about 80 points per game, Mikan each of those seasons averaged about 28 points to lead the league. In 1948, in the last tournament of the decade-long run of the World Professional Basketball Tournament in Chicago, Mikan's Lakers won. That tournament included the best Black teams in the country as the Lakers defeated the New York Rens. Mikan was a four-time scoring champion, once in the NBL and three times in the NBA; an NBA rebounding leader; champion five times in the NBA and twice in the NBL; NBL MVP (the NBA didn't have the award until after he retired); and eight times all-NBL or all-NBA first team. Mikan went on to become ABA commissioner and introduced the red-white-and-blue ball and the three-point shot. Mikan was voted the basketball GOAT of the first fifty years of the twentieth century.

**PJ:** The centers actually were some good-natured guys—Shaq, Johnny "Red" Kerr was an affable guy. He liked people and communicated with people. Mikan was a friendly guy.

**SAM:** What was interesting, given the way the game evolved, was that when Mikan was coming along, the view was basketball was a small man's game, that these big guys were galoots, goofs, and the game was fast and to be played by smaller guys. I guess that thinking came back seventy years later.

**PJ:** Did you ever hear the story with the Celtics? They used to make fun of Mikan. Ed Macauley would walk down the street and bump into a light pole and go, "Oh, excuse me, George."

**SAM:** Red's trash-talking influence? Couldn't beat him. Red was in Washington with the old Capitols till going to the Celtics in 1950.

**PJ:** The element of race was a much bigger factor at that time. Boston was one of the notorious racial cities. It was just almost like an insult to the community by Red. Red said, The hell with it. They're playing the best players, we're going to put them on the court. Willie Naulls kind of made that group. Heinsohn was injured and then retired, and Red put Willie in, the all-Black starting lineup. And then Satch came in. Heinsohn and Cousy retired almost simultaneously, so he fleshed the team out with the talent that he had. And the Celtics' attendance was like five thousand.

**SAM:** Naismith's grandson was bringing the original rules of the game around at one time, before he sold them.

**PJ:** The real thing about Naismith that's interesting is he was a physical education teacher and he never expected this game to be a spectator game. This game was a participation game, envisioned for the ethnic neighborhoods, guys barnstorming, and towns playing towns. Basketball's had to make rules to keep the game fair and competitive. One of my complaints is they haven't done it anymore. They haven't changed the court or the dimensions of the game.

**SAM:** They're not going to do that, even though the courts probably weren't standardized until into the sixties because of all those neutral-site games. They can charge so much for those courtside seats. Not giving that up.

**PJ:** That's not true at all about the lost money for courtside seats. You could have more sideline seats, more people on the sideline who could pay whatever. Make it a hundred-foot court, fifty feet wide. Extend the court six feet. They made the apron bigger already, didn't they? Guys are so much bigger and faster.

# Dolph Schayes

Dolph Schayes probably was the NBA's first big free agent, and the Knicks blew it by being outbid for the New York native and NYU star by the franchise in Syracuse. The Knicks weren't a financial behemoth then. Ned Irish was the team president in the Knicks' early years and, like most of the U.S., more of a college basketball fan. He is credited with the college basketball double-header phenomenon and would say even after the leagues merged in 1949 to form the NBA that the Knicks were a tax write-off. The six-eight Schayes still was a practitioner of the two-hand set shot even as the game evolved to the higher-scoring model with the advent of the twenty-four-second shot clock in 1954. When Schayes retired, he was second all-time in scoring and the first player to accumulate 15,000 points and 10,000 rebounds. Schayes became the 76ers' coach, which was a common career path then, as the top players after they retired often were named coach, mostly to roll the ball out and watch—though with an aeronautical engineering degree, Schayes was a bit more informed. He was a Jewish kid from the Bronx in an era when it was not uncommon for the top sports figures to come from Jewish backgrounds. The first great twentieth-century basketball team was the Philadelphia SPHAS, their name derived from the South Philadelphia Hebrew Association. Schayes was known to shoot from long distances that would be three-point-worthy in this era. Once the shot clock went in, he averaged more than 20 points per game for six straight seasons, was an All-Star and all-NBA twelve times, led the league in rebounding once, and averaged more than a dozen rebounds per game for his career. He was top five in MVP voting three times. Schayes played in 706 straight games, surpassed eventually by his Syracuse teammate Johnny Kerr, who played in 844 straight games. Schayes led the league in free-throw shooting three times, twice shooting more than 90 percent for the season.

**PJ:** That's Charley Rosen's favorite player. I don't think I'd put him in the same category with Bird, but a good player. Broke his wrist and played with one hand in a cast an entire season.

**SAM:** They put a cast on it and he didn't miss any games and played the rest of the season lefty, which gave him great use of both hands driving the ball. It was not unusual in that era. So you hear all these things about how those guys could not match up to today athletically and physically, and they couldn't. But they played through everything.

**PJ:** I did see Dolph play once on TV. They used to show Wilt all the time. There was one time they showed Syracuse. But Bob Pettit stood head and shoulders above him as a player. I would put Bob ahead of him, more in a class with Larry Bird. A really good shooter who could get to where he wanted, well-built athletically.

**SAM:** Schayes got that coaching job when Alex Hannum wouldn't relocate with the team from Syracuse to Philadelphia. Maybe he couldn't get out of a snowbank. Alex knew coaching as Tex's teammate and went to the Warriors to coach Wilt, and they got to the Finals, and when Schayes lost in the first round in '66 and clashed with Wilt repeatedly (which hardly made him unique), Hannum came in to reunite with Wilt and finally knock off the Celtics with that historic '67 Philly team. But Wilt did lack the coaching stability of Boston, which made a difference. Chicken or egg? Rotating coaches or Wilt being tough to coach?

**PJ:** It's been said recently that the hardest job in the NBA is picking the coach. I think because the coach has a relationship that's intimate with the team, and if you're on the outside, how do you know what that is? How do you know how a coach actually handles the locker room? I think every coach has a little different type of a relationship, a way of dealing with players that brings them together as a community. I think you have to have that now. One of my friends in coaching was Bill Musselman. He played this eerie, frightening music in the locker room before the game. Bill Fitch told me some guys are good people, they're good basketball minds, but they're just not head-coaching material. One thing that I was capable of doing is somehow or other not favoring the favored or blessed ones but bringing along the whole group, and particularly the people that were the same ilk as I was when I played, the level that I was. I think that's the other thing about coaches: A lot of them who were star players never made good coaches.

**SAM:** That baseball manager thing with the backup catchers. I guess you look at the NBA's best—Auerbach, you, Riley, Pop, Larry Brown, George Karl. Though there also was Lenny, who I'd say was more blue-collar star.

**PJ:** Red Holzman saw that about me. I used to think, "What is it that this guy saw in me that made me the spokesperson?" Like, "Phil, tell this team what you and I talked about yesterday." I would have conversations with him. He sat next to me on the airplane. He always would say, "If you only carried another twenty-five pounds or so, you'd have been a great center in the NBA." Sometimes I would think, "If only I had a better back, if I hadn't had a spinal surgery," things like that that went on. But the thing that gave me a chance of looking at teams with an inquisitive eye was having sat out—sitting next to Red Holzman, being in the locker room with him and him saying, "What do you think about Cazzie Russell playing defense on Mel Counts?"

# Paul Arizin

Paul Arizin was so good he made the 25th, 50th, and 75th teams, and who is he, anyway? A lot of the NBA gets lost in time, especially before the start of the so-called modern era, as defined by the introduction of the twenty-four-second shot clock in 1954. But for his time, beginning in 1950, "Pitchin'" Paul Arizin was Dirk, Nique, KD, Gervin, Harden: He could score. The springy six-four Arizin didn't invent the jump shot, and there's widespread disagreement about who actually did, from Kenny Sailors at Wyoming in the 1930s to Hank Luisetti and Arizin's NBA predecessor, "Jumpin'" Joe Fulks. They did love alliteration back then, and as "Sudden" Sam Smith, I approve. But Paul Arizin is a pioneer in where he took the jump shot. And it's notable that his two scoring championships (averaging more than 25 points both years) bookended two years in the Marine Corps during the Korean War. And then when his Philadelphia Warriors moved to San Francisco after the 1961–62 season, he retired to continue more lucrative offseason work at home in Philadelphia for IBM. Who really wants to live in San Francisco? Arizin then played three seasons in the Eastern Professional Basketball League for the Camden Bullets, where he was MVP and won a title, this after being an NBA All-Star in all ten of his seasons.

**PJ:** Obviously, I never saw him, but when this guy was in college he was the one who came in and shocked everybody at Madison Square Garden, the holiday tournament game. He scored like 30 points when the games were like 40-, 50-point games. And they were like, Who is this? A number of people have come and said, No, no, he's not the first one to shoot the jump shot, but he's the one who really was the first to be famous for it.

**SAM:** Not that I saw Arizin much, but I did a few times in the Garden in the early sixties with my GO card and seventy-five cents for those amazing hanging balcony seats. He was known for this asthma condition, if that's what it was. But with all the smoking in the arena back then, it's hard to imagine everyone else wasn't panting, running up and down like he did. Amazing as it seems, they never really diagnosed anything then. Guys just played. Mickey Mantle blew out his knee in the 1951 World Series and basically was the fastest player in the majors the next decade and the strongest hitter, and he played with an untreated ACL the whole time. Just play, baby. Arizin was known for the running jump shot. He explained that he started playing—he didn't even play in high school before going to Villanova, where I think he had a 90-point game or something—on dance floors, which were slippery. That was not uncommon back then, so he started to pull up and jump and shoot, and what do you know?

**PJ:** I had a lot of things revealed to me when I came to the Bulls because of Tex and Johnny; they'd seen so much. Tex was the guy actually writing the rules. Tex told me one time where the names *forwards* and *guards* came from. Why's a guard called a guard? Where did we get that terminology? "Well, guards were the first people that defended you, and they were the ones that attacked the ball." And because there wasn't a whole lot of dribbling then, it became, like, you had to send your guards up to stop the ball carriers. And that's how they got that name. Not sure where the forwards come from, because, really, they're behind, but they were forward. On the offensive end, they're ahead, forward.

**SAM:** Ooo, ooo, call on me! Center in the middle? Arizin was a big-time scorer, really, an unusually fluid and athletic player for the era. When his Warriors won the title in 1956, his first series he averaged more than 30 points against Dolph Schayes and then in the Finals 27.6 against George Yardley, who probably was the other superstar of the time, other than Mikan. Then Arizin just walks away with the highest scoring average in league history at the time. I remember John Paxson saying that his dad, who played two seasons in the NBA as a top three draft pick and averaged a reasonable about 10 points his second season, retired to go into the insurance business to make enough money to support the family. So I guess you'd have to say Arizin truly had the love for the game, ten seasons at less pay than IBM, and then three seasons of even lower pay in the minors.

# Bob Cousy

Bob Cousy wasn't the most dominant player of the early NBA; that was George Mikan. Cousy couldn't win the big prize until Bill Russell came along. But Bob Cousy was the first major star of the NBA, perhaps not so coincidentally because he played more like the Harlem Globetrotters than anyone else in the NBA. The Globetrotters weren't always those clown princes of the game, though they became relegated to carnival acts because of the segregation in the NBA until 1950. But the nascent league survived in part thanks to the Globetrotters' exhibitions, often pregame or at halftime to attract fans not only for their antics but also for the remarkable ballhandling skills of players like Marques Haynes and later Curly Neal. And then came Bob Cousy, nicknamed "Houdini of the Hardwood," the kid who eventually became a basketball phenomenon. Though not before being cut twice from his high school junior varsity team. He sustained a broken arm in high school from a fall, and that helped, as he learned to try everything left-handed. It began the legend of the behind-the-back, no-look passes, the through-the-legs creative dribbling that begat Pete Maravich, Magic Johnson, Isiah Thomas, Jason Williams, Allen Iverson, and Kyrie Irving. Cousy wasn't just a performer. The thirteen-time All-Star was a league MVP, twice All-Star MVP, twelve times all-NBA, and eight times league leader in assists. And for the first half of his career there was no shot clock forcing the offense. Cousy also was an activist and sponsor, starting the players' association that eventually led to the negotiation of free agency and refusing to stay in cities where his Black teammates were not welcomed.

It wasn't instant pro stardom for the six-one guard from Holy Cross with the slight lisp and long arms. Initially skipped over by the Celtics in the draft despite Boston having the number 1 pick—Red Auerbach said he wasn't concerned about going after the local yokels—Cousy eventually came to the Celtics literally after a drawing out of a hat when the Chicago Stags folded. They'd traded for him when he couldn't come to a salary agreement with the Tri-Cities Blackhawks. But with Bill Russell and eventually the handoff to K.C. and Sam Jones, it meant the greatest American sports dynasty of all time before Cousy went on to coach Boston College and the Cincinnati Royals.

**PJ:** Supposedly Cousy modeled his game after Bob Davies, who was the forerunner, a really terrific guard. Went behind his back, the stuff they talked about eliminating in basketball clinics. Cousy was a perfect type player for the Celtics. A hundred shots a game. That was their motto. Think about that in forty-eight minutes: What, two a minute? That was the Celtics. Then Cousy came back six or seven years later to play with Cincinnati and coach. That wasn't a good situation.

**SAM:** I'd talked to Oscar about that. There was such a buildup with Oscar coming into the NBA after that big game in New York. The press asked Cousy about this great point guard and, competitor that Cousy was, he said, "Well, Jerry West is better." I think Oscar as point guard threatened Bob some. Not Jerry as shooting guard, though those distinctions didn't exist then. Cincinnati always was losing money and likely hired Cousy to coach as an attraction. It was a classic case of really not being ready to coach pro players. Remember the famous Dick Barnett observation that if Oscar's got a twelve-footer he'll get a ten-footer, if you give him that he'll get an eight-footer, and so on. Cousy wanted to run, push the ball, a hundred shots like you-know-who. And then came the famous Knicks game.

**PJ:** I missed that season and was watching the game. We'd won seventeen straight and were going for the record eighteenth.

**SAM:** Coach Cousy puts himself in and I'm watching at home too, and it's look-away stuff, painful, because we all loved Cousy even though we hated the Celtics. It was his Willie Mays Mets moment, stumbling around in the outfield, the greatest fielder ever, and now the greatest ball handler, the magician, can't make an inbounds pass. Cousy had played bits of seven games as Royals player/coach, averaging less than a point. But the Royals did win most of those. Eighteen straight for the Knicks would break the all-time NBA record of Cousy's Celtics. So Cousy reactivated himself for that game at home. It became Bird stealing Isiah's pass. Cousy botches up two possessions with turnovers and the Knicks get number eighteen. The Knicks lost the next game. But thanks, Coach. So what does make a good coach if even Cousy can't do it?

**PJ:** The ability to sell, or persuade. I once wrote a piece called "Transformational Coaching and Transactional Coaching": That's the demarcation. This is stuff that I was into in graduate school. I ran into two psychologists who were teaching this idea of transformational therapy, which was about providing a safe space, group activity that gave authority to the participants of the group. As opposed to transactional coaching, which is more Pat Riley: I'm the only one who talks. You do it my way or you're gone. Both of them work. One of them is salesmanship, which Riley can do. I think Jimmy Butler was really the case for him. **Here's a guy who's kind of a renegade.** He's kind of a guy everyone knew was going to be difficult. He's bounced here, bounced there. He chose to go to Miami. He chose to go under the discipline of that system because he knew he needed it. There's something to him that said, If I go into that system, I'll be able to succeed. I think one reason my relationship with Michael was so good was because I never got in the Michael Jordan fan club, never had an autograph, never anything. Everyone's asking him for something. I played the guy thirty-seven, thirty-eight, forty minutes a game, though, that's for sure.

**SAM:** Yeah, we thought it would be tough-guy Thibs in Minneapolis for Jimmy, but Jimmy blew that up. Thibs isn't the confrontational guy he looks like or the public thinks. Not like Larry Brown. Of course, even Riley couldn't make it, let's say forty-eight minutes, with Jimmy.

**PJ:** You kind of knew Larry was going to be a good coach because of how he was playing in the ABA. You also knew he was eccentric. Doug Moe and I had a conversation. He was coaching Denver at the time. He said, "I got a call. Larry calls me up at eleven thirty. What's the problem? Larry says he can't get along with this guard. He goes on for a half hour. I say, 'Larry, you're seven and two and I'm two and seven.'" Larry was never happy. Complaining that Reggie can't get a shot, always needs all these picks to get open. That's also one of the things I learned about coaching: You don't disable players by your attitude toward them. Like Kwame Brown couldn't catch the ball below his waist. Well, don't pass him the ball below his waist. Don't see them at their most limited level; see them where they can be the best of who they are. Like Popovich with the guy he had stand in the corner, a great defensive player. I called him Edward Scissorhands because he was always karate-chopping players. Popovich was great with him. Kept him at what he could do. Make a cut, stand in the corner. They never won those back-to-back championships, though they were good enough, if Robert Horry hadn't made a couple of shots.

**SAM:** The famous Larry story everyone loves is he's nagging Carl Scheer all season in Denver he's got to have George McGinnis: "Get me George McGinnis." First practice Larry goes to Scheer—I think George stopped to have a smoke—"You've got to trade George McGinnis." I think Scheer left for a two-month scouting trip after that. By the way, Bruce Bowen with the Spurs—the guy they created the landing rule for, because he was always sliding under jump shooters—Kobe fumed about the guy. Kobe would always say Tony Allen was his toughest defender to get back at Bowen. Bowen liked that. Shane Battier was the other guy created as a Kobe stopper, always putting his hand in Kobe's eyes. And then Kobe would average 30 against all of them.

# Bill Sharman

I s this man the greatest sports figure in American history? Consider the ré-
sumé. He was a professional baseball player and a professional basketball
player with four championships. He coached championship teams in three basketball leagues, the NBA, the ABA, and the ABL. He was general manager of a
two-time NBA champion team and then team president for three more titles,
making it ten NBA championships as a player, coach, and executive. Did you
guess Bill Sharman? Probably not, but Bill Sharman, in addition to being the
first great shooting guard in NBA history, was the man who basically laid the
foundations of American sports, from scouting to training and nutrition. And,
perhaps even more impressive than all that, he was able to get Wilt Chamberlain to wake up early. That was when Sharman was coach of arguably the greatest team in NBA history, the 1971–72 Lakers, who won thirty-three consecutive
games and the NBA title with a then-record sixty-nine regular-season wins, finally enabling Jerry West, after so many years of frustration, to be called a
champion. And Wilt got that elusive second.

Sharman retired from the NBA and the Boston Celtics in 1961 after eight consecutive All-Star game appearances in the first superstar backcourt with Bob
Cousy and, to the chagrin of Red Auerbach, went to the new rival American Basketball League of Abe Saperstein. Sharman immediately took the Cleveland team

to the title with Dick Barnett and Larry Siegfried, and the league then folded during its second season. Sharman went to coach college before moving to coach Rick Barry and Nate Thurmond to a surprise NBA Finals in 1967 with the Warriors before Barry jumped to the ABA. Sharman was then off to the Los Angeles Stars of the ABA, who moved to Utah, where they won the league's 1971 title with Zelmo Beaty, and the following season back to LA with the Lakers with Wilt and Jerry West, boldly benching an ailing Elgin Baylor nine games into the 1971–72 season and cruising to all-time records and yet another championship as coach. No surprise, actually, considering the mighty oak of a coaching tree he came from at USC, where his college teammates were Alex Hannum, the only other coach to win a title with Wilt and Tex Winter, who was a Phil Jackson assistant and master of the triangle offense with nine Bulls and Lakers championship teams. All studied the offense's concepts under Sam Barry at USC. But Sharman's goal was to be a Major League Baseball player. And he was on the bench for the Brooklyn Dodgers, unfortunately watching Bobby Thomson's baseball "shot heard round the world" to win the 1951 National League pennant in a playoff series. Sharman was alternating with basketball, where he excelled as the game's shooting specialist of the era. He led the league in free-throw shooting seven times, three times at more than 90 percent. He once made fifty-six straight free throws in the playoffs. Sharman perhaps is most known for originating the NBA morning shootaround to prepare for games. But at a time when players still were smoking cigarettes during breaks in games, Sharman exercised, practiced strict diets, maintained note-card scouting reports on every player in the league, which no team even did, and, according to roommate Bob Cousy, unpacked and hung up his clothes in order on hangers in closets and folded his clothes in drawers even on one-night trips. This was an organized and meticulous person. Which also obviously contributed to his disciplined teams. The six-one Sharman was seven times all-NBA in an eleven-season playing career and an All-Star game MVP.

**PJ:** Bill strained his larynx and had to give up coaching. Was kind of a Bill Cartwright voice. So he had to learn how to speak from his diaphragm instead of his vocal cords. He'd say, "You're doing a fine job, Phil. I'm supposed to be giving you some criticism." I don't know if he was an original two-sport guy. Bud Grant, the coach for the Minnesota Vikings, he was football and basketball.

**SAM:** I guess Jim Thorpe. OK, a few more. Gene Conley may have done both the longest. DeBusschere, obviously. Bo Knows and Neon Deion, Michael? Danny Ainge, Dick Groat, certainly others. Does wrestling count? Rodman?

**PJ:** Football and basketball are tough to be two-sport. Baseball and basketball were conjoined, skill sports, opposite seasons. Basketball season was over in March. Tournaments were end of February, early March. Baseball started and we were heading south for three weeks after playing baseball indoors. They were thinking I could be two-sport. I had a really good curveball. I was playing at thirteen with the junior legion team with guys sixteen, seventeen years of age. We won state. At that time I was throwing a big curve, was really lanky. I pitched in the Basin League after my junior year. We played a professional team, the Aberdeen Pioneers, class C minor league. I realized I wasn't gonna be able to throw my fastball by people at that point.

**SAM:** I love the story with Bill when he invented shootaround, and Wilt told him, I come to the arena one time a day, you choose which one. But Bill did get him to come.

**PJ:** Bill talked Chamberlain into that. Because Chamberlain stayed out so late at night, he said, "We're gonna have shootarounds in the morning." He thought, "If I get him out of bed, get him moving, maybe we'll get some productivity out of him instead of him taking a quarter to get ready to play."

**SAM:** So Wilt gets his two titles with a triangle coach, Jerry his only one, Michael six, Kobe five. I know no one's listening. They're practicing the high pick-and-roll.

# Bob Pettit

There are many modern NBA eras, from when Bob Cousy brought the ball-handling magic to the game to Bill Russell's elevation on defense, Wilt's dominant offense, Oscar's versatility, and the NBA/ABA mid-seventies combination that merged the playground with the profession. There also was the coming of the multifaceted big forward who eschewed the set shot and shot the NBA into the era of Elvin Hayes, Kevin McHale, Dirk Nowitzki, and Tim Duncan. Bob Pettit started all that in the dying era of the slow-paced game, and carried it past the invention of the shotclock into the superstar 1960s with career averages of 26.4 points and 16.2 rebounds. Pettit played eleven seasons and was an All-Star every season, retiring in 1965 despite averaging 22.5 points and 12.4 rebounds because a banking career was much more lucrative than staying in pro basketball. Pettit was Moses Malone first as a relentless tracker of offensive rebounds. Pettit isn't in the top ten of all time for rebounding, because he played just eleven seasons. But in rebounds per game he's third all-time to Chamberlain and Russell with more than 16 per game. Pettit was the first NBA Most Valuable Player in 1956, one of his two wins, both a league scoring and rebounding leader, four times All-Star MVP, and all eleven seasons all-NBA, ten times first team.

NBA basketball was almost unheard of that far south in Louisiana, where he was from. Pettit was cut from the high school team as a freshman and sophomore. But in a familiar story he grew, developed coordination, and excelled. Playing mostly in the post in a dominant collegiate career at LSU, Pettit, then about two hundred pounds, moved to power forward with a deft face-up and running jump shots to complement his relentless pursuit of the ball. A few years before Pettit was drafted by the Milwaukee Hawks, the franchise—then in Tri-Cities on the Illinois-Iowa border—drafted Bob Cousy, but traded him. How that might have changed the NBA. Pettit appeared in the Finals four times, his St. Louis Hawks winning the title in 1958 as the last all-white team to do so. Pettit closed it out with the first 50-point game in a Finals. Boston after the 1958 Finals loss defeated the Hawks in the 1960 and 1961 Finals before the Lakers took their place as the Celtics' annual Finals victims. Pettit averaged 30.1 in the 1957 Finals and never fewer than 25 in his four Finals series. He is one of four players to have averaged at least 20 points and 20 rebounds for a full season; even Russell never averaged 20 points in a season. Pettit in 1962 averaged 31.1 and 18.7 for the season, mostly unnoticed, as Wilt averaged 50.

**PJ:** One of those guys like Jerry Lucas, Dennis, the great rebounders, who tracked the shot. Dennis knew the angles, where the rebound was going to come. But he didn't have the hands that Jerry had. Sometimes he'd juggle a ball even if he had it.

**SAM:** Obviously Wilt did, but bigger guys like Shaq and Kareem always were criticized for not putting up rebounding numbers.

**PJ:** Shaq's too big, Ewing's too big. Sometimes it's harder when you're standing underneath the basket basically from that center position as opposed to being out ten to twelve feet, seeing the shot, having the angle you're going to get it.

**SAM:** The awkward thing with Pettit—and everyone seemed to love the guy, Southern gentleman—was the Cleo Hill story. Pettit took a lot of grief for that even back then, though perhaps not so much in St. Louis. Remember, that was the American South, pre–civil rights and voter registration laws, governors blocking the schools to keep Black students out, separate water fountains, Black people can't go to restaurants and hotels, all the horrors we heard. St. Louis, after all, did trade the rights to Russell for Macauley and Cliff Hagan. You're not keeping the NBA prospering in St. Louis as a civil rights advocate in 1956.

**PJ:** Robert Lee Pettit Jr.

**SAM:** Hill's the predecessor at Winston-Salem to Earl Monroe, big scorer for Big House Gaines, exciting player, Oscar is praising him in preseason. The coach, Paul Seymour, was a big advocate. It gets to the point where Seymour accuses his Big Three, Pettit, Hagen, and Clyde Lovellette, of freezing out Hill, though Lenny Wilkens was also on that team and playing a major role. I remember reading Hill saying it wasn't about racism but about points. The Hawks players were saying Hill's throwing off the chemistry and being selfish for a team that has won. Seymour believed Hill, with his high-scoring, athletic play, was the appropriate response to Boston and Russell. Seymour said if they didn't involve Hill more, he's benching guys. The game was changing, but those guys also were proud former champions and wanted to keep their jobs. Seymour was fired and replaced by interim coach Bob Pettit. Hill never played in the NBA after that first season, going to the Eastern League and then coaching and teaching in New Jersey, where he was a successful community college coach. Different times, especially in that part of the U.S.

# Bill Russell

There's the "greatest player" debate, generally between Michael Jordan and LeBron James with some veteran sentiment for Kareem Abdul-Jabbar. There's the "most dominant" debate, in which Shaq makes the case versus Wilt. There's the point guard debate between Magic and Oscar, the modern debate between Magic and Bird. There's "best shooter," which Steph Curry seems to have locked up. Unless you maybe saw Bill Sharman. There's ballhandling, which Kyrie Irving tries to make the case for if you haven't seen Pete Maravich. And as for "best teammate," at least on the court, because no one surpasses what Jack Twyman did for Maurice Stokes off the court? On the court it has to be Bill Russell, who turned a Boston Celtics team without a portfolio—or a championship—into the greatest dynasty American team sports have known, with eleven championships in thirteen seasons, including the last two with him as player/coach, the first Black head coach in the NBA, a six-ten, 220-pound defender, distributor, and inspiration whose presence, persistence, and principles led the NBA to permanently retire Russell's number 6—like Major League Baseball with Jackie Robinson—for what he meant to the game, its history, and its place in American society on and off the court. Russell stood up equally against injustice and opponents, in one instance boycotting a Celtics exhibition game in Kentucky when his Black teammates were denied service at a local restaurant.

The Celtics with Walter Brown, Red Auerbach, and Russell were the league's most progressive organization, the first to draft a Black player, to start five Black players, and to hire a Black coach. All despite playing in a notoriously racist city for the northern United States.

Russell was known to be both moody and aloof, perhaps because of his horrendous experiences with racism, though he could be generous to white teammates, like inviting rookie Mel Counts to live with him when Counts couldn't find housing, and quick with a joke or a laugh, with his famous high-pitched, infectious cackle. But none of it would have mattered if he hadn't produced, not only with his presence as a premier defensive player who revolutionized basketball but also with championships, MVP awards, and historic clutch performances. His series-saving chase-down block in the 1957 Finals was the first of its kind. His teams were undefeated in ten playoff Game 7s, in which he averaged 18 points and 29 rebounds. In Boston's 1960 Game 7 win, Russell had 22 points and 35 rebounds. His Celtics effectively invented the fast-break game thanks to him. In the 1962 Finals, Russell led the Celtics in overtime with 30 points and 40 rebounds in Game 7. In the previous game, he had a triple-double with assists that probably would have been a quadruple-double if blocks were counted in that era. Leading the Celtics from the first 3–1 playoff deficit to victory over rival Wilt Chamberlain and the Philadelphia 76ers in 1968, Russell saved Game 7 in the last thirty seconds with a block, rebound, and steal. He and Wilt are the only NBA players with 50-plus-rebound games. The Russell/Chamberlain rivalry remains the greatest in league history, even compared with Magic and Bird.

Russell's story is even more compelling given his humble start in sports, at first serving as his high school's team mascot, owing to his lack of coordination and offensive basketball abilities. Then Russell had the growth spurt from five ten to six eight. With long arms and track abilities that would have made him an Olympian in that sport if not for basketball, Russell got himself at least to a modest basketball program at the University of San Francisco, which became a power because of Russell and teammate K.C. Jones, winners of fifty-five straight games and back-to-back NCAA titles. The legendary collegiate and big-man coach Pete Newell, who coached USF before Russell's arrival, offered Red Auerbach a scouting report: "He can't shoot to save his ass, can't hit the side of a barn, and he's the best player I've ever seen." Despite the success Russell brought to the Celtics, he was often condemned in Boston, vandals spray-painting racial epithets on his house. Russell would, after retirement as a player, accept a ceremony for his number to be retired only if fans weren't invited; it was done pregame. He didn't attend his Basketball Hall of Fame enshrinement, though later in life he softened his anger, attending ceremonies and a statue presentation. Though Chamberlain averaged 30 and 23 against him to Russell's 15 and 22, the Celtics were 57–37 against Wilt's team and 29–20 in the playoffs. Russell led the Celtics to the first 60-win season in league history. So intense a competitor was Russell, he was famously known to vomit before every game—sometimes Coach Red Auerbach would hold off team introductions until after Russell vomited. Mostly Russell made the opposition sick. Russell was five times MVP, twelve times an All-Star, and eleven times all-NBA. He was rebounding leader four times in the Chamberlain era and among his eleven titles had two as player/coach.

**PJ:** I don't know if I would call Cousy a great athlete, but he had great stamina. The whole thing about the Celtics was they had six plays: high post, low post, and various sequences off that. They ran that for fifteen years basically. Bill was a passer out of the offense, not a big scorer. Not a very good shooter, very left-handed. But they had this little play for him to get points. On the defensive end, you'd be shooting a free throw and Bill would be on a defensive rebound position on the inside of the lane. They would stack the side Bill was on. Havlicek or whoever else was a defensive rebounder. The power forward is rebounding the other side, which could have been Bailey Howell or Nellie, maybe. Whoever else was power forward picked the center that was sitting next to him. They'd throw it up ahead to the next guard, and Russell had the speed to beat the center, and they'd just block the center. Russell would be all by himself down at the other end with a guard, and he'd run and lay it in. The thing with Bill on defense is he was so smart and had everyone looking over their shoulders.

**SAM:** He invented that vertical jump to block a shot we all take for granted now.

**PJ:** Bill could block your shot, but also what he'd do is sort of lie in wait like he wasn't there, behind a guy or quartering, and then spring at them from behind or the side. Intimidating. Bill would not sign autographs. He had a mood about him; you felt the same way with Oscar, a wariness or lack of acceptance from what they went through. But in older age I'd make Bill laugh, and his laugh was infectious.

**SAM:** I wasn't around him, obviously, when he played, but got the stare when he was Kings coach in the late eighties. But he could really be funny. There's a famous story that he's coaching a bad Kings team and looks like he's sleeping in the stands at practice. Something gets said, and he responds that if they weren't so boring, he wouldn't be falling asleep.

**PJ:** When he was coaching in Seattle, if they lost, they had to run around the court so many times for how many points they lost by. That's what Boston did: They ran those few basic plays, and no one could stop them because of Bill.

# Sam Jones

S am Jones was Mr. Clutch before there was a Mr. Clutch. Maybe also the Father of the Bank Shot. Only Bill Russell was part of more championships as a player in NBA history. And it wasn't just "Hop on Russ's back and follow me." Jones waited his turn, along with K.C. Jones, to seamlessly keep an elite Boston Celtics backcourt humming with the handoff from Bob Cousy and Bill Sharman. Though it wasn't Sam's first choice. Red Auerbach, with his insider connections with former players, discovered Sam at the HBCU North Carolina Central. Sam was drafted into the military in 1954 despite being in college, because Black students in North Carolina didn't get student deferments like white students. Sam said a cousin was drafted and inducted with him despite missing one eye. Once discharged in 1956, Sam planned to teach, especially when he found out he was drafted by the team with Cousy and Sharman. So Sam negotiated. If the schools increased their $5,000 offer by $500, he'd pass on the NBA. They wouldn't, so he went to Celtics camp. But supporting youth long remained a commitment for Sam. He mentored a kid from his neighborhood in Boston and paid for his tuition to private school to escape the rough neighborhood. The kid was future NBA number 1 overall pick Jimmy Walker. Sam's famous backcourt partner, like John Havlicek later, was pursued by the NFL. But when K.C. Jones was injured in an LA Rams exhibition, he contacted Auerbach for a tryout and got a job warming the bench with Sam. They eventually replaced the great Celtics Cousy/Sharman backcourt, and Sam went on to make some of the biggest shots and have some of the most elite games of the Russell championship era.

Sam earned his ten championships. There was the time he outscored the indomitable Oscar Robertson 47–43 in Game 7 of the 1963 Eastern Division Finals to advance toward another title. Jones scored 35 points in the 1962 Finals Game 6 to even the series and then had the big Game 7 second half. The humble Sam usually didn't have big regular-season numbers until they were needed. In their 1969 finale, in Game 4 with the Celtics trailing 2–1 and heading back to Los Angeles, it was Sam who made the jumper from the top of the key with a second left for the one-point win to even the series. And then for good measure making ten of sixteen shots—who said those guys couldn't shoot?—for 24 points in the famous Game 7 with the balloons poised in the Fabulous Forum. Sam Jones was a ten-time champion and five-time All-Star, known as Silent Sam for his modesty—but not when he was needed. Though a career 17.7-points-a-game scorer, six times in playoff series Jones averaged more than 25 points.

**PJ:** Sam and K.C. went on without missing a beat. That's a great story about Sam Jones being, what, twenty-four or twenty-five when he first started to play. He sat on the bench behind Sharman. They stepped into that vacuum and they kept winning.

**SAM:** Really the most gentle guy, also, for playing in that era and succeeding. I remember reading Wooden once said the bank shot was the most accurate, which I guess Duncan learned. Gets drafted by the Lakers after he's in the service but decides to finish school, small North Carolina Black college, so he goes back in the draft. The Celtics don't even know who he is. But Red has this network of former players, and

Bones McKinney kept insisting Sam is the best in the state. So Red drafts him and stashes him on the bench. I read one time that Sam's pants length was the same as Russell's. Unusually long legs and arms to get that shot off. My other favorite Sam memory: It's 1962, the season Sam makes the winner in Game 7 with two seconds left to knock out Wilt and then has that clutch Finals. It's Game 5, and Sam is getting into it, verbally anyway, with of all guys Wilt. Sam says Wilt elbowed him on a drive and he elbowed Wilt back. It's on. Sam grabs a photographer's stool and is waving it menacingly at Wilt. Sam's retreating with the stool. Guy Rodgers grabs the stool from Sam, but Sam's teammate Carl Braun, of those awful Knicks teams I grew up with, steps in and Rodgers punches him in the mouth. Loscutoff charges Rodgers. Police are all over the place. Next day the Celtics go back to Philly for Game 6. The night before Game 6 Sam gets to his hotel, and Wilt comes by to pick him up and they actually went to Wilt's mom's house for dinner with Wilt's siblings. Sam explains to Wilt's mom that her son was trying to kill him, but no hard feelings. Wilt the next night in Game 6 laid out Sam coming into the lane, and it was over. And it always was Boston again.

# Elgin Baylor

In golf they always talk about the greatest player not to win a major, and they're never famous guys, like Rickie Fowler or Colin Montgomerie or Steve Stricker. Not like the most famous NBA player never to win a title, Elgin Baylor. Charles Barkley, Patrick Ewing, and Karl Malone all get mentioned because they were denied in the Michael Jordan era, and Oscar Robertson was denied a long time by the same Boston Celtics until he hooked up with Kareem in Milwaukee. And then, nine games into the 1971–72 season, Coach Bill Sharman benched the knees-ravaged Baylor, who'd played only two games the previous season. And with Wilt and Jerry West enough of a Big Two, the Lakers went on the all-time thirty-three-game winning streak and rolled to West's first and only championship as a player. For the transcendent Elgin, it was eight losses in the NBA Finals. That was the fate of Elgin Baylor, along with a long and tortured executive relationship with the dysfunctional Los Angeles Clippers that dimmed Baylor's star amid the success of the twenty-first century's best and brightest, like Kobe, Shaq, Duncan, and LeBron. But Elgin Baylor basically invented modern NBA offensive basketball with hang time, statistical improbabilities, and the wow factor. Bill Russell was amazing in a team sense and Wilt was dominant in an individual sense. But it was Elgin Baylor who began the alchemy that produced the entertainment/sports spectacle that led to Dr. J, MJ, and so many others like Kobe and Nique. Baylor had the numbers, a 71-point game against the Knicks just before Wilt scored 100—so, again, overlooked. Baylor was in the active reserves in 1962 and could play only on weekend leaves, and he still averaged 38 points and 19 rebounds in forty-eight games. He holds the record with a 61-point Finals game. He played with West, but all those years in the sixties the Celtics had Russell and six or seven other Hall of Famers, and that was the difference. By the time the Lakers got Wilt, Elgin's knee surgeries were making him a part-time player.

Amid all the scoring and huzzahs, Baylor was also standing up for social justice. He remains the only player in NBA history to sit out a regular-season game, played out of market in West Virginia as teams did then for attendance bumps, because he was denied restaurant service. He stood up to the owners during the labor boycott of the 1964 All-Star game. He instructed the tentative West to stand behind him: He had this. The six-five forward wasn't recruited, because the big schools didn't come to recruit in Black-dominated Washington, DC. Elgin started at the College of Idaho on a football scholarship. But he played basketball and averaged 30 and 20. And then basically invented basketball in Los Angeles when the troubled Minneapolis Lakers moved to LA. And, by the way, was all-NBA ten times, averaging more than 27 points for his career and more than 30 points per game his first seven seasons, before knee problems hit, and, oh yeah, about 16 rebounds per game those seven years.

**PJ:** Elgin had that twitch; it looked like he was having a stroke sometimes. An unintentional head fake. Effective. He'd operate right around the pinch post just inside sixteen, seventeen feet and going at you, beating you left and right, so many shots he could make, though I don't remember him using his left hand much. The Black players in the fifties weren't allowed to play like that; Elgin changed things.

**SAM:** Yeah, the old "three Black players on the road, four at home, and five if you are losing" thing. The Civil Rights and Voting Rights Acts were not until 1964 and 1965, and the South still was enraged that Black people, what, get to vote? There still were Southern NBA cities, Cincinnati and St. Louis, and soon Atlanta, and there still were stories in major publications like *Sport* and *Sporting News* about whether there were too many Black players in the NBA. Hardly anyone was like Red Auerbach. The thing they did with the Black players before Elgin, and somewhat afterward with guys like Bill Bridges and especially the early guys like Sweetwater Clifton—he'd cruise Michigan Avenue as a taxi driver in the eighties and I'd always take rides from him to hear the stories—they'd make sure they were role players, rebounders and defenders. Then they couldn't score as much and thus would not have to be paid as much.

**PJ:** Elgin never did break through against the Celtics. Their defensive player who wears the bow ties, Satch Sanders, was tough. Elgin was beyond defending man-to-man, which was how we had to play then. You needed multiple players to help to be effective; you had to crowd his space and get him off his spot and hope the center came across to challenge.

**SAM:** I recall once Elgin had like 45 or 50, and Cousy afterward tells Sanders, seriously, how great his defense was on Elgin. You know my Elgin story with Donald Sterling. I'd gotten to know Sterling and, no, I never heard any racial stuff, but it was time for him to go. I was always giving Donald trade ideas, which was my hobby, and when the All-Star game was in Minneapolis in '94 and it's freezing and you can't go out, he says he needs me as an adviser. Of course, I think he said the same thing to his barber. Anyway, I'm not doing anything since it's so cold, and I have all these meetings with him and Elgin, and he keeps asking Elgin about my trade ideas and Elgin clearly wants to be anywhere else. Sadly, that's the vision we got of Elgin all those years.

**PJ:** Sterling liked his players. I know he was also a scalawag, the lawsuits here in Santa Monica, rent control, pushing people out. Buss bought the Lakers from real estate he sold to Sterling. Buss did the tax shelters popular in the sixties that Reinsdorf also did. Two huge apartment complexes to put money up for the Lakers. And he also got a ten-thousand-acre ranch, the Kings, and the Forum. Jack Kent Cooke was going through a divorce and needed the money.

**SAM:** The Elgin story with the Minneapolis Lakers and that plane crash, the only time an NBA team had such an incident, is a remarkable story: flying in an ice storm, electronics out, pilots literally leaning out their windows scraping ice off, guided in by farmers putting the town lights on, landing on that ski-packed snow in the Iowa cornfield, amazing piloting really. Elgin was a garrulous nonstop talker, really a funny guy. Slick Leonard, who became a longtime Pacers broadcaster, said Baylor joked as the plane descended that he was lying down to save burial costs.

**PJ:** One of the trips I had to make from Albany was to Bangor, Maine, and they had a team up there where the university is. Young man that was running that franchise ended up being the commissioner of the CBA and died in that plane crash.

**SAM:** Jay Ramsdell. I got to know him some; such a sad story. High school whiz kid who becomes the team's PR director when he's still in high school after doing an article for the school paper on the team.

Becomes CBA commissioner, enthusiastic guy, selling the CBA all the time. He and his deputy Jerry Schemmel are on that flight. Schemmel survived with hardly a scratch and Ramsdell died. The fatalities were so arbitrary.

**PJ:** I think the pilot was laying on the floor pushing the pedals with his hands so that they could guide the plane down. It was a giant plane.

**SAM:** I especially loved the sports minor leagues, like the CBA, with the good-enough-to-dream kids like I hoped to be.

**PJ:** They may not have had all the talent, but they had all the desire. I cut a kid one time and he dropped to the floor and started crying. It was like his dream was to play in the CBA. I cut him and it was like heartbreak for him. I said, Come on, someone else will pick you up. Just keep playing. Crushed their dream. You have to figure a way out of it, and there are so many who just don't get the chance.

# Hal Greer

Hal Greer is the prototype for the argument that players in the fifties, six-ties, and seventies could have shot the basketball as well as or better than anyone in the current era, which is to take nothing away from Steph Curry or Damian Lillard, who, like Greer, were undersized and unappreciated and from small colleges. West Virginian Greer was the first Black player at Marshall University, after attending all-Black schools growing up in segregated West Virginia. The six-two Greer was the master of the midrange shot, so proficient at the fifteen-footer that he attempted his free throws shooting a jump shot and had a career mark of more than 80 percent. Imagine this guy moving a few feet back without someone bumping into him on every shot, as they did then. Hardly known despite being the second-leading scorer on Wilt's 1967 champion 76ers and the team's leading scorer in those playoffs at about 27 a game, the soft-spoken and laconic Greer mostly gets lost in NBA history. He was a ten-time All-Star and seven times all-NBA. How great a history with scoring stars did the 76ers have with Wilt, Erving, Barkley, Dolph Schayes, Iverson? The 76ers' all-time leading scorer? Hal Greer.

**PJ:** What a wonderful player he was. Hal was the perfect triangle player. Had that little jump shot. Chamberlain just had to screen for him.

Like Sharman had Wilt do in LA and Hannum in Philly. Supposedly Hannum got into Wilt's face in Philly; he's gonna fight him, wanted to go outside and fight.

**SAM:** Wilt fought discipline but really wanted it. That's why he did best with coaches like Hannum and Sharman. As we've discussed, the triangle won a lot; I thought the NBA was a copycat league.

**PJ:** The triangle is just an overload that creates an isolation on one side of the floor, creates multiple options and lots of freedom. I see elements of it with Steve, Nick Nurse. It's just not a three-point shooting offense.

**SAM:** And there's the rub.

**PJ:** No idea why coaches don't at least explore it. They don't want a clogged center; they want a space to dump in there. Coaches complain to me, We don't have time to teach the fundamentals necessary; these kids from AAU don't have the skills. So we have to do too much teaching of just passing and footwork. OK, I'll accept that. Hal was a really good shooter. They ran a simple offense. Maravich wasn't as great an outside shooter. Great ball-control guy. Adrian Smith was a good shooter who paired up with Oscar. Lou Hudson midrange. Oscar was a good shooter, but he would get down to eight to ten feet.

**SAM:** Because he could, right? Sharman was a great shooter. Over 90 percent at the free-throw line.

**PJ:** He got famous for bringing Wilt to the arena in the morning.

**SAM:** Another Sharman innovation like scouting notebooks, vitamins, training table, weights—because that created the NBA power nap.

# Wilt Chamberlain

One of the biggest highlights of my youth was the arrival of Wilt Chamberlain. It was like how you'd see all those people in the Japanese horror movies with the anticipation of Godzilla. Like everyone waiting for the outbreak of war. Wilt was coming! We'd heard, but no one had ever seen. He was playing college ball in Kansas, wherever that was, and imagine what they paid to get him there from Philly. But we knew basketball. It was the city game. There was Mikan against the Knicks on the Madison Square Garden marquee, the college betting scandals involving the city schools that were the NCAA champions then. Oscar came into the Garden in '58 and outscored the entire Seton Hall team with 56 points, more than any collegian or pro had before in the Garden. Russell saved the Celtics and they finally won the championship, but he wasn't even the team's most popular player. That was Cousy. But all that was supposed to be nothing compared to the coming of Wilt, the giant, seven two and who knows how much, and a track and field star. Imagine what this guy could do. Scored 90-something points in a high school game. Dunked from the free-throw line. We've gotta see this! And then on opening night in the Garden, he plays every minute and beats the Knicks—no big deal back then—with 43 points and 28 rebounds. And before long he's scoring 100 points in a game. Impossible!

History hasn't been as kind to Wilt because of the unfavorable comparisons to Bill Russell, whom no one defended as much as Wilt. But Russell's teams won. Having Red Auerbach and the most structure and stability and the best rosters of the era helped. Red, running the summer athletic program at the Kutsher's Catskills resort, once tried to get high schooler Wilt to attend Harvard so the Celtics could select Wilt as a territorial draft pick, the NBA's carrot-and-stick attendance scheme then to try to increase local interest. Philadelphia eventually prevailed when their owner, Eddie "the Mogul" Gottlieb, convinced his fellow owners that high school was territorial enough if you were a wizard in Kansas. Would Wilt have won the same in Boston as Russell? Of course he would have, being surrounded by Cousy, Sharman, K.C. and Sam, Hondo and Heinsohn, and with Red managing things. Wilt didn't do himself any favors with his various publicity outrages: threats to retire over rough play, feuds with his coaches, trades to California and back. The result was two titles, to eleven for Russell. There were all the stories with women, the book about the supposed twenty thousand conquests, and Wilt did live with actress Kim Novak and date America's sweetheart, Doris Day. Wilt was a bit too numbers driven. But who could blame him, as the most productive offensive player ever, seven times scoring champion, including averaging 50 points for an entire season when he also averaged more than forty-eight minutes per game with the overtimes, leading the league eleven times in rebounding and once in assists? Ten times all-NBA, thirteen times an All-Star, and four times an MVP, all when Russell played, and the players voting then liked Russell better. Most Valuable Player when he also was Rookie of the Year. No one lives up to the hype. Except Wilt. He doesn't get into the "greatest" debates because of only two championships; they are the tiebreakers the way the game is analyzed. But there never was anyone as dominant, as feared, and as misjudged, no one more welcoming to media and fans. And flight attendants.

**PJ:** Uncle Wilt and Russ, they were very different guys. Uncle Wilt was kind of a maverick, just a guy going in his own direction. His gardener found his body after the weekend. He'd had a stroke and passed away. I was in a hotel that weekend in LA and these guys came in. "Coach, come and join us and have a drink." "I can't, I'm with my daughter. I'll be back later." They were in town for Wilt's memorial, party guys. They said they used to have these big parties at Wilt's place, bringing in showgirls. They asked me if I wanted to come to the memorial. I had some stories, but I didn't know Wilt personally. All the stories were variations of "Just don't get him mad, just let him play, it's just basketball, a business, he's doing what he's doing."

**SAM:** Yeah, just let him get 50?

**PJ:** I made the mistake when I was a rookie of blocking his shot, came up from behind. Then he was like, I'm hunting this guy down. He made it so I could do nothing in the lane. I challenged him and that was stupid. The ball obviously went in to Wilt a lot. They'd get jump shots from Hal Greer. Wilt would reach back to do his dipsy doo, and I timed it and blocked it. So he started tracking who I was. I'd embarrassed him by blocking his shot. It became a thing. We'd play them eight times, but it seemed my rookie year like we were driving to Philly all the time. It was kind of loose then, but when Red came in, he said we go as a team and come back as a team. So Cazzie shows up and Red says, "You drove down? How much did the turnpike tolls cost? How about the Ben Franklin Bridge? OK, take that off your hundred-dollar fine, and next time you travel with the team." Wilt could run the 440, high-jumped, played beach volleyball. He had those skinny legs, was more developed in his arms and shoulders. I don't think he was much more than 250. Shaq was 60, 70 pounds heavier. But Wilt would take everything as a challenge.

**SAM:** I once heard when Walt Bellamy, your future teammate, came into the league—big guy, first pick in the draft in '61—now Wilt's supposedly got a rival his size. Bellamy lines up for the jump ball and Wilt says to him he's not getting a shot off in the first half. Bellamy gets every shot thrown back in his face, and then after halftime Wilt tells him, "OK, now you can play."

**PJ:** Wilt never took a shower after games, like Dennis Rodman. Showered before the game, put his deodorant on, drank a few, but didn't drink that much. He would drive these cars a hundred miles an hour cross-country. Insane stuff. Cars with like two hundred gallons of gas stored in the trunk; they'd have races. I don't think Wilt liked Philly that much. He lived in New York when he played in Philly. Built that huge house in LA that Jimmy Goldstein now owns. Was always, "Come on over." Russell used to have Wilt over for Thanksgiving. They really were close, but then everyone would accuse Wilt, like they did with Michael, of conning him. But I think Russell understood what Wilt was going through. These guys were supportive of one another.

**SAM:** The players seemed to have more respect for Russell.

**PJ:** I think they did because of the moxie he had. It was all about defense. He'd let you go in and he'd have a little bit of fun. You thought you were there and he'd block you from behind. Then he'd show up and scare you, and you're looking around like, Where is he going to block my shot from?

**SAM:** I know the 100 points defines Wilt, but also it's sort of the negative that he scored and Russell won. It didn't even get that much attention at the time because of the huge numbers he was putting up every game.

**PJ:** Everyone told me Hershey had these playground rims; you hit the front and it falls in. Wilt made 28 of 32 free throws; it's the only way he could make that many. His free-throw shooting was not that bad compared to some guys today, shot 60 percent that season he averaged the 50. At All-Star games, Wilt would stand at the top of the key and shoot against guys like Sam Jones, shooting contests. He could shoot it, but he couldn't shoot free throws.

**SAM:** I remember the stories Tex told about him. He had that famous overtime game when his Kansas State team beat Wilt. That was the real triangle with the three guys Tex put around Wilt. Tex said he went to watch a Kansas freshman/varsity game and Wilt took off from above the top of the key, jumped at the free-throw line—remember, Olympic-level high jumper—and dunked the free throw. Tex goes to the NCAA rules meeting to tell them about this play Kansas is running where they are throwing the ball over the backboard and Wilt catches it on the way down and dunks it. Tex says he's putting chicken wire above his basket. So they outlaw both plays, change the rules.

**PJ:** Tex's defenses frustrated Wilt. That's why he left college a year early. So he had to play for the Globetrotters for a year because of the four-year rule. Then he's saying he'll stay with the Globetrotters. Wilt was always in the headlines.

# Oscar Robertson

There's a quote from a book written by the adventure novelist Clive Cussler that speaks to why Oscar Robertson these days often slips off the list of top ten players in NBA history: "Time is a thief. It steals our memory." You had to see Oscar, and there just aren't that many around anymore who did, and many of those who did see him did so during his slower days in Milwaukee, where he was in a supporting role around Kareem Abdul-Jabbar. And where he finally was part of an NBA championship team. As these things go in this statistics- and analytics-driven era, the tiebreakers are the championships. Fewer saw Robertson during his prime in the 1960s playing in Cincinnati, where even his own ownership was sabotaging his title chances in the name of attendance and thus finances because the white fan base in that Southern city just wasn't interested in watching too many Black people play basketball. It's sort of where the cliché got going about the white-guy tenth man. The Royals made sure at least the reserves were white. Robertson did become known for his unique triple-double average statistic, rivaled by Russell Westbrook, though Robertson also averaged at least 30 points and his teams were in more serious playoff contention against the greatest dynasty in NBA history, the 1960s Celtics with Hall of Famers coming off the bench. And in an era without the three-point shot and when once you received a pass and dribbled, the assist was wiped away. And given no one had invented the term *triple-double* yet or counted them, there was no pursuit of the statistical holy grail as there has been in recent years. Robertson was the first of the big guards, a physical advantage he had at six five and maybe 220 pounds, able to bull his way anywhere he wanted on the court. Robertson never played Boston without three guards attacking him to limit and try to tire him. It never much worked: Red Auerbach's message always was to try to keep him under 40. But despite his heroics, Oscar couldn't win a title with the Royals; the Celtics had Bill Russell and Oscar had Connie Dierking. Then Cincinnati, preparing to move to Kansas City, began unloading parts and Oscar got his championship with Kareem in a Finals sweep. Those Bucks couldn't repeat against the sixty-nine-win Lakers, but they did end the Lakers' record thirty-three-game winning streak. Oscar's first five seasons in the NBA he averaged a combined triple-double at more than 30 points per game. Jerry West said it was Oscar's image and not his that should be the logo for the NBA, given the combination of Robertson's skills and his activism on behalf of the players. Robertson had a brief national broadcasting run that was silenced when owners objected to the player who had sued them commenting on games. Then—talk about the assist of a lifetime—Oscar donated a kidney to save the life of his daughter.

Robertson grew up in segregated Indianapolis, where his high school became the first all-Black team to win an open-state title. Which led to just one in a lifetime of indignities: The winner traditionally paraded around the downtown Monument Circle, but not Robertson's team. Robertson ended up at the University of Cincinnati, where he was refused hotels when the team was on the road and had to stay in dorms. Black cats would be thrown into the locker room. As with Bill Russell, a lifetime of insults can alter a man's mood. But it didn't inhibit Robertson's play. Oscar took on the NBA with his demanding personality and perfectionist ways, which could frighten teammates. Bill Walton said Bill Russell told him Robertson was the smartest player he'd ever played against or seen. Even six-eight Wayne Embry, known as "the Wall" for his massive physique, said he feared Oscar's wrath, not unlike the demands Michael Jordan often put on teammates. Robertson seemed to have a unique ability to know where players were even behind him, that "sense of where you are," as John McPhee put it in his book about Bill Bradley. Robertson, like Chamberlain, was a track star. Robertson was an excellent shooter, with several seasons at close to 90 percent on free throws. Robertson was all-NBA eleven times and first team nine times. He led the league in assists six times and, along with Tiny Archibald, was the only player to lead the league in scoring and assists the same season. Robertson was All-Star game MVP three times back when that game mattered and season MVP in 1964, when Wilt averaged 37 and 22 and Russell averaged 15 and 25.

**PJ:** You gave him the ball at the end of the game. I came in to watch him on doubleheaders. I would be on Jerry Lucas. Lucas would bend me over, put me in an arm bar; he's like 250 at the time. He had some back issues, got too heavy. Oscar was the one down in the post. Don't let him get down in the post. We had a big guard, Dick Barnett, and Barnett idolized Oscar. Oscar won all those high school tournaments in Indiana. Dick was in Gary and Oscar was in Indianapolis. Oscar was always barking at guys on the court, telling them where to go. If they fucked up, he's giving them shit. He just didn't expend energy. He played at his pace. Used to play forty, forty-five minutes a game. No double-teaming in that day. So he'd back somebody down and he had Lucas sitting up there, who could shoot jumpers like crazy, and he had Adrian Smith. And Twyman and Embry at center. DeBusschere had to play guard because of Oscar. Everybody went big. He's the one that kinda brought that into play. Are *you* gonna guard Oscar? So everybody started getting big guards.

**SAM:** Like the Magic effect, when everyone had to go back to looking for big point guards again, where you had the era of Isiah, Cheeks, Norm Nixon, Stockton, John Lucas, Tiny.

**PJ:** Oscar was a back-to-the-basket guy who manipulated you in the post and made the defense react to him and find open guys; he really controlled games. West didn't control a game at that level, and he had Baylor, who was superior to anyone Oscar had, could elevate and shoot that jump shot. But such an ass Oscar could be. The racism for a lot of these guys growing up and what happened in our country, you could understand them being poisoned by it, it making them bitter—excluded at swimming pools, like Oscar was in Cincinnati. Jerry West's effectiveness was different.

**SAM:** Oscar was understandably always compared with West, coming in the same year, leaving the same year with one title, but LA versus Cincinnati makes a difference, and you can get to the Finals if you don't have to go through Boston. But then you just get to the Finals.

**PJ:** One of the remarkable things during my tenure with the Lakers, West gave me a call and said he'd gotten a call from Kobe. Kobe wanted to know how West and Elgin could both have averaged 30 points per game. "How did you do that?" Jerry told him it was a different game then, a speed game with more open shots and not the same element of the game we had now, a more wide-open game. With Oscar and Jerry, I wish I'd seen some film of that '60 Olympic team, a really potent team.

# Jerry West

Jerry West represented and personified the NBA so perfectly and ideally that when the league decided to create a logo to embody its play, it approved a silhouette image that most resembled Jerry West. Which was fitting enough, since West was as complete a player as the league has seen, ten times all-NBA first team. He led the league in scoring one season and another in assists. He holds the Finals scoring record of almost 40 points per game in 1969 when he was voted MVP despite playing for the losing team. And no one has ever averaged more in a playoff series. He was so reliable under pressure that the six-three guard earned the nickname "Mr. Clutch." West as a team executive was regarded, along with Red Auerbach, as the best in the game's history. West's eight championships as an executive go along with the one he finally won as a player with the Lakers in 1972 when that team won thirty-three consecutive games and a then-record sixty-nine games. West also was a consultant with the Golden State Warriors during two of their title runs, honored three times by the Basketball Hall of Fame as a player, contributor/executive, and member of the 1960 Olympic gold medal team.

Long and lean, with a powerfully springy jump shot and unusual leaping ability, West was an NBA constant for accomplishment. His sixties Lakers with Elgin Baylor, the basketball Mr. Inside and Mr. Outside, lost six Finals to Auerbach and Bill Russell's dynasty Boston Celtics in the 1960s. It wasn't until Russell retired and Wilt Chamberlain was acquired by the Lakers that West finally got his elusive championship in 1972. West averaged 37.9 points and 7.4 assists in the 1969 Finals loss. In that Game 7, West had a triple-double with 42 points, 13 rebounds, and 12 assists. In a 1965 playoff series against Baltimore he averaged a record 46.3 per game and more than 40 for the entire playoffs with another Finals loss to Boston when teammate Baylor was injured. West was an All-Star all fourteen seasons of his NBA playing career and four times averaged more than 30 points per game for the season. Twelve of those fourteen seasons he was all-NBA. He was an uncannily accurate shooter at a time when play was centered inside. Despite the recent high-scoring era, West still is top ten of all time in career scoring average. He led the league at 9.7 assists in the 1972 championship season. In his last four seasons combined, he averaged 9 assists per game. West attended East Bank High School. As part of an annual tradition, the school changed its name to West Bank for a day because of West's exploits.

**PJ:** The series we won in '70, Baylor, West, and Chamberlain should have carried them. They had Garrett as off guard, a rookie. They lost some players in expansion, Hazzard, Goodrich.

**SAM:** Jerry told me he was most upset with the Lakers for trading Dick to the Knicks. Between the expansion drafts and then the Wilt trade that cost them Archie Clark and Jerry Chambers and losing Barnett, the Lakers were basically out of guards. So Jerry did have to do it all from the backcourt. Frazier just wore him out in 1970.

**PJ:** It was Barnett's defense. We played full-court pressure defense on Jerry. You could be body on body then. Dick wasn't fast, but laterally he was really good and could get his body on Jerry. Plus, Dick had been with the Lakers and knew Jerry. Dick was a talent. Everyone knew that when the Knicks traded for him. Then he tore his Achilles, and that changed his life.

**SAM:** That was before the '70 title season. Dick averaged like 23 his first season after the trade and then tore it. But he was back and played eighty-one games the next season.

**PJ:** We had this reunion of the '73 championship team and Dick was at my table with Jeanie. Jeanie asked him what was his impetus to get his PhD, and he said he went to school not for academics out of Gary, and when he tore his Achilles he said to himself, "Is this basketball all I really have? So I have nothing if this is the end of my basketball career." No one came back from an Achilles then. Luke Jackson tore his a year later and that was it for him, Larry Costello a year earlier. But his defense that year on Jerry West really was the turning point for us in that series. Jerry never seemed happy, he was tormented.

**SAM:** No one knew, but everyone knew. Like the subtitle of the last of his memoirs, *My Charmed, Tormented Life.*

**PJ:** June's into astrology, and she loved to give me all these characteristics of people I knew, and she said Jerry was the perfect Gemini: two personalities, the good Gemini and the bad Gemini. That's Jerry. We had those affable talks and he couldn't be nicer to everyone.

**SAM:** I'll attest to that. When I was working on the Robertson free-agency-suit book, he took a day to spend with me, talk about the suit and Oscar, tell me if anyone should have been the logo of the league it was Oscar. He said his greatest disappointment in his NBA career was when Elgin had to retire early in the season and they finally won the title and he couldn't be there to share it with him.

# Lenny Wilkens

The 1992 Dream Team was famously the greatest ever, though it's not likely they would have beaten the 1996 USA Basketball Olympic team with Scottie Pippen at his personal zenith, a healthy John Stockton, Charles Barkley, Karl Malone, and David Robinson, and with the additions of Hakeem Olajuwon, Grant Hill and Penny Hardaway, Reggie Miller, Gary Payton and Mitch Richmond, and Shaq for Christian Laettner. There likely never was more basketball talent on one team. So Shaq had a question for coach Lenny Wilkens. "Hey, Coach," Shaq asked, "you ever play at this level?" The phlegmatic Wilkens looked at O'Neal with a wry grin while Pippen burst out laughing. Wilkens responded that he had. Shaq said he went home and questioned his stepdad, Phillip Harrison, whom he called Sarge. Shaq reported back to Wilkens. "My dad said you were a bad man." Bad as in good enough to once be runner-up for league MVP to Wilt Chamberlain, ahead of Elgin Baylor and Oscar Robertson. Wilkens is among the rare individuals enshrined in the Naismith Basketball Hall of Fame three different times. He's in the player and coach rankings for all-time greatest. He was nine times an All-Star as a player and a championship coach, perhaps the Mensa of the NBA as a player/coach for two different franchises. The six-one, 180-pound, left-handed Wilkens was one of the most elusive drivers of the ball, who taught through his play and his voice.

Wilkens came out of Brooklyn, the then-rough Bedford-Stuyvesant neighborhood, and Boys High, which featured the likes of Connie Hawkins. The studious Wilkens had dreams of being an economics teacher while dabbling in basketball. At Providence he was MVP of the 1960 NIT even though his team lost to Chet Walker and champion Bradley. Wilkens was drafted number 6 overall in 1960 by St. Louis, then the most Southern of the NBA cities. Even though the pictures of every starter, of which Wilkens was one, hung in the window of the restaurant across from the arena, Wilkens was denied service there because he was Black. But he basically helped integrate the last all-white NBA championship team, the 1958 St. Louis Hawks, with the franchise's last Finals appearance in his rookie season. Wilkens was traded to expansion Seattle, where he settled following his career. There he set his career-best scoring average of 22 per game in his first year, became the team's most popular player, and added coaching to his duties when the general manager noted he was running the team anyway as point guard. He was traded to Cleveland and then to Portland, where he also was player/coach during Bill Walton's injury-plagued first few seasons, and then returned to the SuperSonics as coach, with the team 5–17 to start the 1977–78 season. With a disparate group without an All-Star player, Wilkens guided Seattle to the NBA Finals and a seventh-game loss after being ahead 3–2 in games, and then the franchise's only NBA championship in 1979. Wilkens then coached two rising franchises in Cleveland and Atlanta along with the Toronto Raptors and the Knicks, accumulating more than 1,300 coaching victories to rank as the leader when he retired and third into the mid-2020s.

**PJ:** Lenny being a player/coach reminded me a little of my start when I finished my playing career with the Nets and Kevin got thrown out of like fourteen games and he'd ask me to coach the second half.

**SAM:** Lenny had done the player/coach thing, but when he went to Cleveland after that, Fitch was always having him take over when Bill was thrown out, even though Jimmy Rodgers, who was with Bill in college, was still with him. Bill could see it in Lenny. It was Lenny, really, who invented Riley's "Disease of Me" with his Sonics when two seasons later they didn't even make the playoffs. Lenny called it "Championship Fallout."

**PJ:** My coaching began when I got a call from this guy that's the county commissioner in Albany. He said, "We're really struggling here, we've got a rookie franchise, we're brand new, we have the All-Star game. We only have seventeen games left in the year. It's March 16th and we need six weeks for someone to come in and take over. Dean Meminger's our coach and he's having a real struggle. Would you be interested?"

**SAM:** Why you?

**PJ:** New York Knicks, I'd been assistant coach for a couple of years with the Nets. So I called up Dean and I said, "Dean, what's going on?" And he said, "I'm outta here. But I want to try out for the team." We're struggling a little bit to meet finances with June for the health club we were opening. Give us a little financial relief for the health club. So I went out there and coached them. I had some success, and so they said, "Would you come back and do it again?"

**SAM:** And eleven rings later? That Cavs team Lenny coached, as you'll recall, was supposed to be who your team became. Magic called them the team of the nineties when they swept you 6–0 that season of "the Shot." Price, Harper, Williams, Nance, and Daugherty were good, if not tough, which was part of the downfall.

**PJ:** I moved out to Woodstock, where June's sister was living. We had friends there. Charley Rosen was there. They gave me a rental car to drive back and forth to Albany. If the team was going south to Lancaster or wherever, they'd pick me up on the way down and I'd drive the rest of the way.

**SAM:** Not exactly like Lenny's path, but we all travel different ones. One Lenny story for who he was. Lou Hudson was a Hawks rookie and basically is running against Dave Bing for Rookie of the Year. Players voted for awards then but couldn't vote for teammates. So Hawks coach Richie Guerin tells his players to vote for someone other than Bing to give Hudson a better chance. Lenny objects and says he wouldn't do that because it was unfair and perverted the process. The Hawks labeled Wilkens a troublemaker and traded him. Lenny would never sacrifice his values. Probably cost him some jobs.

# Dave DeBusschere

D ave DeBusschere is among the most accomplished sports figures in American history. Obviously not in terms of championships won, though he did star with two New York Knicks championship teams. He pitched Major League Baseball and had an ERA under 3.00. He served as the youngest player/coach in NBA history, an executive with the Knicks and Nets of the ABA, and commissioner of the ABA. And talk about your tough guys. Nobody ever messed with Dave DeBusschere. When the NBA finally introduced the all-defense team during his career, he made it all six times until he retired when he was thirty-three and was the leading vote getter those last four seasons at a time when other top defenders included Wilt, Kareem, John Havlicek, Walt Frazier, Norm Van Lier, Jerry Sloan, and Nate Thurmond. The six-six, 220-pound DeBusschere was the classic final piece in the trade of Walt Bellamy that put the Knicks on their final glide path to six years as perhaps the most admired, team-oriented, unselfish group in NBA history.

**PJ:** Perfect trade. Red had a formula that he used when he came December of my first year. Before Red was hired, Bradley had just shown up. He had to do this whole stint in the air force reserves. We never saw hide nor hair of him, but Dick Barnett was always, "When's Superman showing up? When's this Superman gonna come and rescue this team?" He was always talking shit in the locker room.

**SAM:** Maybe players don't feel it as much as fans, but that buildup for Bradley was like Elvis coming home from the army. Bradley had that famous 58-point game in the NCAAs playing for, jeez, an Ivy League school and was Final Four MVP without winning. Media is writing he's the white Oscar Robertson with some Jerry West thrown in. They still had the territorial rule, and Princeton is a mile closer to New York than Philly. But the Knicks have to wait two years while Bill takes a Rhodes Scholarship in England and plays weekends in Italy and wins a title, and he's coming to save the Knicks like Babe Ruth saved the Yankees. But he stinks. I remember Bill telling me fans were throwing stuff at him his first game, he was so bad, couldn't play guard. Finally the Knicks traded Cazzie, against whom he was competing, and that's another sort of final piece of the unselfish, ball-movement, man-movement, everyone-can-shoot Knicks.

**PJ:** Howie Komives was starting and Dick Barnett was starting. And Reed and Bellamy. Then the second unit would come out and play and we were, defensively, the dogs. We were on people. It made a difference. Red wanted to play that style of game. So the next year we got off to a start that wasn't very good. The writing was on the wall: Clyde was going to be a starter really soon. But he and Dick, neither one of them were lead guards, really. Bradley was kind of a guard type and so was Cazzie. DeBusschere played guard at Detroit. He had been a six-six guard, and as a consequence we had four guys that could handle the ball. Willis and I were on the one-dribble rule, basically. We could dribble once or twice and that was it, or we had to call it quits. I used to rebound and try to drive the length of the court and get it taken away or whatever; things wouldn't happen great.

**SAM:** I hate to admit it, but there'd be a collective groan in the stands when you began dribbling. Here comes a turnover. "Pass it, Phil, pass it!" Everyone was yelling at you all the time.

**PJ:** It was best said by Jack Marin, who said, "Dave DeBusschere, it's like playing with a guy that has Velcro on his chest. You think you're gonna jump and turn around and shoot your shot, and all of a sudden you can't leave the floor, because he just puts that chest on you. He just puts you down back on the floor." The first few times I played against Dave when he was in Detroit, I was looking at the referee: "That's a foul." I went for my hook shot and couldn't get off the floor. He was really good against guys like Elgin Baylor, Gus Johnson, big scorers of the time, Chet Walker in Chicago. When we would go to Chicago, Dave's best friend was a guy who lived in Chicago, who owned these Stop and Go grocery stores. Greek, a great character named George. I asked him, "How'd you guys meet?" "Well, Dave was pitching with the White Sox, and Dave says, 'It just so happened I pulled my car out and he was on the street,' and George says, 'Hey, big guy, come on, I'll take you out for a couple beers.' So I got in the car and we had this relationship." Dave's father was a beer distributor and bar owner. One day Dave's friend George gives Bradley a check for $10,000. He says he wants Bill to go out and buy him a work of art he thinks is worth it. So we get a George Bellows painting of Billy Sunday delivering a sermon in Chicago. Anyway, George dies, and I go back for the funeral and I ask what ever happened to the painting me and Bill got. It's behind the couch by the wall.

**SAM:** Dave would have been with another regular guy.

**PJ:** We would get into Chicago and I'd stop by on Rush Street and Dave would be in there with his friend, and he would be like, "Have one with us. And then go home. You're gonna have to guard Chet

Walker tomorrow." He was having a late night. Distance shooter, too, before they had the three. Defensive player like that, one of the best shooters from distance, strong, tough, amazing player. DeBusschere-type guys were difference makers; they are the guys who carry the water. When we lost to New York in '94, they beat us up physically the final game, Mason and Oakley. I know they talk about the bad foul call against Scottie, but we got an ass kicking in the seventh. You need to have a guy willing to go into it, and we didn't. Like Michael did with Xavier in '92. Michael could do that, too. Scottie was intimidated by Detroit early on, the concussion putting him out of a last game. The intimidation factor was there, and you'd have to have guys who confront that. Bill Bridges was one of those guys. He and Lonnie Shelton had an historic fight, just mayhem, trading blows.

**SAM:** I remember that one in '84, swinging away like one of those MMA cage fight things they have now. I think each got a one- or two-game suspension.

**PJ:** That's also why Houston had such success against us with Otis Thorpe. Horace could not deal with him. Hakeem was a dominating physical presence on the floor, and Michael would go into the middle and that team would take him down all the time. It wasn't just Detroit—Houston had a lot of success against us. There was nobody on that Cleveland team to take care of Price when the Pistons beat the shit out of him. They let Mahorn take him out. Mahorn's going to do this and nobody is doing anything. The league still was pretty much wide open. Oakley carried the water for the Knicks. Ewing had bravado and was physical, but he wasn't that ultimate threat; there's still a place for them, unfortunately, in basketball. Red used to like the fact I had that physicality. I didn't have the power or strength to back it up, but I had the instinct. I remember I was in third grade and my buddy in fourth grade was challenged, and I had to fight the fourth-grade guy. That was maybe part of who my character was. I had this big fight with Jack Marin. He was a cocky guy, kept saying Bill was a pinko and communist. We had this rivalry with Baltimore. Conservative Duke-type guy; he was feisty. I knew how to get his goat and did. I'd elbowed him in the neck and put my hand on his neck and tried to jump. He came down the court after me and I kind of laughed at him, got his goat. We ended up at half-court rolling around awhile. Unseld came up behind me, chested me, and knocked me down. Next year Marin waited and gave me an elbow I never saw coming. I went down; I never had been knocked out like that. I was coming in to offensive rebound, didn't see him. He turned around and punched me. When you had Dave with you, though, you never had to worry. They knew they had to be watching, too. Dave got him back.

# John Havlicek

I 've always been convinced John Havlicek was the inspiration for Forrest Gump. Remember Forrest's famous run across the United States and back without stopping over three years, more than fifteen thousand miles? Fondly named "Hondo" after the John Wayne character, Havlicek was the absolute blue-collar superstar, lacking the flair of Russell or the offensive production of Bird. He just started running and never stopped from the day in 1962 he signed with the Celtics and went on to so many memorable moments. Havlicek didn't have a classic shooting form or graceful driving ability; perhaps mostly by force of will, he made the most crucial shots of the era for the Celtics, the driving layup in the 1976 triple-overtime game against Phoenix, baskets to force each of two overtimes in Game 6 of the 1974 Finals, one of two Havlicek-led titles for the seventies Celtics. In all, he played for eight championship teams while spending almost half his career as a sixth man and going straight from that to team captain. Knicks-Celtics games were classics of the early seventies, and Havlicek and Bill Bradley running nonstop were the marathons of the era. In Boston's 1968 series against the defending-champion 76ers, Havlicek led the Celtics back from a 3–1 deficit with near triple-doubles, scoring more than 20 points in games 5 through 7 and playing all forty-eight minutes in the last three games, including the Game 7 clincher in Philadelphia. Those seventies Celtics lacked the superstar personalities with Dave Cowens, Jo Jo White, Paul Silas, and Don Nelson. They were defined mostly by Havlicek's blue-collar relentlessness. The humble six-five Havlicek was an All-Star thirteen times, eleven times all-NBA, eight times all-defense, and a Finals MVP. The rugged frontiersman from Ohio played at least eighty games in seven straight seasons and all eighty-two in his final season. He averaged almost forty-six minutes per game during the 1974 playoffs.

**PJ:** The problem with Havlicek was that when I had to guard him, I couldn't. He ran around too much. He was constantly in motion, using picks from Silas, an insidious offensive rebounder, effective at what he did. He'd get second chances for his team, so many offensive rebounds. Good enough to have always been a starter, but sacrificed for his team. Had a little bit of a crooked shot. Made some big jump shots against us in Game 5 in '68. Went back up there for Game 7 and we got that one.

**SAM:** That was the sixty-eight-win Celtics the year you won in '73. Havlicek hurt his shoulder in Game 3, came back and had a big Game in 5. They always say in Boston that was their best team of the seventies.

**PJ:** I felt we were destined to win that year. We were a really good team. Willis said that was the best team he played for, better than '70. The '70 team had more flamboyance. Howard Cosell was following us around, and we had parties in all the high places and we were the toast of the town. We'd lost Cazzie and Stallworth, but the addition of Meminger was big, who was an extremely good player, especially defensively. He had elevation going to the hoop. He was not a great shooter. John Gianelli had some big games for us in the playoffs, even Harthorne Wingo.

**SAM:** You're breaking the hearts of Knicks fans. They talk about 1970 like Bears fans do of 1985.

**PJ:** Willis was limited that season, so he split minutes with Lucas, which was a nice situation. Luc and I would go in the game at the end of the first quarter, eight minutes or so, and Willis would come back in and play maybe three, four minutes into the second quarter. Jerry had maybe eighteen, twenty minutes where he could be effective by then. That team had six guys averaging in double figures. Barnett was coming off the bench, but what was remarkable was Red was up to all his old tricks still in Boston. He put us in a different locker room every game, visitors' locker room, hockey locker room. Then finally one outside the ring by the court so you walk through the door and people are yelling at you, throwing things. People are throwing beer on us. There are these New York kids in the stands right there fighting the Boston kids because of all the New York kids up there going to college.

**SAM:** Probably not Harvard. The irony, of course, regarding Havlicek was that he probably was the most moral, upright, straight, and fair guy, the last guy who would want an unlevel playing field or someone sticking a victory cigar in your face. They did get you the next year in five when Havlicek basically never went out of the game when the Knicks' run was ending.

# Jerry Lucas

Jerry Lucas has escaped the memory of most, which is delicious irony because no NBA player—or perhaps anyone ever—remembered more than Jerry Lucas. He was a successful and accomplished collegiate basketball player, renowned in his time but hardly remembered like Walton or Alcindor. He rebounded like few ever in the NBA, but who remembers anyone on the boards but Russell and Wilt, or Moses Malone and Dennis Rodman? Jerry Lucas was a marvel. He might have appeared on TV to be a magician as much as a basketball player, especially considering he was playing much of his NBA career in Cincinnati and before that for the ABL Cleveland Pipers. Lucas had a dazzling mind—he could shock you in the most mundane ways, like reciting a full page of the New York City phone book. Any page; he knew the whole thing. Pick a card, any card. But it was no trick. Lucas was the original player/investor and built a business empire while he was in the NBA. His interests lay so far beyond the sport that, even though he was the best collegiate player in the nation for three years, according to teammate John Havlicek, his acolyte, he said professional basketball didn't interest him and he probably wouldn't play professionally. He tried to save a new basketball league, the ABL, started by Globetrotters impresario Abe Saperstein, and to play for the team owned by Cleveland shipbuilder George Steinbrenner. The league failed quickly and Lucas went to the Cincinnati

Royals under the old territorial draft. Cincinnati had secured his rights when he was a high schooler. The six-eight Lucas was a prodigy whose southern Ohio high school games were promoted and attended like those of LeBron James years later. Lucas was labeled a next Wilt. His college team at Ohio State went to three consecutive NCAA Finals with Havlicek and future NBA players Larry Siegfried, a Havlicek teammate with the Celtics, and Mel Nowell, who played for the NBA Chicago Zephyrs. Their winning streaks were UCLA before UCLA. Lucas was the first collegiate athlete to be Sports Illustrated Sportsman of the Year. He was Bill Walton East. In a professional career limited by back problems and curiosity, Lucas became the only noncenter with a 40-rebound game and one of only four NBA players—along with Wilt Chamberlain, Bob Pettit, and Nate Thurmond—to have 20/20 seasons. Lucas had the most 20/20 games other than Chamberlain, and Lucas is fourth all-time behind Chamberlain, Russell, and Pettit in rebounds per game. Jerry made seven All-Star teams and was All-Star MVP. He was five times all-NBA and the rare instance of a champion in college, the pros, and the Olympics, the latter with the famed '60 team.

**PJ:** Jerry was my roommate for a while. We did really well when he came to us for '71–'72. He'd gone to San Francisco and came back heavier, like 250. He was bothered by back problems, and the Knicks were willing to trade Cazzie for him. Jerry lost weight and saved our ass that year.

**SAM:** Jerry had this wild run in the pros starting in that ABL, and then he says he was not going to play and tries instead to buy an NBA franchise with business guys he knew. But that also falls through, and he finally goes to the Royals and supposedly is going to be this savior coming finally to beat Boston for Oscar Robertson. But Jerry's the same size as Wayne Embry and really not a center, which was big in that era, pun intended. It's a disaster of a franchise in the NBA South. The one season Oscar told me he felt they were better than the Celtics, they get rid of future All-Star Bob Boozer because they have too many Black players for Southern Cincinnati and pick up a small white guard for the bench. Attendance boomed when Lucas came, but then they're scrambling and playing home games around the state, and he's more into his investments, and he's having knee and back issues, and they can't beat Russell. Then Cousy comes in to coach the Royals, and he wants Jerry and Oscar gone so Cousy can re-create the fast-breaking Celtics. But Jerry, like Oscar, has a no-trade—I recall they first tried to trade Oscar to Baltimore and he rejected that—and Jerry picks to be traded to the Warriors.

**PJ:** He was great. He had the inside game. He could stay in there and shoot hooks and turnarounds, and his defense was so good. He held down Dave Cowens. We had to go through those teams to get to the '72 Finals. Chamberlain was too big for him. We won the first game, and then Jerry came outside and screened for Bill. We had one other overtime game that we lost in that series, lost the series 4–1. That overtime game was a big thing. We woulda won that game, we woulda made that series 2–2. Then they beat us up the last game.

**SAM:** Jerry had to start most of the season for Willis and had a great season, something like 17 and 13. He really was fifty years before his time playing center and shooting what today would be threes with that high, arcing shot; everyone said he'd be too small, but the big centers couldn't get out to him. And he was strong, having put on that weight. And he could rebound. Shot more than 50 percent that season, and you know those were mostly twenty-five-footers.

**PJ:** It was funny. DeBusschere didn't like him because he said he was full of hot air, always had a plan, always talking. Memory stuff that he was going through. Give him a word and Jerry could put the letters in alphabetical order for you faster than you could spell the word. So if you said *losing*, he would put the letters in alphabetical order faster than you could spell l-o-s-i-n-g. . . . That kind of stuff he was very effective at. He's teaching Scripture now to people in the Christian church, how to memorize Scripture. Cheri was a minister's daughter. It was a match made in heaven for the two of them. Bill put together this panel for the big Allen & Co. Sun Valley conference one year. Barnett, Lucas, five of us; Monroe had heart issues and could not make it. Warren Buffett said it was the best panel he'd been to in thirty years. Lucas sold his memory school. I don't know why it hasn't been adopted in our educational system; it's about learning how to think.

**SAM:** I remember seeing Jerry on TV those years doing that stuff, the visualization. I think he was even on *Ed Sullivan*. Like the HOMES thing to remember the Great Lakes, Huron, Ontario, Michigan, Erie, and Superior, think of it like that. It got me through the Great Lakes but never any phone books.

**PJ:** Memorization works well, but if you want to learn how to think, you have to teach different ways, he'd say. There was the story of Bobby Fischer, the chess champion, challenging Jerry Lucas. Fischer got phone books *A* to *M* and *M* to *Z*, and Jerry is repeating each column, and Fischer keeps asking him how he's doing it, can't believe it. Jerry could pass the ball, massive hands. Really great touch. It was a joke. The game was too easy for him. He retired when normally guys play two or three years longer, but he retired at an early age. I think it was too easy and he was going through some physical difficulty. He,

Reed, and DeBusschere all retired the same year. Left a real hole in our team. He taught me how to shoot a jump shot. I was shooting and he said, "Come here. Let me show you how to shoot a jump shot. You gotta get the ball underneath your forearm. Gotta get the ball here. Can't be shooting like this, because it's all about elevation, getting the ball up in the air. The angle comes down by gravity, so it's gonna create this opportunity for it to go in and it's gonna have touch besides." We did it one day. I was like, "OK, I'm into that. I can practice that."

**SAM:** I heard that talk one time from Johnny Bach about how you shot artillery and there was a higher arc which cut down the angle and seemed to make the target bigger.

**PJ:** Jerry saw the game kind of like Walton. He saw the game in perspective, how it's happening. But he didn't have that same competitive drive that Bill had. Or the edge. His team won a ton of games when he was in college. Three years in college they're probably like 90–8 or something. So he wants an audience with me when I'm with the Bulls. Calls up, gonna drive up from Ohio to Chicago. Can I talk to you? Sure. Now his scheme is he's selling golf clubs. He won the pro-am one time in Pebble Beach. That's how talented he was. He had scores, whatever the margin is called, the handicap, that seemed unfair. They end up winning by like twenty strokes. His handicap was like maybe for an 80, 82, and he was, like, a scratch golfer. That's what they call it: sandbagging. But he probably hadn't played that often. He wasn't trying to cheat. He was just a natural; he didn't have to play regularly. He was Mr. Everything at Ohio State. I don't think he played baseball, but he had a ton of talent, extremely smart, quick, the first person in his family to graduate from high school.

**SAM:** He was from Middletown, which was a basketball hotbed near Cincinnati, but rural. I remember reading his games would draw more than ten thousand when places didn't have that much population.

**PJ:** His grandfather Pappy Lucas was from Kentucky, and he had twenty-two children from three wives. He had a child at age seventy, something like that. Luc's grandpa was a deputy sheriff in some place in Kentucky and went and arrested the local Ku Klux Klan leader in the community because they burned down a church, set fire to a cross. He came up to the cabin and went in and he said, "I'm here to take old Joe." They said Joe was in his bedroom taking a nap. "I'll go in and talk to him." Grandpappy never carried a gun. He was a deputy sheriff without a gun. He went in and said, I gotta put you under arrest. And the guy went along with him. And he booked him and that was it. That was the reputation he had. Jerry played with John at Ohio State. John was a multitalented guy, right-handed dominant. Luc was multiple. We'd talk about passing. He'd get the ball in what we call triple-threat position. Shoot, pass, or dribble. Lot of people think it's down here so you can dribble. That's the most important thing of a triple threat. Not about passing or shooting. He'd be right here and he would just look at the basket, and all of a sudden he'd drop a bounce pass to you and it's, like, right there. When I first played against him, I would get on the post and he would just lean his weight and buckle me. I would be trying to hold my spot. Couldn't stand. He was that heavy, was 250, and he would arm bar you in the middle of the back. Would guide you with his big old hands because hip checking was in vogue. He wasn't that active or mobile when he was a forward. But then we moved him to the center spot when it was downsized to small centers in the East. It was Unseld and Elvin Hayes. Who else? Cowens, McAdoo, Philadelphia I believe had LeRoy Ellis, Atlanta had that kid that was known for rape, lasted one season and that was it for him. And then they had Tree Rollins, Boerwinkle. Dearth of big centers then.

**SAM:** And Kareem was forcing his way out west. Too bad Luc and Willis broke down; you coulda been contenders. Oh, right, you did win it the next season when Willis came back and split time with Jerry and you guys beat the Lakers in the Finals.

# Nate Thurmond

N ate Thurmond was so old-school you could call him a one-room school-house. The six-eleven-and-a-half, 225-pounder lacked the athletic grace of the great centers like Kareem Abdul-Jabbar, the quickness of Bill Russell, or the power of Wilt Chamberlain. Facing all of them in his era, and even teaming with Chamberlain for two seasons as the first so-called Twin Towers center front line, Thurmond eschewed dunking. "I suppose I could make a reputation for myself by dunking the ball and other stuff, but what would it get me?" he once told a reporter. He always talked about a life goal of owning his own restaurant. His Big Nate's BBQ became a San Francisco standard, and his fare still sells at Warriors games. He was blue collar in the tuxedo time for centers. He was physical, possessed excellent timing, and was strong. Abdul-Jabbar, never expansive with praise, was insistent that no one defended him better than Thurmond. "When I score on Nate, I know I've done something," Abdul-Jabbar told the *Los Angeles Times*. "A lot of guys beat on me and said they played good defense, but Nate could actually do it." When they met in the 1972 playoffs, even though Abdul-Jabbar's more powerful Bucks won, Thurmond, in that one-on-one era without help, averaged 25 and 18 to Kareem's 23 and 19. Abdul-Jabbar's two poorest-shooting playoff series were against Thurmond.

Thurmond never was part of a championship team, often because of bad luck. Two years after he joined forces with Wilt, the Warriors traded Wilt because they needed the money. It wasn't until Thurmond's ninth season with the team that the Warriors got an arena in Oakland. Before then in San Francisco, they played in the Cow Palace, the Civic Auditorium, the War Memorial Gym at the University of San Francisco, and various arenas in Oakland and San Jose. Thurmond said players would check the schedule to see where they were playing, not when. Though noted for his rebounding and defense, Thurmond, with a baby jump shot, averaged at least 20 points in five consecutive seasons, 20/20 combined over two of those, and was among five players to average at least 15 rebounds per game in their careers and have a 20-rebound season. Thurmond paired with high-scoring Rick Barry and went to the 1967 Finals. Then Barry jumped to Oakland in the ABA and spent years trying to fight his way back to playing with Thurmond; he acknowledged leaving him as his greatest mistake. The NBA didn't count blocks until the 1973–74 season, and in 1974, in his first game after being traded to the Chicago Bulls, Thurmond collected the first recorded quadruple-double in NBA history—apologies to Wilt and Russell, obviously. After being unable to adjust to Chicago's forward system, Thurmond went home to the lowly expansion Cleveland Cavaliers for the their first great season, what they called the Miracle of Richfield, for their first playoff appearance, and then went to the conference finals and lost to the eventual champs, the Boston Celtics. Thurmond's contributions to stabilizing the franchise were so important that his jersey number was retired, despite his playing just two seasons in Cleveland. Thurmond was an All-Star seven times and five times all-defense.

**PJ:** I laugh because the first times I played against Nate I put the shot up after a rebound and he blocked it. I thought he fouled me, but he was known as a shot blocker. So I ran the referee down on the court. And I end up in the commissioner's office about my actions on the court for running down the referee. There was a belligerence about the referees. You had to earn your stripes; then they let you play. I can't tell you how many times I thought I blocked the great Philly jump shooter Hal Greer. He liked to pull up at the free-throw line. I'd just block his shot. "Foul!" "No, that's not a foul! All ball." Hal had that fifteen-footer down. Kojis was another one with that jump shot from the free-throw line.

**SAM:** My late buddy Don Kojis, original Bull in '66, leaping white guy who started the backdoor dunk with Guy Rodgers; they called it the Kangaroo Kram. Kojis has a good season with the Bulls. One of the owners goes to represent the Bulls at the expansion draft to stock the new San Diego team. Gets drunk on the plane and loses the expansion list and mistakenly puts Kojis on it. That was also the NBA then.

**PJ:** I don't watch much NBA anymore, but I was watching on YouTube the highlights of a Bulls game with Cleveland, and the coach from Cleveland had them in the triangle a number of times, taking advantage of the size, throwing it over the top. This young kid Mobley was scoring pretty much in the first half like he was a force. Could become quite the force for Cleveland. Nate probably wishes he could have, being from Akron.

# Willis Reed

There have been tough players in the NBA and there have been determined and spirited players. But few in NBA history symbolize the essential elements of competition like Knicks center Willis Reed. Reed has the honors from an injury-shortened career: seven All-Star games, all-NBA and all-defense first team the same season he became the first—and just Michael Jordan since—to earn the triple crown of NBA awards, the regular season, All-Star, and Finals MVP, along with an NBA championship. Reed had plenty of individual highlights, like averaging 28 points and 12 rebounds against Kareem Abdul-Jabbar and the Milwaukee Bucks to get the Knicks to that 1970 Finals. Reed had a 53-point game and a 33-rebound game, and one for 46 points as a rookie second-round draft pick. For five consecutive seasons, Reed averaged at least 20 points and 13 rebounds per game. For both of the Knicks' only two championships in franchise history, he was the Finals MVP. Those seven All-Star games were in his first seven seasons. But by thirty-one he was retired after knee problems, playing fewer than twenty games two of his last three seasons.

It was just two games that perhaps both defined and introduced Willis Reed, the Knicks' undisputed captain, for what he represented on the basketball court and to the larger community of the human spirit. Both are iconic moments in NBA lore, Reed's Game 7 in the 1970 Finals, a metonym for resilience, tenacity, and courage, and Reed's brawl with the Los Angeles Lakers in an era when fighting wasn't uncommon in the NBA, coming to represent standing up to greater odds and a bigger opponent. That 1966 fight began simply enough for the era, with the Lakers' Rudy LaRusso elbowing and pushing and eventually taking a swipe at Reed in the Knicks' home opener, but right in front of the Lakers bench. Reed responded and then, with other Lakers joining in—or, as they claimed, attempting to break up the fight—Reed, in seeking out LaRusso, found himself in combat with virtually the entire Lakers team, several Lakers backing away from the merciless Reed. Reed had once been held back in a college fight at Grambling and been sucker punched. Never again. Reed, not the aggressor, just the finisher, got an ejection and a fifty-dollar fine along with LaRusso. Reed, with a torn thigh muscle, was not expected to play in Game 7 of the 1970 Finals, being barely able to walk. But as the introductions began, he limped out of the tunnel onto the Madison Square Garden court, where fans said they never heard the Garden so loud for so long. Reed had just two baskets in the game, both early, but his presence and audacity so inspired his teammates—and seemed to deflate Chamberlain, West, and Baylor and the mighty Lakers—that the Knicks jumped out to the lead, 14 points after the first quarter and 27 at halftime, and rode the wave of the unrestrained New Yorkers' joy to the team's first NBA championship. When someone plays valiantly through injury and hardship, it is often still called a Willis Reed moment. The six-ten, 235-pound Reed, with his superb left-handed midrange jump shot and rebounding prowess, went on to coach both the Knicks and the New Jersey Nets and serve in an executive position for the Nets. Performing valiantly and never giving in has become synonymous with *Willis Reed*.

**PJ:** Willis commanded a certain amount of respect, like, Pay attention to this guy. If he spoke, it was important. I don't remember him being an outright spokesperson. Bill testified at this trial he had. He got in an altercation with an off-duty policeman; it was a Black/white thing. About a parking spot. He got there first and the policeman wanted to bogart it from him. And he was not having any part of it. And then there was an assault charge or an intimidation charge or something. And it went to court. Bill came in as a character witness. Dick Barnett played on this in the locker room. He called Willis an original American.

**SAM:** I remember Frazier tell this story of Willis picking him up at the airport when he was a rookie, like Red, before he was head coach, picked you up. So they're driving into the city and Willis gets stopped for speeding or something and is out arguing with the police. Frazier, being from the South, says he's thinking, "Here comes a shooting." Back comes Willis, no ticket, and on they go.

**PJ:** When it all changed for the Knicks and Willis was the major fight with Atlanta when they first moved there. It was the fight that led to the rule that if you come off the bench, you'll be suspended. The fight just went on and on. It was early November 1968. Atlanta had won maybe sixty games the year before, and they were disappointed, obviously, that they hadn't gone to the Finals. They had a stacked team. Lou Hudson was coming off the bench. They had Bridges and Zelmo Beaty, big guys, both really good ballplayers. We met them six times that season. We had a couple of dustups in the process. When I was a rookie, they were still in St. Louis. I started a game against them because they had a big front line. There was a loose ball and I went down to get it, and so did Bridges. I have really sharp elbows. I literally broke a kid's nose in college with my elbows. There's a term for it, trainers would tell me: pointed elbows. I wear through shirts. I broke a vessel in Bridges's forehead. He had a pool of blood around him. Zelmo said, "Get that motherfucking rookie next time." They were in

85

Atlanta and they got off to a poor start the next season. Lenny was gone. Hazzard had come in. At halftime, one of the last plays before half, the clock was running down and I posted up Paul Silas, who was burly. It was Silas, Beaty, and Bridges. Silas hits me in the back of the neck. I don't know if he hit me behind the ear or what happened, but I went down ass over teakettle. The half ended and we walked up this tunnel in Georgia Tech's field house. Komives was bitchin' at them: "You shoulda been thrown outta the game."

**SAM:** I was watching that game. There were a bunch of fights. Like yours in the first half, there'd be a fight, they'd work it out, free throws, then another fight.

**PJ:** The ball boy had seven cigarettes in his hand lit for the players to smoke while he went up the ramp to the locker room. He'd hand them out; they were in between his fingers. They were lit. I don't know how he did it. Players smoked in the locker room, which were bare-bones, just shoulder-high partitions, in the field house. We could hear Richie on the other end talking about how tough we have to be, how physical we have to be, slamming lockers. "You gotta get out there and fight for what you gotta do." They had kind of lost the soul of the team, losing Lenny. Lou Hudson came back to a pick that Willis was setting for Barnett. We picked for Barnett, but Bells used to pick like this, stick his ass out. He had a big bubble ass. Then he didn't have to roll. Willis was setting a hard pick and Lou just came back and punched him. Didn't come to the pick. Just came back to punch him, which I think his reputation would have been spread around the league this time. Because he had been in a couple altercations around the league. Known as a rugged guy who's gonna stand his ground. So everything went to shit right after, because Hazzard jumped on Willis's back and Willis threw him off. And then everybody was in on the fight.

**SAM:** I read about it years later, and the *New York Times* reporter who was there, the NBA historian Leonard Koppett, described it like a dance scene from *West Side Story*.

**PJ:** I was like, Where's Silas? This is a guy that's taken me on twice now in my career. Nate Bowman wrapped up Bridges, which is the smart thing to do. This is an old-time field house that had a lower floor. There's a balcony railing all around the oval. Bridges just walked Bowman over to the railing and started slamming him against the concrete wall. This woman came down and started hitting him with her purse. There was so much going on at the time. Anyway, Bells did not get up off the bench, and that was the story. Walt Bellamy had these unbelievable statistics. Every year his average went down to like 32, 30, 28, 24, 20 . . . every year descending. Never seen anything like it. The game resumed after fifteen minutes of mayhem, but it was also televised back to New York City. We met the next day before we flew out. Red called the meeting and confronted Bells. "Why didn't you get up? Why weren't you part of your team?" He said, "I didn't think there was anything worth fighting for in basketball." That was it. At that moment we were gonna move Bells, and we had to move Komives, too, to do it. That became the trade for Dave.

**SAM:** And the puzzle solved. Willis could move back to center, where he was better, could pull the big guys out and was tough enough to play them. And Dave made everything work with his defense and toughness, the corner shot and now everyone's—once Bradley gets Cazzie's spot—a playmaker and shooter. The New York basketball nirvana. So sometimes fighting works out. Bells's pacifism creates the championship Knicks. Now, kids, don't try this at home, eh?

# Rick Barry

Rick Barry may have been the most polarizing NBA player ever, and he didn't need a TV show like LeBron James. There have been guys who were loved, hated and loved, like Kobe, Wilt, Kareem, and LeBron, but Barry was different. No one knew quite what to make of the nonstop-talking Rick with the underhand free throws, who remains one of the game's greatest shooters, the player who began the war between leagues, who set clutch playoff scoring records that still stand. Rick was the ultimate Mr. Know-It-All, but he could back it up like few others. He probably invented the point forward position with his unique alchemy of shooting, ballhandling, passing, and defense, the latter better than advertised. He probably got cheated out of the MVP award in 1975. He was second in scoring to winner Bob McAdoo and first in steals. That also came just after Rick was the lone NBA player during the contentious Oscar Robertson suit to testify in Congress against the NBA players. Rick desperately wanted to get back to the NBA from his odyssey in the ABA, though he became that league's greatest scorer, surpassing stars like Julius Erving, George Gervin, Artis Gilmore, and George McGinnis. He ran around like Havlicek and shot like West. Rick was a champion in both leagues, with eight NBA All-Star games and four in the ABA. He led both leagues in scoring and was the only player ever to lead in those two and also the NCAA. He averaged 40.8 points in a six-game losing effort in the 1967 NBA Finals and averaged more in the Finals in a career—over 36 per game—than anyone else. And he was a Finals MVP. When the three-point shot was first introduced in the NBA, in what was his final season, after multiple operations he still was among the top ten in percentage and led the league in attempts. Forget those arguments about how players from previous eras could not compete these days; with his six-seven size, elusiveness, and shooting skills, Barry would have rivaled anyone in today's game. And then he would have let you know.

**PJ:** My all-complaint team: Barry, Heinsohn, Oscar, Elgin, Hayes, and Wilt.

**SAM:** Historically, anyway. You left out LeBron and Dončić. Probably have to include Laimbeer, Chris Paul, and Draymond, the latter for this era.

**PJ:** Rick was terrific. So quick, with this high twitch. Tough to guard. He made this move and had this hesitation or jab step in which he could go by you right or left. I saw a lot of Rick when he was with the Long Island Nets. I thought he was unhappy. Shot a lot, a gunner; didn't shoot a high percentage, but he scored. Wanted the ball in his hands.

**SAM:** I loved the story your buddy Charley Rosen tells about Rick: when he got himself to the Nets with all his craziness in the ABA, jumping what could have been a great Warriors team with a young Nate Thurmond for the Oakland Oaks because his father-in-law was coaching, then the team moving to Washington, as ABA teams went broke every few months then, and then to Virginia, and Rick pisses everyone off saying in an interview he's got to get out because he can't envision his kids growing up saying *y'all*. Charley said Rick was becoming so disgusted with the league and wanting to get back to the NBA—and you know he didn't suffer fools well—he told all his Nets teammates that when he signed, he'd play them each one-on-one for two hundred dollars, and anyone who beats him keeps the whole pot. No one beat him. Perhaps apocryphal.

**PJ:** The Phoenix Suns took them out in the conference finals in '76, the year after the Warriors won the championship. Phoenix had that tough little guard who challenged them physically all the time.

**SAM:** Future Bull Ricky Sobers. That was the famous seventh game when Rick and Sobers got into a fight right when the game started. Supposedly Rick stopped shooting after that because he was mad at his teammates because they didn't run to help him. Like that playoff Game 7 when you came back to the Lakers and Kobe didn't shoot in the second half and you lost after being up 3–1.

**PJ:** There was a game where Kobe didn't take a shot in the first half against Sacramento, and it became kind of big news. He came to me about it and said, "I thought we were playing a team game." I didn't even notice. It wasn't like I was going to take him out, but they were attacking him inside. Maybe he just conformed to it, and it was another level of coaching that I wasn't concerned about this guy.

**SAM:** That was '04 when you and Kobe were at the end for the first time. Rick Barry haunted us in Chicago. That Bulls team was going to the Finals in 1975, and that Warriors team with maybe one All-Star in Rick then sweeps the Bullets for the title after beating the Bulls. The seventies Bulls were this great underrated team because they never won. Never could get by the Bucks with Kareem and the Lakers with

Wilt. So it's '74–'75, Kareem gets pissed off preseason getting poked in the eye and punches the stanchion and breaks his hand. The Bucks finish last and Kareem is demanding a trade and is off to the Lakers after the season. Wilt has retired. The Bulls pull off a deal to get Nate Thurmond, and he gets the first—OK, Wilt and Russell probably had plenty, but they didn't count steals and blocks then—quadruple-double, 22 points, 14 rebounds, 13 assists, and 12 blocks, and Chicago fans are counting a championship already. But Nate was not the same guy. The Bulls were ahead 3–2 in the conference finals in '75 going back home for the golden ticket to their first Finals. The Bulls lose Game 6—the Mother's Day Massacre we still call it in Chicago—and then, the Bulls, leading at halftime by double digits in Game 7 back in Oakland, Rick goes six for seven in the fourth quarter for the Warriors to pull away. It took till '91 for you and Michael and everyone to save the city. Though I have to add, I loved spending time with Rick. Always accessible and cooperative, great stories, photographic mind, one of my favorites ever.

**PJ:** I remember one story I heard when I came to the Knicks. Rick took the ball away from Willis after he grabbed a rebound, and Willis just punched him. Nothing was called. I remember coming to San Francisco for a game and standing around with some players and asking about the Oakland Oaks, and they're saying it's not going well. After I retired, in '82 I went to China with a team Monroe put together with this congressman from Queens, who became New York City comptroller, Then he went to prison. I was coaching in the CBA. So they say, "Phil, you be the coach." We had Cazzie, Bobby Dandridge, Dennis Awtrey, Pistol Pete. Anyway, we get over there and Rick's the only one who brings a partner. Said we're gone twenty-six days and he has to bring his wife, second wife. No one else could. He's like, "I'm not good by myself." Anyway, we get to Hong Kong and then we're going to Canton, Beijing, and we end up in the Philippines. Easter Sunday we're in Hong Kong, beautiful hotel. It's five thirty in the morning and Rick calls me. "Can I come to your room and dry my hair?" What's the deal? He says he doesn't want to wake up his wife. We're leaving for a television appearance at six thirty, so I'm up and you're all screwed up on sleeping anyway. He starts telling me that he had this reputation for hunting women and has been really faithful, so he wants to bring his wife. We continue the conversation, which is dominated by him. That's the first time I really got to know him as a person. Then we ride to the TV studio and do a promo for the game and run into Nancy Reagan, who's also doing a diplomatic thing. Lot of diplomacy on that trip.

# Billy Cunningham

Billy Cunningham was a unicorn, a high-flying playground-phenom white kid from Brooklyn, nicknamed "the Kangaroo Kid," who jumped so high he landed in the NBA-ABA tug-of-war, like Rick Barry. Cunningham became the 76ers' marquee star after they traded Wilt Chamberlain. Billy's career wasn't long because of injuries, capped by a career-ending ACL rupture when he was thirty-two, back when they couldn't do anything with those things. Without any prior experience, he went on to coach the Moses Malone–inspired "Fo', fo', fo'" 1983 champion 76ers, whose motto since the disappointing 1977 Finals loss to Bill Walton and the Trail Blazers had been "We owe you one." Billy later became a part owner of the expansion Miami Heat. He started off his pro career as a high-flying sixth man for the historic 1967 champion 76ers and then post-Wilt averaged more than 23 points and was all-NBA four consecutive seasons before jumping to the ABA Carolina Cougars to play for fellow UNCer Larry Brown. Cunningham, like Rick Barry, signed back with the NBA trying to return, went to court, and lost. So he had to play two seasons with the Cougars. He was ABA Most Valuable Player when Erving, McGinnis, Artis Gilmore, Dan Issel, and teammate Joe Caldwell were flying around the ABA. Cunningham got back to the 76ers in 1974, but early in the 1975–76 season the six-six jumping jack was grounded for good by the shredded knee.

**PJ:** That series we had with the 76ers when Billy got injured was at the time of Martin Luther King's assassination. I remember Barnett saying what a shame it was the league still was playing.

**SAM:** After the 76ers beat you guys, I know they considered a boycott, and Chet Walker always told me he regretted playing, but activism wasn't so welcomed then in the NBA. Game 2 was delayed until after the funeral, and Wilt and Russell attended the funeral. Leonard Koppett wrote about it being the "eeriest, most subdued" sporting event he'd ever been at.

**PJ:** That was also the year the Spectrum roof collapsed and we had to play at the Palestra. Played another game somewhere else, Convention Hall. We had that two-overtimes game where Cazzie got 40 points and we lost; he was incredible. Cunningham drove to the basket, hit the standard, and broke his wrist and was out the rest of the playoffs. We still lost in six. Cazzie scored a ton of points and Bellamy fouled out, and then Willis fouled out—fouling Chamberlain on purpose—and I ended up playing a little bit at center. We won the next game. The next game we played in another different building; we didn't play in the Spectrum. Then they came back and beat us on our home court to take the series 4–2 and Hal Greer had this big game. Cunningham was a really effective player, all drive left and hanging; he had a little bit of an Elgin-type game. He'd chase his own rebound down if he missed—the Kangaroo Kid.

**SAM:** I remember talking to Billy about the New York playground game once. He said when he got to Philly he thought they shot better, but the New York kids were better drivers because of the wind. No indoor gyms to play in, so everyone played outside. He went to Erasmus Hall High School, where Jerry Reinsdorf went, though Jerry couldn't jump. That's why those great New York City guards couldn't shoot. They were always attacking the basket because it was too windy. Though when I think of Jerry and his basketball, I always remember the story he tells of complaining about why your guys were missing so many free throws, and you told him that's all the little Jewish guys would talk about because that's all they could do in basketball. I have to admit that mirrors my experience.

# Dave Bing

Just think how good Dave Bing would have been if he could have seen properly. Bing's probably just on the edge of the top-seventy-five vote, but perhaps grandfathered in like Bill Walton as a top-fifty guy. That sentimental NBA. When they counted the votes for the top seventy-five, it seemed like they didn't want to embarrass anyone by dropping them after being in the top fifty. Which seemed reasonable, though they might have kept in Joe Fulks and Bob Davies from the twenty-five-year team, who didn't make the cut to fifty. Bing has historic credentials, seven All-Star teams, Rookie of the Year, a scoring championship, and All-Star MVP. Though perhaps superseding all that are the groundbreaking elements, an NBA renaissance man if there ever was one, founding a multimillion-dollar steel company and conglomerate and becoming mayor of Detroit. This was a man who could see the future. If not always peripherally. At five years old it didn't seem like he'd see anything anymore. His left eye was pierced by a nail during play, his family in Washington, DC, too poor to afford surgery. So they relied on, and hoped for, natural healing. His vision became good enough for Bing to earn a basketball scholarship to Syracuse, where he became one of the nation's leading scorers. He quickly made the Detroit Pistons get over their disappointment when they lost the first draft coin flip in NBA history and the chance to draft Michigan star Cazzie Russell. Player/coach Dave

DeBusschere worked the rookie into the starting lineup, and Bing averaged 20 points to become Rookie of the Year, then 27 per game as a sophomore to lead the NBA. Then, after being among the league's leading scorers the next three seasons, during the 1971–72 preseason Bing was poked in the other eye by a teammate and suffered a detached retina. The medical advice was to retire or risk losing his eyesight. He played on and didn't miss a game the following season, averaging 22.4 points. After a financial dispute, he was traded to Washington in 1975 and finished his playing career in 1977–78 with the Boston Celtics, which for Dave Bing was just the end of the beginning.

**PJ:** Dave Bing, nice speedy motor, solid player. I did like his game, but they didn't have the team to put it together. Hard dribble and into his shot, a little like Jerry West. Eddie Miles, the man with the golden arm, was there. I remember having to chase him down and him having the speed, and you'd have to run him down, which Cowens did to Frazier all the time, except Walt had this trick. He'd slow up and Cowens would run over him, foul, and ride him to the basket for the three-point play. My teammate Dave DeBusschere was coach when Bing was drafted.

**SAM:** I know there was Oscar and Lenny and Guy Rodgers, but wasn't there still this taboo, at least a little and certainly in football, that Black players couldn't run a team?

**PJ:** Lenny and Oscar were at the peak of their games when I came in the league. Bing led the league in scoring. Guy Rodgers was leading the league in assists that year.

**SAM:** With the expansion Bulls, actually. Still the only season-assists leader they've ever had. Guy invented the backdoor lob with Don Kojis.

Which takes me to my go-to that Johnny Kerr remains the greatest omission from the Hall of Fame debate. Johnny was three times an All-Star playing in the same conference as Wilt and Russell—he was the original iron man, an NBA champion who finished with more than 10,000 points and rebounds, a career double-double, and went on to be Coach of the Year, recruited Dr. J and George Gervin to the ABA, and was the ultimate NBA toastmaster who never met a hotel bar he couldn't dominate. Oh, right, you were saying, DeBusschere.

**PJ:** Dave was going through a lot there. They'd just moved to Detroit. Didn't they have a guy that was also a referee that was their coach? He also invented that game where you push a button and the ball pops out of the hole in the board. What was his name?

**SAM:** Charley Eckman, a few coaches before Dave. Eckman officiated the All-Star game, and a few years later he was coaching the West team after his Pistons made the Finals in back-to-back seasons. The Pistons fired him in Detroit twenty-five games in, and he went back to officiating.

**PJ:** I do know Dickie McGuire was with the Pistons, a little earlier. He told me a story of this kid who jumped straight from high school to the NBA, a seven-footer, who was banned from the league for various situations, a street kid who was talented.

**SAM:** Reggie Harding, one of the classics in the NBA. Was briefly with the Bulls in their second season, then tried the ABA for a bit until he was released for threatening to kill the team's GM while doing an interview. That was Mike Storen, who started in the NBA selling tickets for the expansion Chicago Zephyrs and eventually became ABA commissioner and was part of the merger. One of his children, Hannah Storm, has been a longtime ESPN anchor. The famous story was that

Reggie as a kid in Detroit was doing stickups. He hit the same store a third time and the manager goes, "C'mon, Reg, I know it's you." Reggie goes, "It ain't me, man." Reggie was known to fire a gun at the feet of teammates to see if they could dance.

**PJ:** Reggie used to sit in the stands and yell down to the players, "I'm coming, I'm getting you next year, I'll be back in the league." The stories surrounded him. DeBusschere's the coach, twenty-four, twenty-five years old.

**SAM:** The next season DeBusschere is traded to the New York Knicks, and he is the final piece, and Dave Bing is on the way to national Minority Small Business Person of the Year and the cleanup of Detroit continues. Reggie Harding was shot to death on a Detroit street in 1972.

GEORGE MIKAN. George was from the Chicago area and played at DePaul for Ray Meyer, the teacher who created an NBA monster. George may have impacted the game more than anyone in NBA history. He was so dominant, the league extended the lane from six to twelve feet and actually played a regular season game with a twelve-foot-high basket—instead of the regular ten feet—as an experiment that lasted one game in an attempt to counter George's effect.

DOLPH SCHAYES. One of the last great practitioners of the two-hand set shot who made Syracuse the most famous basketball city in New York State at the time. He began the succession of elite rebounding and scoring front-court players that continued with Bob Pettit through Elvin Hayes and Tim Duncan.

PAUL ARIZIN. The first of the great jump-shooting scorers who, when his Philadelphia Warriors moved to San Francisco (Golden State) because of NBA economics at the time, remained in his beloved Philadelphia to retain his executive job with IBM despite being an All-Star in every one of his NBA seasons. Talk about love of the game, Arizin then played professional minor league basketball for several years and was Eastern League MVP.

BOB COUSY. Known as "the Houdini of the Hardwood" in the nickname alliteration era, Cousy basically was, at least for the NBA post–Harlem Globetrotters, the inventor of entertainment basketball, with fancy passing and ball handling for the dynasty Boston Celtics of the 1960s.

**BOB PETTIT.** He was the prototype power forward who essentially began the modern era at the position, with a relentless scoring and rebounding game that enabled his St. Louis Hawks to be the only team ever to defeat Bill Russell's Boston Celtics in the NBA Finals.

**ELGIN BAYLOR.** Look where he is: well above the rim as the first great athlete of the game to begin the mirage of being suspended in midair that became the legends of Dr. J and Michael Jordan. Elgin was the first acrobat of the game, who performed the amazing feat of averaging 38.2 and 18.6 in 48 games in a season during which he was in the military and could only play on weekend leaves.

HAL GREER. One of the best pure jump shooters in NBA history who could put 'em up there with the likes of Steph Curry, because no one maybe ever attempted more jump shots, Greer even shooting them on his free throws. He also was the mostly anonymous second leading scorer to Wilt on the famous 1967 Philadelphia team that stopped Boston's run of eight straight titles.

WILT CHAMBERLAIN. The amazing Wilt of the 100-point NBA game and averaging 50 points for an entire season almost didn't go to the NBA. With a four-year "college" requirement, Wilt left the University of Kansas after three years of quadruple-teaming and played one year for the Harlem Globetrotters, then a bigger basketball draw than the NBA. Wilt occasionally returned in summers to play for the Globetrotters.

BILL RUSSELL AND WILT CHAMBERLAIN. The game's greatest rivalry. If you watched the NBA in the sixties, that's what you saw since Wilt vs. Russell was the NBA's TV offering basically every week. Like Wilt once griped, no one loves Goliath. It was the classic Goliath against the determined army of Davids, Wilt in the matchups scoring twice as many points as Bill Russell. But Russell and his Celtics were 86–57 in the matchups between the two.

LENNY WILKENS. The crafty left-handed playmaking guard was enshrined in the Basketball Hall of Fame as both a player and coach and was also the rare player/coach. He was celebrated for his star playing in the NBA's then south in St. Louis, where, despite All-Star status, he wasn't permitted in restaurants with his teammates, and later, as a coach, directed one of the great championship upset runs for the Seattle SuperSonics.

DAVE DeBUSSCHERE. He played Major League Baseball and in the NBA during the same years and still was pitching in the minors when he became player/coach for his NBA Detroit Pistons. His trade to the New York Knicks in 1968 galvanized that franchise as the so-called final puzzle piece that led to two championships in the Knicks' best run in their history.

JOHN HAVLICEK. He was the iron man with endless stamina who would run all day, the everyman forward of eight Boston Celtics championship teams and a bridge between the Bill Russell and Dave Cowens title eras, who was involved in some of the franchise's most legendary plays, including the famous 1965 "Havlicek stole the ball!"

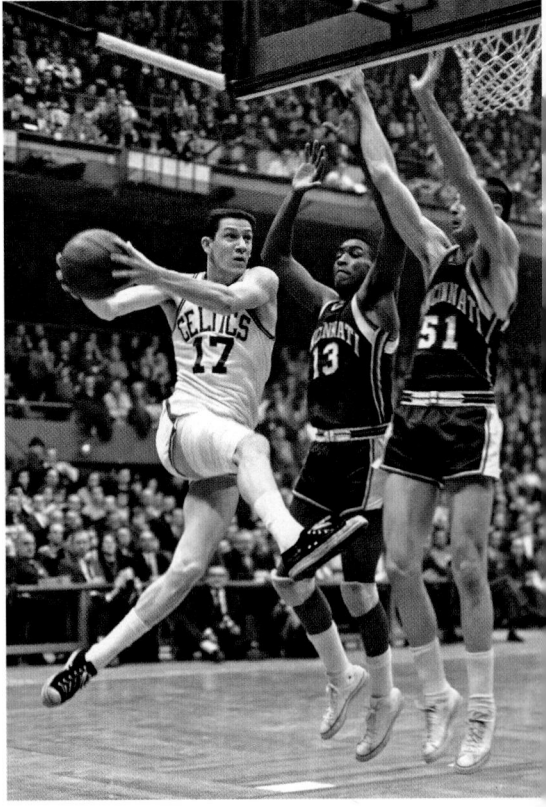

JERRY LUCAS. He was one of the most awaited and celebrated prep players and eventually an NBA champion with the New York Knicks as an elite rebounding and shooting forward who was even more well-known as a memory savant who'd appear on network TV memorizing the New York City phone book or spelling words backward faster than you could spell forward.

WILLIS REED. The famed captain of the legendary championship 1970s New York Knicks, whose courageous return for Game 7 of the 1970 Finals remains the stuff of NBA and New York legend; a mild-mannered man who was the toughest guy on the basketball court.

**EARL MONROE AND WALT FRAZIER.** The exciting guards eventually became unexpected teammates for the champion 1973 New York Knicks. But the matchups of the übercool Clyde in New York and the white-hot "Black Magic" Monroe for the Baltimore Bullets were among the best of the era.

**ELVIN HAYES.** He played in perhaps the most famous collegiate game, the first big TV production in the Astrodome, beating UCLA's dynasty and Kareem Abdul-Jabbar, then Lew Alcindor. He was one of the game's most prolific rebounders and scorers with a reputation for coming up small at the biggest times.

**KAREEM ABDUL-JABBAR.**
His sky hook is considered the
most unstoppable shot in basketball
annals. His fluidly efficient play
masked by a practiced detachment
generally leaves him out of where
he belongs, in the debate among the
greatest ever in the game.

**DAVE COWENS.** He helped
popularize the era of the small
big man, his oft-televised
legendary head first sliding
across the court chasing a
loose ball, typifying his manic
play. A sporting iconoclast
who took odd jobs, like taxi
driver, during his playing
career to experience what fans
went through often proved
as perplexing for his team as
opponents while leading the
Celtics to the first post-Russell
titles.

BILL WALTON. The greatest coulda, shoulda, who woulda been in that debate with Jordan, LeBron, Kareem, and maybe Wilt and Russell, if not for more than thirty foot surgeries. The seven-footer was a bygone-era Nikola Jokić, capable of being the best scorer, rebounder, and passer in the game. Through high school and college his teams went undefeated in more than 140 consecutive games. Injuries shortened his pro career after a 1977 title with Portland, and he then overcame a lifelong stutter to become one of the most verbose sports commentators for multiple networks.

PETE MARAVICH. The Lakers invented Showtime for a franchise, but the moniker was most appropriate for the Louisiana kid with the floppy socks and mop of hair. The highest scoring collegiate player ever, averaging 44 points without a three-point line, Maravich was the greatest showman of the game, equal parts Globetrotters and Houdini.

**GEORGE GERVIN.**
The jazz-cool scoring
guard became known
as "the Iceman" for his
languid scoring style
and smooth finger roll
shot. Most of his points
came in the old ABA
after he was essentially
blackballed by the NBA
after a fight in college as
he had to work his way
out of the basketball
minor leagues.

**MOSES MALONE.** The first
modern-era player to go directly
from high school to the pros—then
to the nascent ABA—was one of the
greatest rebounders despite being an
undersized center at six ten known for
his relentless pursuit of his own team's
missed shots. Though playing for ten
teams in his career, he was a three-
time NBA Most Valuable Player.

**LARRY BIRD.** Bird's rivalry with Magic Johnson often is credited for an NBA revival to the prosperous modern era of the game. Bird was an insouciant master of the jump shot, the pass, and the playful so-called trash talk that stretches from the playgrounds to the pros.

ISIAH THOMAS. Thomas and buddy Magic Johnson elevated the game with their All-Star highlight shows that captivated fans when the midseason games mattered. Thomas was the leader of the infamous Detroit Pistons Bad Boys, who won consecutive championships and the enmity of opponents, and he is often considered the game's greatest little man at barely six feet.

MICHAEL JORDAN AND SCOTTIE PIPPEN. Often considered the most dominating two-player combination in NBA history, Jordan the best offensive player in his era and Pippen often regarded as the best defender, the yin and yang of Bulls basketball that produced six championships in eight seasons. There was Shaq and Kobe and Steph and Klay, but none rivaled Jordan and Pippen.

SHAQUILLE O'NEAL AND KOBE BRYANT. The Lakers' star-crossed stars, the game's then most dominant center and most creative and exciting guard, were on the way to a longtime dynasty with three consecutive titles before internal rivalries caused a bitter divorce, with O'Neal moving on to a championship in Miami and Bryant eventually recovering with two titles with Pau Gasol in LA.

DIRK NOWITZKI AND STEVE NASH. Their pick-and-roll game when they were teammates in Dallas set the template for NBA play for years to come, Nowitzki eventually winning a title with the Mavericks and Nash being traded to Phoenix, where under coach Mike D'Antoni began the small ball, three-point shooting NBA revolution.

TIM DUNCAN AND DAVID ROBINSON. The San Antonio twin towers, both league MVPs, began a run of five championships for their Spurs that bookended the Lakers' era with Shaq, Kobe, and Pau. The voluble Robinson and the taciturn Duncan were two of the most resourceful big men in the game.

KEVIN DURANT AND LEBRON JAMES. The two most prolific scoring players of the NBA's twenty-first century didn't produce a rivalry because they didn't meet in the playoffs often enough, as both changed teams frequently in the James-inspired peripatetic era. But they stood out for their scoring, with each winning multiple championships.

STEPHEN CURRY. The game's greatest ever shooter, no longer much debated, led the change in the game to the three-point era despite being an undersized, six-two guard who was a weak defender and supposedly too small for shooting guard and who couldn't pass well enough for point guard—to then become the all-time three-point-shooting leader and arguably one of the game's ten or fifteen greatest ever.

CARMELO ANTHONY. The longtime Knicks and Denver Nuggets forward was one of the best scorers in the game, averaging more than 20 per game in each of his first fifteen seasons and for USA basketball in the Olympics trailing only Kevin Durant in career points and rebounding.

# Walt Frazier

Walt Frazier's nickname came from the sixties movie *Bonnie and Clyde*. Frazier admitted he was two different guys. The shy kid from Georgia with the house filled with sisters, the small college guy who came to the big city, like Clark Kent, put on a fedora, and became Clyde, the cat burglar of the basketball courts, the man with the fastest hands and vocabulary since Ali, whose brilliance lit up New York. And then he was gone like heat lightning. But it was brilliant to see, a pair of NBA championships, one of the ultimate partnerships with "Black Magic" Earl Monroe, six times all-NBA, seven times first team all-defense, the star of the famous Willis Reed Game 7 in the 1970 Finals when Willis limped out to make two baskets and Clyde took the baton for 36 points, 19 assists, 7 rebounds, and 6 or 7 steals—though they weren't officially counting them then—denying Wilt and Elgin and Mr. Clutch yet again in one of the most historic games in NBA annals. Frazier had six straight seasons averaging more than 20 points. Then, slowed by injuries—he never was the big-time, high-flying athlete type—a few years later he was surprisingly jettisoned by the Knicks for Jim Cleamons, to Cleveland where they didn't much appreciate fashion. Or his game, anymore. But what a game it was. Clyde was the gentleman thief of basketball, slowing up on the fast break so Dave Cowens would plow over him, timing the flops in Pistol Pete's mop of hair so that when it dropped over his eyes Clyde would snake in for the steal. He was Joe Willie in short pants on the court and sable or chinchilla off. His game was poetry, and then he expanded his couplets to the broadcasting booth with the lyrical touch of his game.

**PJ:** Archibald and some of those other quicker guys gave him trouble. Not a lot of lift, a lot of lateral movement. He had an arthritic big toe, and that limited what he could do. I don't know if he sprained it, had turf toe, or whatever happened, but he used to put this liquid heat on it before he'd go out and play. His locker was right next to mine. I was in between Willis and Walt. We had some great battles with the Bulls, Van Lier and Sloan, who Walt knew from college, same conference. Van Lier, if you're not careful, would step in front of you and fall down, draw a charge. Walt developed an ability to shoot. He was a workman about his game. He knew how to drive. Could go either way. He was really good at getting guys off the floor. Walt was living down there in the Garment District, stayed at the Claremont, right there on the corner of Thirty-Eighth. Stayed there for a number of years until he got an apartment up on the East Side.

**SAM:** Not an Algonquin Round Table guy?

**PJ:** It was the evolution of Walt. I remember training camp. It's midnight. "Walt, want to play cards?" "No, see you in morning." He was practicing vocabulary; he was reading the dictionary and thesaurus. Had a bit of a speech impediment and had five sisters, so wasn't likely able to get a word in edgewise. I'd always kid him about being slow to speak, deliberate. Yet he had these catlike capabilities, particularly defensively. He was physically strong, six three, six four, not tall but a big guard. For the most part, people didn't want to play Walt. He was right in the Garment District. *Bonnie and Clyde* came out, and that became a moniker for him. He became Clyde.

**SAM:** I remembered that story. Danny Whelan, the trainer, supposedly called him that when Walt comes into the locker room one day with that fedora, technically a Borsalino hat, which was rabbit hair, fancier. Barnett supposedly kept asking him if he was shopping at Goodwill now.

**PJ:** There was a furrier down there who had his number. He got an elephant coat, a seal coat. Had maybe seven or eight. Mink, ermine, elephant. That elephant coat must've weighed twenty-five pounds. You had to be a man just to put it on. The Garment District was much bigger than Wall Street then.

**SAM:** Walt became famous for that Game 7, though.

**PJ:** I was at the game but couldn't play. He had like 36 points and whatever, assists and steals, maybe 8. He had to guard Jerry West. You thought the building was actually rocking. I was always hanging out in the locker room that season, and I did color broadcasting with a guy Wolff, who was a famous broadcaster. Did Don Larsen's perfect game. I'd had back surgery. I was supposed to be back maybe in December. They had that run when they won eighteen straight and they were leading the league and everything was going hunky-dory. And then expansion was coming up, three teams coming in. So they just kept me on the injured list so they wouldn't have to put me on the expansion list.

**SAM:** You came in with Clyde, right?

**PJ:** Frazier and I walked into San Francisco from Oakland one time, walked the streets in San Francisco our rookie year. Walt got approached on the street by a guy, a hustler, who was going to sell him a ring. He was a little naive, Georgia, Southern Illinois, shy. "I got a diamond ring here." Walt took it into a telephone booth to see if it could scratch the glass. He bought the ring for like ninety bucks. But it was fake. Now we get to the game that night, our legs were dead, two guys not very sophisticated. Bellamy on the road would invite us up. Bellamy had skis for feet. He had his foot taped—it was like a mummy's foot—and then he wore like four pairs of socks. So he had, like, these pillows in these shoes. So he could run straight forward, but he wasn't much of a lateral guy. So Red would put Willis at center, myself at power forward, Cazzie, small forward, or Dick Van Arsdale, a great defensive player, and Frazier and Emmette Bryant at guard. And we played pressure defense. And we had the best record in the NBA the last part of the season after Red came in. The first day Red gets the job, Red goes, "These plays, I wipe my ass with them and throw them in the garbage can. That's not gonna win games. What's gonna win games is defense." And from that day on, we played full-court pressure defense. The next year, it didn't go that well, and that's when we made the trade for DeBusschere.

**SAM:** That's when you lit up the city; New York was always baseball first with the three teams, but basketball was the city game.

**PJ:** I remember the day I came to New York. Red picks me up at the airport. Got in the car and drove down the Van Wyck, going underneath an overpass, and a kid leaned over the top of the railing and threw a rock and broke his window. Red took a breath and said, "Ya know, living in New York is not always that easy. Sometimes things happen that are very disrupting, but we carry on here." He told me you live in the suburbs, you make sure you have a chore you can also do. Selma was in the car and had a lampshade to take in to fix. So he dropped me off and said goodbye.

**SAM:** But he really was the one who gave you your coaching base.

**PJ:** One time I look at Red and said, "Where did you get such a deep tan?" He said, "Well, I coach in Puerto Rico in the summertime." He's an assistant coach, so he needed to make money down in Puerto Rico. He ended up coaching the team that Tex Winter had coached in Puerto Rico. Tex and Johnny Bach were the first two coaches in Puerto Rico. Red brought back some of Tex's teachings and I followed.

# Earl Monroe

Before there was the Pistol and Doc and Magic, there was Black Magic, the man who brought the playground, the entertainment, the style, and the reality to the NBA. Earl Monroe was far from the first Black player when he entered the NBA a decade after Bill Russell and almost two after Chuck Cooper. But Monroe, Black Jesus in South Philly and to Spike Lee and Denzel Washington in *He Got Game*, represented the beginning of the change in the NBA from the corporate world to the people. You'd pay to see Earl Monroe play, as you would for just a dozen or so over the history of the NBA, the players who had you jumping out of your seat with those "Did you see that?" moments. Michael, Pistol, Julius, Steph, Kobe, Nique, Hawk, and not too many others. One was Earl Monroe, the jazz aficionado whose play was similarly improvisational. After his career Monroe even started a record label named Reverse Spin. It was Monroe's dribble, something no one had seen before or since, hand on top of the ball and never palming but spinning with the dribble right and left—his drive to his little pull-up shot was as indefensible as any of the great shots.

Too street for the college game in the segregated sixties, he couldn't get a serious basketball scholarship and ended up at Division II Winston-Salem in North Carolina, where a rumpled scout named Jerry Krause, who'd developed a relationship with Coach Big House Gaines, was touting the phenomenon to his

Baltimore Bullets. With burly center Wes Unseld, the dean of the outlet pass-ers, drafted the next year, the Bullets became a force and something to see, Unseld on the wing to Earl. NBA television was rare in those days and surely for a team in Baltimore. So Monroe's legend just grew as fans clamored to get a glimpse. His Bullets' playoff matchups with the Knicks became lost classics, arguably the greatest five-on-five rivalry matchups in NBA history. It was Mon-roe versus Frazier, Kevin Loughery and Dick Barnett, Jack Marin and Bill Brad-ley, Gus Johnson and Dave DeBusschere, Unseld and Willis Reed, All-Stars at virtually every position, eight of ten Hall of Famers, nobody to play off, the greatest isolations back and forth. They had a pair of classic seven-game series before Monroe jumped the Bullets in a salary dispute, common in the era with the ABA bidding wars. And so the unimaginable came: Monroe was traded to the rival and hated Knicks to pair with Walt Frazier in what was called the Rolls-Royce Backcourt; both drove Rolls. Critics insisted it never could work as both were ball-oriented players. Monroe was sitting in but allowing Clyde to have the solo. Then Red Holzman told Monroe, "We want you to be great, so get your ego back and play how you used to play against us." The Knicks then went on to win the 1973 NBA title. Knee problems, likely from too much street ball on those concrete playgrounds, caught up with Monroe. He was Rookie of the Year, four times an All-Star, and one of a handful of players in the history of the NBA whom you had to see.

**PJ:** Earl had to accommodate the rest of the Knicks and be part of a team rather than be the scorer or star. He came in the league, leading scorer in college, and had this game. It really was accentuated the next year when Unseld came to the Bullets. Great rebounder, and he could throw it to half-court, where Earl was there and he could do what he wanted to do against the defense before the rest of the team could get down. That was their key. He needed space because he was a spinner, and we always tried to keep them in the half-court. I showed the film of one of those playoff games to kids at a camp I was doing, and I asked them, "What did you think about that, you guys? There wasn't one dunk in the game." No one dunked the ball. That wasn't part of the game.

**SAM:** No dunking, no trash-talking?

**PJ:** First kid I remember trash-talking was a Long Beach player, and then he was in Seattle maybe for two seasons. Then the guy became a bodyguard for Idi Amin and disappeared.

**SAM:** John Brisker, legendary ABA stories guy, pulling guns on teammates, ending practices chasing guys with a gun. Nothing like the ABA.

**PJ:** Earl had this little dance. I think playing soccer had a little something to do with it, like a soccer player dribbling the ball, coming at you, and all of a sudden he was around you. There was a guy at Duquesne who people talked about when I got to New York, an NBA player for a short time who was very flamboyant, Black kid who was six four. But at that time it was all about the jumpers, like Pogo Joe from Arizona. Cazzie Russell was supposed to be the next Oscar, but Cazzie was a face-up player.

**SAM:** The Duquesne guy was the famous Sihugo Green. He was a talented guard but a trivia answer in a negative way, because he was the guy Rochester took with the number 1 pick in '56 ahead of Bill Russell. That was the agreed-to deal. Red wants Russell, so he trades Ed Macauley and Cliff Hagan to the Hawks, who aren't paying Russell anyway and don't really want the Black guy in St. Louis for the number 2 draft pick. Rochester has number 1 and are cash-strapped so probably can't pay Russell, who has a big offer from the Globetrotters but doesn't want to play there. So supposedly the Celtics owner offers the Rochester guy the Ice Capades for a few weeks so he can fill his arena in Rochester if he'll pass on Russell. He's got Maurice Stokes, who they figure is as good as Russell and is averaging like 18 and 18 but has that accident in the playoffs for Cincinnati a few years later and is paralyzed. Rochester needs a guard to run with Stokes, who was a LeBron-type guy for that era. And Green was pretty good. His team won the NIT, which then was bigger than the NCAA, and he averaged something like 24 as a senior when Duquesne was a big-time program. I'd heard one time that Earl, who went through a lot, sometimes wore one black sneaker and one white.

**PJ:** I never felt any kind of racial animosity from Earl. It kind of bristled off Cazzie.

**SAM:** Cazzie was South Side of Chicago, so no surprise what he might have gone through back then. I remember hearing this heartwarming story Bradley told about how all those years after him replacing Cazzie and you guys winning and thinking Cazzie was bitter and how overcome Bill was to see Cazzie at some function and Cazzie was embracing him.

**PJ:** Bellamy was the humorist who used racial innuendos all the time. Nate Bowman, too. I remember Natalie Cole was traveling with him for a while. We were always going up to Harlem and hanging out, meeting up with Dean Meminger and Earl.

**SAM:** I don't think it still was the quotas anymore. But stuff went on in the Southern cities, Cincy and St. Louis or Atlanta.

**PJ:** I roomed right away with Walt Frazier. We had this one white player, Howie Komives, who used to get into the racial arguments with Cazzie. They'd be in the middle of the floor jawing at each other. Howie would retort, "Don't tell me your tough life. My mom was a widow. She raised her boys. Had to work two jobs." He was, like, the leading scorer in the nation in college. Tough guy. So we're having this dinner, Van Arsdale, Komives, myself, another teammate, eight of us in the party. Komives doesn't show up. Then he and his wife come in about a half hour late and he's got a bloody nose. You might remember New York was an antagonistic place. People would accost you on the street. He says, "This guy came and held me up. So I just started fighting with him. And the fucking guy took my wallet anyways. Got away from me. But I got a couple good punches in and stuff." I'm like, "Howie, just give him the money and walk away next time."

**SAM:** Fun city.

# Elvin Hayes

There may not have been a more paradoxical great player in NBA history than Elvin Hayes. Hayes just about never missed a game, playing in more than thirteen hundred in his regular-season career and thus missing just nine games in sixteen seasons, the first twelve of which he was named an All-Star. But his reputation was to almost never excel in big games, frustrating teammates and coaches. The durable Hayes was a shy kid with a speech impediment, but he spoke loudly on the basketball court. He played fifty thousand minutes over those sixteen seasons and never fewer than eighty games in a season. He was all-NBA six times and all-defense twice and a league scoring champion and twice a rebounding leader. He burst into the league when the Rockets were in San Diego, averaging about 28 points and 17 rebounds for a team rarely even getting close to making the playoffs. Hayes in his thirteenth game as a rookie scored 54 points in the third game of a back-to-back-to-back, the previous game on the road in Chicago when he had 40 and 20. He played forty-eight minutes in both games. But with Hayes challenging coaches, his Rockets teams never reached .500 until he practically was given away in a trade to the then–Baltimore Bullets for Jack Marin. Then, teaming with the fierce Wes Unseld, who beat out Hayes for Rookie of the Year despite Hayes averaging 28.4 points and 17.1 rebounds, Hayes finally got that NBA championship in 1978.

There may never have been a greater rebounding duo than he and Unseld, the way Hayes could track a ball like Walton or Rodman. In college, Hayes was the star of the Game of the Century in the Houston Astrodome in 1968 when his Houston team, with Hayes getting 39 and 15, ended UCLA and then–Lew Alcindor's forty-seven-game winning streak. UCLA won the rematch later that season. But that first game was attended by more than fifty thousand, and the national TV extravaganza was considered the beginning of the age of big-time broadcast collegiate sports.

**PJ:** Elvin was one who just didn't like the pressure of the game. I had a lot of trouble when he hit that turnaround jump shot, would bank it off the backboard. He'd drive to his right when he turned round, fade off the block. Shoot a little hook shot going to the basket. Great scorer, let's face it.

**SAM:** Had that fadeaway shot, which a lot of great players did, like Wilt, Garnett, LeBron. But you also wondered if they were shooting it to avoid going to the line, having to stand there in front of everyone. I loved the story you told me when they were moving to Houston, and Tex was Rockets coach and is trying to persuade Elvin that it's great to come back home to Texas, and Tex is saying Elvin will love the cafeteria buffets. But Elvin killed Tex; probably ended Tex's NBA head-coaching career. Would refuse to go into games, always complaining. But then he actually completes the Bullets, though it took a few years because they needed Bobby Dandridge to make the clutch shots. Gene Shue, then Bullets coach, would joke that it was not a straight-up trade. He'd say they got Elvin's psychiatrist, also. Elvin was so frustrating no one hid the barbs. So the Bullets win and owner Abe Pollin puts together a trip for the players to China, and Elvin is cranky again.

They get to the Great Wall and Elvin won't get off the bus. He says he's seen walls before.

**PJ:** Dick Motta had me down to his camp in Dillon, Montana. He has a summer home in Bear Lake just south of Yellowstone Park. He had a little basketball camp up there. Hundred kids or so. I drove down. "Congratulations, Dick, you won the championships, da da da." He says, "Never would have won it if Elvin Hayes hadn't been in foul trouble." He said, "Fortunately we had Mitch Kupchak and we had Wes." Mitch got a big contract after that championship.

**SAM:** Mitch actually was one of the first big free agents after the Robertson suit settlement. Magic was pushing for him. Said if they got him, Boston was done. Then Mitch gets hurt and is out almost two years.

**PJ:** Our crew was sliding. We still had the guys, but we were decimated by '76. Elvin almost didn't play in Game 7. They played this guy Kozlofski.

**SAM:** Tom Kozelko, played a few seasons off the bench from Toledo, the basketball powerhouse.

**PJ:** Elvin says he was sick Game 7. He was OK the day before. Said he had the flu.

**SAM:** K.C. was coaching that year, and the story was Elvin asked out early in the game in the second quarter and Kozelko scores 11 points to keep the Bullets in it, though Elvin did play a lot in the game, just didn't do much. Dick, when he talked about it years later, said he thought Elvin just couldn't deal with the pressure of that kind of game on the road.

**PJ:** I don't even know how we won enough games to be ahead of Washington. They had Phil Chenier, Hayes, Unseld; that little guard, Kevin Porter, came in and saved that crew of guys.

**SAM:** We had no idea who he was, Kozelko. Gets 19 in that Game 7, Elvin has 12. You always said Gianelli gave Elvin trouble. Look, Elvin was the Big E; he could score, but you always heard all this other stuff. I remember the joke Motta used to tell about Hayes, that he had this recurring dream. He'd be jogging peacefully and suddenly from nowhere out jumps Elvin Hayes. But Dick also wasn't the most popular guy when he was Bulls coach. Basically blew up that seventies Bulls team, turning on players who held out prior to that season, like Van Lier and Love. Said if they didn't, they would have won more than Golden State and had home-court advantage for Game 7. Told the other players to deny them playoff shares. Dick was always getting fined by the league for his outbursts. One of my favorites was he gets suspended, so to show up the league, he makes the trainer interim coach. Trainer goes 2–1. He was tough, but I do think he deserves to be a Hall of Famer.

# Wes Unseld

**W**es Unseld developed an empirical philosophy about basketball when he was one of the most sought-after prep players in the nation, averaging 25 points and 21 rebounds for two state-title teams, and then as a college freshman at Louisville, where he averaged 36 points and 24 rebounds per game when freshmen were not yet eligible for varsity play. Everyone was happy when the team won, but everyone was really happy when they scored and felt they contributed to the team's success. So Westley Unseld, the burly six-seven son of a former boxer and Negro League baseball player, reasoned that anyone could score, but not everyone could rebound, set screens, and pass the ball. So Wes Unseld set out to become the purest of fundamental NBA players, the ultimate player who made his teammates better. He did it by rebounding the ball for them, sixth all-time at 14 per game; by his unselfish play, sixth all-time in assists for a center; despite his career being limited by knee problems, the greatest outlet passer in NBA history; and setter of some of the most powerful screens, which looked almost cartoonish the way players bounced off like crash dummies. And when called upon, like when the then–Washington Bullets won the only championship in franchise history in 1978, it was Unseld with a follow-up score getting his team to the Finals against the Seattle SuperSonics, and then in Game 7 in Seattle with scoring star Elvin Hayes long fouled out, it was Unseld, a relatively poor free-throw shooter, making the two pressure free throws for the victory.

The Washington franchise that began in Chicago in 1961 and traveled through Baltimore never could match the Unseld playing years. They'd never won more than thirty-eight games until Unseld was drafted number 2 overall in 1968 after Elvin Hayes. Who, by the way, then became the only player other than Wilt to win Rookie of the Year and MVP in the same season. Perhaps no player, other than Bill Russell, Michael Jordan, and LeBron James, has had such an effect on an NBA franchise. Unseld was Finals MVP in 1978 even though he averaged 9 points in the seven games, the fewest ever for an MVP. He was an All-Star five times, and in his first five seasons, before knee problems, Unseld never averaged fewer than 15.9 rebounds per game. After his playing career, the stoic, fierce-looking man with the biggest heart was a longtime executive and head coach for the Bullets/Wizards. Perhaps his greatest assist was funding the private K–8 Unselds' School, one of the players, along with David Robinson and LeBron, who started a school.

**PJ:** The best guy at throwing an outlet pass I'd ever seen. No one has ever seen it like that. Next guy that was really good at that was Benoit Benjamin. Throw it to half-court on a line.

**SAM:** That got Pearl cookin' with his spin drives in transition. I remember Wes saying he'd check the wing guy for a pass, but if he saw the defender overplaying his guy, he would know to release and he'd flick it full court. Walton was great at that and Kevin Love did it, maybe not quite that good. Jokić now. People would be surprised to hear Benoit. Got a bad rap with his attitude. Wes always seemed aloof and unapproachable but typically selfless with the mentality of a point guard. He'd say it was embarrassing to talk about himself.

# Kareem Abdul-Jabbar

There are perhaps three players in the history of the NBA in the conversation to be considered the GOAT, the Greatest of All Time: Michael Jordan and LeBron James, about whom the popular debate continues, and Kareem Abdul-Jabbar. Abdul-Jabbar isn't much included in the bar and talk-radio debate, less for when he was in his prime—the 1970s and early 1980s—than for his adversarial relationship with, well, people, those who wrote and talked about the NBA and those who watched. Abdul-Jabbar really wasn't the aloof, grim polarizing figure he's often depicted to be. His Bucks teammate Jon McGlocklin said Kareem could be a merry prankster around teammates, often switching shirts in lockers, once slicing off the ponytail of a sleeping media member, one time putting a teammate's son on top of a locker so no one could find him. A Lakers teammate said Kareem once put so much hair remover on Michael Cooper he had a bald spot for months. He once put a pair of panties in a teammate's gym bag when the wife was showing up. Few outside the locker room sanctum saw that sort of thing. There have been better cutups, but few with his credentials: six titles and regular-season MVPs, a pair of Finals MVPs, nineteen times All-Star, fifteen times all-NBA, eleven times all-defense, two scoring championships, a rebounding title, four times leading the league in blocks. Bill Russell won more titles, but primarily from the defensive side. Wilt Chamberlain scored more points but primarily was the offensive guy. The kids debate Michael and LeBron; the old-school veterans often pick Kareem.

**PJ:** I had kind of an interesting relationship with Kareem. I had some Muslim friends when I was with the Knicks who wanted to meet him. So I invited him over; I was living on Central Park West then, had food, not drinks. Nice to sit down and talk with him. That was a great apartment. Bought it for $29,000, which was a steal at the time. Prewar building, no air-conditioning: They'd tell everybody to open the windows. I sold it for $65,000. My neighbor upstairs was Zero Mostel. They'd have parties all the time, always something going on. They played and sang. They had a dog and I did too, and we became friendly. He had an art studio and loved to paint. He said, "They keep asking me to do *Fiddler on the Roof*, and it's going to kill me," and it did. The Knicks were the toast of the town then. A few of us did this movie with Woody Allen and then he invited us all to dinner. When June and I got home, she told me he stared at her tits all night.

**SAM:** C'mon, Woody was one of my neighbors from Brooklyn. Funnier, more successful, but it doesn't look like I'm getting thrown out of the country. Sorry, *Take the Money and Run* and holding up that bank with the misspelled note, *Bananas* with Howard Cosell? He made me smile as much as Snoopy. I'm still with Woody. So Kareem?

**PJ:** Yeah, we'd spend time in the locker room before games when I was coaching the Lakers, chatting it up, talking about history, religion. He's a bright guy. He wanted to come to the games. When we got Andrew Bynum, Andrew was like, "Yeah, my hero is Kareem Abdul-Jabbar." "Well, let's bring him in," I said. "He can teach you the [sky] hook." So, anyway, two weeks later, Kareem comes to me and says, "The kid can't shoot a hook. He doesn't have the strength to shoot the hook; he can't go off one foot. He doesn't do anything I recommend; he's not a coachable guy." But you want to talk history, about the jazz age, about religions and popular movements? Kareem's a student. I'd get into it with him politically and about race. The racial politics I knew most about from experience growing up in Montana had to do with Native Americans. LaVonne Swift Eagle was in my sixth-grade class. She was kind of shunned and didn't make it to high school. He'd talk about the year he tried to coach on the Indian reservation. He said they wouldn't let him coach, wouldn't give him the reins. I guess they valued their jobs for themselves.

**SAM:** It seemed obvious to me that Kareem wanted to coach, and as badly as he treated some of us, not cruel, really, but indifferent . . . That stuff haunts you. The NBA remembers burned bridges.

**PJ:** The players would start giving Kareem a hard time because he wasn't teaching Andrew anything. So before long, he'd just come and have a little workout, skip rope or do something to keep active. He was ahead of his time with stretching and yoga. He'd mostly come back with me in the coach's office and we'd talk about that tenure on the reservation in Arizona, in the White Mountains.

**SAM:** Kareem was always the cautionary tale for me when I'd speak with players who were somewhat reluctant to talk. I understood what Kareem went through with the racial attacks, and he had some incredible tragedies, like that house fire that cost him his awards and jazz collection and so many of his prized possessions. He suffered unfairly, as Muhammad Ali did, when he announced he was a Muslim. And remember when the Hanafi Muslims were massacred a few years before in DC by the Nation of Islam in a house Kareem had donated to them? He went through a lot. It's not funny, but when they had the All-Star game in Chicago that year, they came up with an injury excuse for Kareem to miss it, but it was really for security reasons. Jon McGlocklin told me the players, when they came down for games from Milwaukee to Chicago—where the rival Nation of Islam is based—would be moving away from Kareem on the bench. You know, just in case.

**PJ:** That was a really devastating thing, the killings at his house, which really got limited coverage because it was Black-on-Black crime. The media didn't care.

**SAM:** One of my favorite stories involves Kareem just tangentially. It was the famous coin flip in 1969 between the teams with the worst records for the number 1 pick, Kareem. Here's a guy who leads his freshman UCLA team to beat the varsity, who were the defending national champions and favorites. Jerry Colangelo had left the Bulls to take over the expansion Suns and taken his buddy and first Bulls coach Johnny Kerr with him. Jerry calls heads. It's tails. The Bucks guys are screaming over the conference call to New York; there's silence in Phoenix. Finally, Johnny Kerr speaks up. "Hey, Jerry, maybe they'll take Neal Walk." I miss Johnny Kerr, who explained that his defense against Kareem was to breathe on his goggles. Neal was your buddy, right? How do you go from number 2 overall pick to paralyzed?

**PJ:** He never was bitter. Neal would have four tequilas for the pain. He came to my daughter's wedding. Flew up to Montana. He had a tumor in his back, surgery, and was in the wheelchair as a result. Colangelo was great and gave him a community position. Honored at the White House, Jewish hall of fame. Never let that booby prize stuff bother him.

There was a story I remember about Kareem. Not his Kent Benson punch. I saw him after that. I was like, "What's that about?" He said,

"I lost it. I just lost it." Cunt Benson, I think they called him. He was elbowing Kareem, fouling him hard, just, like, one more white guy who can't play basketball. Benson wasn't a bad player, just not mobile. Kareem usually had this self-possession. Yeah, it's a really hard foul, but I'm not going to take offense. Yeah, fans are razzing me, but I'm not going to get upset. He sort of had that zen state.

The thing about Kareem, as good and dominant as he was, he was so uncharismatic he needed Magic to ultimately succeed in LA because he didn't inspire teammates—he was a star without much personality. I don't know if Kareem was a leader. I think his personality was such that he avoided it. Magic used to call him captain all the time, "Hey, Cap, you're the cap." But Magic was the guy in the locker room.

The surprise to me were the famous foul shots Kareem made in the 1988 Finals. Gary Vitti told me he came to the bench, and he was livid. "Fucking, goddamn, damn, damn." "What's the problem, what's the problem?" "I hate getting fouled at this time of game and having to make free throws." He was just bitching about the pressure that was put on him to make these free throws.

**SAM:** The phantom foul? Yeah, the Pistons were pissed, but though it wasn't enough contact for that era, he did bump Kareem. And it was Laimbeer, and who was rooting for that guy? Not that the refs are biased, right? But all that bitching and moaning for all those years, who's complaining that guy didn't commit a foul?

**PJ:** Kareem said he hated being fouled at that time in the game and having to make free throws. But he made 'em and won the game.

**SAM:** My two favorite Kareem episodes were the self-deprecating cameo in the movie *Airplane!* and his incredible open letter to Wilt, who always was taking shots at him, even after Kareem always talked about Wilt as an idol. Let me read some of it: "Why all the jealousy and envy? . . . Your team couldn't win the NCAA tournament. . . . Bill Russell gave you a yearly lesson in real competitive competence and teamwork. . . . People will remember that I worked with my team- mates and helped us win. You will be remembered as a whining cry- baby and a quitter."

All I can say is, "Holy shit." Imagine that letter in this media envi- ronment.

# Nate Archibald

It wasn't quite Wilt's 1961–62 season averaging 50.4 points and 25.7 rebounds in 48.5 minutes per game—c'mon, seriously?—or Oscar Robertson that same season when—what the heck was going on?—he averaged 30.8 points, 12.5 rebounds, and 11.4 assists in a load-managed 44.3 minutes per game. Or Elgin Baylor, who only played forty-eight games and averaged 38.3 points per game, which may have been even more amazing because he scored like that just playing on weekends or other leaves from his military service. Still, Nate "Tiny" Archibald's 1972–73 season, which basically no one saw because he played for the Kansas City–Omaha Kings, was pretty amazing, leading the league at 34 points per game and 11.4 assists in a league-high forty-six minutes per game. It was part of one of the greatest half careers in NBA history, cleaved by an Achilles tendon tear that led to a modest six-year encore that did play a big facilitating role in the Boston Celtics' 1981 NBA title. Archibald made six All-Star teams, three after his Achilles injury. He was five times all-NBA, but he did miss 130 games in the middle of all that. The maybe five-ten or five-eleven New York Rucker Park playground legend made it out despite his brief high school dropout period and academic struggles, unlike fellow legends who didn't, like Joe Hammond, Pee Wee Kirkland, Helicopter Knowings, and Earl "the Goat" Manigault. Tiny's basketball acumen became an inspiration for eventually returning to New York City to teach and earn a master's degree from Fordham. And the NBA wasn't much of a tiny-friendly league when he entered it: His 1970 NBA draft class had Pete Maravich and five centers as the top six selections, with Tiny going in the second round.

**PJ:** A lot of people kind of credit Jack Ramsay with really putting the emphasis on point guards, smaller guards, guys like Tiny Archibald, who were the guys who changed things. Oscar would take the ball inside and clear out and Adrian Smith, a six-footer maybe, would come up behind him for the jump shot. That was a change in basketball, when you had big guards. Motta was also one of those coaches who came from college and brought system basketball into the NBA. Jack Ramsay was Dr. Jack. These were doctors of education, learned men who taught the fundamentals of the game—shooting, defense. These people brought a sense of the game. There's a goal, and you want to get the ball as close to the goal as you can, so what situation do you create to do that? How do you place your men on the court? You can organize your men in position to attack and defend. It always was about penetration.

**SAM:** The art of war, eh?

**PJ:** Nate the Great. Bill had him in Boston even after he got hurt. He was slippery, slender, but really deceptive. A different kind of player.

**SAM:** Before Isiah, Iverson, Kyrie, Curry, these manipulative little guards?

**PJ:** It's exhibition season and we're playing fourteen, fifteen games. You'd have a week of training camp and then go off for twenty days and play all these games. We're going all around New York to build up our fan base. We're playing in Utica and then Niagara and Rochester, Syracuse. In the morning we're doing schools, and it was me and Willis and another guy, and we're giving the "stay in school and study hard" lecture, and there's a question-and-answer session. Calvin Murphy was at Niagara. Someone asks, What are the chances of a guy Calvin's size, five nine, playing in the NBA? Willis says slim and none. Then we had these six-five, six-six guards, and it seemed like it was only going bigger. Then Calvin comes in and he's quick as a dart, limited in some ways, but they became a pretty good team with him, and then it's like, OK, the NBA better take a look at these guys.

**SAM:** Which Motta did with the Bulls. I remember Johnny Bach telling me when he was at Fordham he always went looking to recruit the little guys because they were a bit hungrier. Earlier in the NBA, Bob Davies, Cousy, they weren't big guards. No one did much scouting then, as you know. The draft was mostly done out of the *Street & Smith's* college magazine and some old player recommendations. Auerbach had the best network for that. Got him onto Russell and got him Sam Jones when Sam came out of the military and had decided to work in the school system. So Motta sees Nate and likes him. But his chief scout then is Jerry Krause, and he loves this guy from New Mexico State, Jimmy Collins, who actually went on to a great coaching career in Illinois. The Bulls have number 11 in the first round, and Motta agrees they'll pick Nate in the second round. But Calvin goes first in the second at number 18 and Nate second. For years Motta would introduce Jerry as "the man who talked me out of drafting Nate Archibald." But it worked out OK for the Bulls. Nate went to Cincinnati, where Norm Van Lier had led the league in assists. They decided to turn the team over to Tiny, so Norm gets traded back to the Bulls and was a key part of their great seventies run, averaging more than fifty wins for five seasons. Their problem was being in the West then and having to face either Wilt or Kareem in the playoffs. Tom Boer-winkle just couldn't match up.

**PJ:** Nate was built kind of like Allen Iverson and had that ability to do that one thing that got him to the hoop or got him a shot. I remember Boston beat Philadelphia when Philadelphia was really good. They got the ball to Archibald at the end of the game and he delivered, a critical play, and I thought, "Damn, that guy is still playing?"

# Dave Cowens

Dave Cowens was Dick Butkus at center. Coming at you full speed, a so-called small center in an era with other physical guys in his mold like Wes Unseld, Cowens with his quickness and ability to make a shot flummoxed the big men of the day. He helped revive the Celtics' excellence in the 1970s—less fast break and more breaking whatever was in his way. Cowens was a thinking man's iconoclast for the era, enforcing his own sense of basketball morality while applying the common touch on and off the floor. He once drove a taxicab for a day during his playing career to get the feel of what the fans experienced in their lives. He took an auto-repair class early in his career to fill in time off the court. He didn't apologize for repairs needed on the court. He helped lead the Celtics to championships in 1974 and 1976, in 1974 outplaying Kareem Abdul-Jabbar in the clinching game. John Havlicek was Finals MVP that year, but in Game 7 the six-nine Cowens, with some help from his friends, neutralized Abdul-Jabbar, with Cowens accumulating 28 points, 14 rebounds, a pair of steals, and a block. Kareem had 26 and 13. It was Oscar Robertson's last NBA game. Cowens's sliding belly flop across the floor chasing a loose ball after switching to defend Robertson at the close of a game in that series is the clip shown to define not only Cowens but also hustle in the NBA. Charlie Hustle in the NBA was Dave Cowens. Jo Jo White was the MVP in the famous 1976 Finals with the "shot heard round the world" in the "greatest game ever played," triple overtime with the strategic Paul Westphal extra time-out / technical to force that third overtime in Game 5. The Celtics won the game with 26 and 19 from Cowens. Cowens averaged 20 and 16 in the six games, while White averaged a point more and a dozen rebounds fewer.

Cowens is one of five NBA players ever, along with Scottie Pippen, Kevin Garnett, LeBron James, and Giannis Antetokounmpo, to lead his team in the five major statistical categories—points, rebounds, assists, steals, and blocked shots—in one season. Cowens was something of a pioneering point center and fast-break trailer who was the Celtics' first championship center after Bill Russell, playing the game differently but almost as effectively, like Russell as the hub in handoffs. Cowens went on to coach in the CBA, the WNBA, and for two NBA teams. He was a league and All-Star game MVP, eight-time All-Star, and three times all-defense.

**PJ:** The whole game shrunk in the East. Milwaukee left the Eastern Conference and went west. Nate Thurmond was out there, Chamberlain was out there, and Kareem. It was interesting about the East. It probably goes back to those cramped gyms with the running tracks. You played a more physical game. The Western Conference always was more wide-open, the wild, wild West. Dave was a year behind Neal Walk. Dave at Florida State, Neal at Florida.

**SAM:** That was a heck of a draft. Maravich fell to third because he said Detroit was too cold and maybe he'd go to the Globetrotters, and the

Rockets didn't feel they could pay him. Dave went fourth after Bob Lanier and Rudy Tomjanovich. After Russell left in '69, the Celtics missed the playoffs. There wasn't much scouting then, and Dave was playing in this running offense as a defensive hustle guy. Cowens goes to the summer Kutsher's charity game for Maurice Stokes and is chasing loose balls all over the place.

**PJ:** You'd hear crazy things about Cowens. He slept in Don Nelson's cabana, the swimming pool house. He'd go out in snowstorms and help people who were stuck in the snow. A story from his college days was that at his fraternity house he was assigned to protect the mascot from abuse. Some kids did something to it and he beat the shit out of all of them. Those things followed him to the NBA.

**SAM:** It was a rough time. Didn't you get into it with McGinnis once, the LeBron of his era?

**PJ:** I got this blind punch from McGinnis that knocked me down from behind. I'd tried this little trick on him I'd use once in a while where I got elevation and I'd put my forearm on someone's shoulder. Took the energy he was providing. I could get away with it. It was stuff you'd do. Ball went out of bounds and he gets me, punches me, but there's no suspension, didn't throw him out, didn't fine him. Two free throws. It was more a question of the severity of the injury at the time. That's why the league's response was so severe to Kermit Washington for his punch of Rudy T. George just got me on the side of my head. George was a huge guy like LeBron, six eight, maybe 260. He could push the ball, but he didn't handle it as well.

**SAM:** My favorite Cowens story is the Mike Newlin flop. Dave, for all his aggression, was a purist about the game. He saw the game with a high sense of morality. He once wrote a letter to my friend at *The Boston Globe*, the Celtics' beat writer Bob Ryan. Dave asked it to be printed in the newspaper, condemning flopping: "To once and for all impress upon the referees, coaches, players and fans that fraudulent, deceiving and flagrant acts of pretending to be fouled when little or no contact is made is just as outrageously unsportsmanlike as knocking a player to the floor. I would not and never have taught youngsters to play other than by the rules, morals, ethics and character of the game. . . . [It] makes players think they can achieve their goal without putting in the work or effort that it takes to develop any skill or talent. . . . [It] arouses the ignorant fans who react vehemently to violent gestures. . . . If this practice continues unrestrained or the actor is allowed to utilize this fraudulent exercise successfully, it will gradually become an accepted strategy and will be taught to kids more enthusiastically by their coaches." He named my buddy Jerry Sloan as one of the worst offenders.

**PJ:** He and Nelson would come back after games and drink beer. Then they'd play this game called Head Bonking or something like that. You hit somebody forehead-to-forehead. I don't know what the game's purpose was, but you know how big a head Don Nelson had, right? Don was, like, the champ. Dave split his forehead open playing the game. He had to give it up. You'd run across the lane and Dave would deliver a blow.

**SAM:** Back to the Newlin flop. Dave was playing the Rockets in a game in '76. Twice Mike Newlin steps in front of Cowens and flops. So Newlin is going back up court after drawing the second charge, and Dave is running at him, levels him with a forearm and body block, and sends Newlin flying. Dave turns to the ref and yells, "Now that's a fucking foul."

**PJ:** A couple of times I told him, "Dave, it's no wonder you get fucking hurt all the time. You create it on your own." One of the Boston fans sent me a picture of Dave dunking over the top of me. He was terrific, played with great gusto. You knew he wasn't going to have a long career. Just played too hard. Played the game full throttle. A guy I grew to really like.

# Pete Maravich

When people speak of never forgetting where they were when a certain event happened, they're usually talking about a historic tragedy like Pearl Harbor, the Kennedy assassination, the *Challenger* explosion, or 9/11. Bob Dylan wrote that for him one such event was when the basketball player-as-artist Pete Maravich died. Pete Maravich didn't have the records, though he did score 68 points in a game against the Knicks one time. He didn't have the championships, or even much team success. But if you saw him you never forgot, the dancing hair and flopping socks, and a basketball game with parts of Curly Neal from the Globetrotters, Bob Cousy, Kobe Bryant, and Elgin Baylor. Legendary St. John's coach Lou Carnesecca said Maravich was drawn from the best parts of a combination of Jerry West and Oscar Robertson. Magic Johnson listed Pete as the inspiration for his magical game. When Pete was first trying to explain in the 1960s what he was doing, he called it "showtime," small *s*. Things get capitalized when they get to LA. The basketball star Caitlin Clark revolutionized the collegiate women's game with her pursuit of what they said was Maravich's scoring record. She technically broke it, and she is a true phenomenon. But nobody really will ever come close to what Pete did in college, where he averaged more than 44 points per game in three years in the freshman-ineligible era, when there was not only no three-point shot but also no shot clock. You could run a stall, and Pete still was averaging 44.5 per game as a senior. Pete's Louisiana State team wasn't very good and didn't get to the NCAAs when there was just the conference winner. So he came to New York in 1970, and it was one of the Garden's biggest-ever tickets, like Mikan versus the Knicks. Marquette's Dean Meminger did a heck of a job on him, and Pete got just 20 points. But we saw him. You had to see Pete. It was something you couldn't explain. Pete's life story was tragic in some respects, driven by his dad, Press, a frustrated former player in the old BAA who went on to coaching and was attempting with his son to build the perfect player.

Perhaps it had been tried, but no one before him did the no-look, the crossover-and-between-the-legs with Pete's flair. Sometimes bouncing it off his head. Let the officials decide. Pete shot almost forty times a game at LSU. And he still averaged more than 6 assists per game as a senior. Pete's last home game was a rare-for-the-time syndicated television broadcast. Pete scored 64 points. But it wasn't such a pleasant professional journey for Pete, who didn't necessarily make teammates better. He did make cities better. He probably saved the Hawks for Atlanta and basketball for New Orleans, at least for a while. The aim clearly was to get a white star for a Black sport in the South, and the Hawks' acquiring Pete enabled them to gain community support for a new arena, the Omni. But a tough, blue-collar, forty-eight-win Hawks team fractured with Maravich's celebrity and huge contract. It's like when you are satisfied with your job until the new person at the next desk comes in making double. Bill Bridges, the rugged conscience of the team, forced his way out. Joe Caldwell left for the ABA; a twelve-win decline ensued immediately. But Pete still could please like no one else as a basketball showman, his third season in Atlanta averaging 26 per game and then almost 28 and making back-to-back All-Star teams. And what a dream it would have been: In the midst of Julius Erving's travels to get to the NBA from the ABA, Erving signed a contract with the Hawks and was a Maravich teammate—alas, for only two preseason games before the court ordered Erving back to his ABA team. Now that would really have been a show, the Doctor and the Magician. But the Hawks were going nowhere and the expansion New Orleans Jazz needed box office. Hey, how about Pete coming back home? They put together a package of players and picks that exceeded even the trades for Wilt Chamberlain and Kareem Abdul-Jabbar in what became known as the second Louisiana Purchase, and Maravich returned to Louisiana to entertain, if not succeed. His third season with the Jazz, Pete led the league in scoring for Coach Elgin Baylor, averaging 31 per game. But a few years later when the Jazz moved to Utah, Pete wasn't wanted and was released in January 1980, finishing his career on deteriorating knees with Larry Bird's Celtics. Maravich made five All-Star teams and was all-NBA four times. He died at forty in a pickup game in 1988 from an undiagnosed heart ailment that limited his heart to such an extent that doctors afterward wondered how he even could have had the energy to play at all. What a loss to basketball that would have been to never have seen Pete.

**PJ:** One time I was like, Pete, "What's the deal with you handling the ball?" He said he'd go to practice—I don't know, he's ten, eleven—his dad was coaching the team and driving the car going twenty miles an hour, and Pete'd be dribbling the ball. "I'd be dribbling and it'd come up spinning. I was with the ball all the time. Then I'd go to practice and I was with the ball." Unfortunately, his dad coached him in college. Which you know led to him being the most prolific scorer, I suppose. They'd be on TV. He told me one time John Wooden—he's always this kind of guy that goes to church, Christian, clean image—Pete played against UCLA, and Wooden was like, "Pull your fucking socks up! What the fuck is that!" Pete said, "He was cursing at me. I couldn't believe it. Took me out of my game. Had to reset myself." Very funny but that musta been very upsetting to John, because John was about teaching people how to put their shoes on, how to put their socks the right way.

**SAM:** The big, floppy socks thing. I once saw where Adolph Rupp said Pete made him change his basic philosophy of "You never get up in the air and pass the ball."

**PJ:** Yeah, I taught that: Don't leave the floor when you're going to pass the ball. But we also taught centers when a double-team was coming, you might have to get in the air and pass and release the ball over the top. So there were times when you broke the rule, but that was a habit.

**SAM:** Johnny Bach used to talk about the seven rules for a good shot, what had Doug wary of the triangle, that you can't shoot unless guards can get back, teammates aware of the shot . . .

**PJ:** We had seven rules for everything, for sound offense and defense. Seven was a kind of holy number. That trip to China was when I got to know Rick Barry. Pete was part of that team. We were sponsored by Puma and Winston cigarettes. They smoke like crazy in China; everybody's spitting and hacking.

**SAM:** So I go in January '04 to China to pick up our daughter, who we adopted, and they give you three days' orientation in Beijing first to get the feel for the country; also to sell you stuff. You know, here come the capitalists. Made sure we went to some jade factory and wouldn't let you get back on the bus until you bought something. At nights we were on our own, so I decide I've got to try Peking duck in Peking. Like you said, it's smoky, and this is 2004. I walk into the restaurant and the guy says, "Smoking or nonsmoking?" Hey, I'm surprised. "Sure, no smoking." Sits me down at this little table right in the middle of six tables with people all puffing away. But you couldn't smoke at my table.

**PJ:** We went to Taiwan to play. It was, "OK, Phil, you be the coach. You've been coaching." Cazzie was also on the trip, but I became the de facto coach. We're playing the Taiwan team, and there's a huge bet on this game between the two publishers. One was a benefactor of our trip, publisher of the Taiwan paper, and the Hong Kong paper—they have a competitive thing going on. We know it's $50,000, supposedly. These Taiwan players are playing a zone and they're physical and it's their referees and it's their building and we're not getting anywhere. So Pete comes over to me and says, "Give me a chance to go at these guys. I can do some things." So he scores 22 points in the second half and we win by 4 or 6. I don't think we covered the spread, but he was magnificent. I hadn't seen him play like that in the NBA.

**SAM:** He got van Breda Kolff one time as coach, and you know he's not letting Pete put on a show. Pete started with Richie Guerin, who was a crew-cut marine. Then I think Pete's coach was Cotton Fitzsimmons in Atlanta, who told Pat Williams to get him out of there. No imagination. The NBA still was stuck in the pre-ABA patterned game. The seventies was the NBA at its most boring, losing all those high-fliers to the ABA. A little like when Bill Russell came into the NBA. They criticized him because you weren't supposed to jump on defense. No one did. You played on the ground. Bill said, The heck with that.

**PJ:** The next team we play it's quiet, so we gotta do something to excite the crowd. They're sitting on their hands. The Chinese people are a nonexpressive audience. They'd just sit there like a church. So at halftime, Pete says to me, "Let me put on a basketball demonstration for them. Just two or three minutes to get them involved in the game." So he went out, did all these tricks, spinning balls, throwing the ball up and bouncing it off his head and putting it through the hoop. And he got them laughing, got them enthusiastic about the game. After the game, we go to Pearl Island in the Pearl River. At the time, the Americans came in because of the lack of industry and did clothing. So all these guys are there from the Garment District in New York, Clyde's guys. We're up till midnight or more after traveling all day to get down to Canton. We're drinking these shots of, like, pure grain alcohol, toast after toast. We got up in the morning and we had to fly to Beijing, and everybody's doing tai chi in the parks, and on bicycles. We gotta come through Canton again to get out. There are no direct flights to Taiwan. Going to Taiwan and Philippines afterwards. The airport is small, and one of these guys who was a merchant in the Garment District comes over to me. I know him from hanging out. He comes over and says, "See all these guys here? I've been coming here for four years. These guys all have submachine guns, Uzis on their shoulders. Now, they used to have pistols in their belts. We used to be able to give them bicycles for what they did as our hosts. Then it became sewing machines. Now it's televisions. In a matter of five years, you watch out for this group. They're going to climb the economic ladder really fast. They really know how to grab on to this."

**SAM:** So you're telling me it's Pete and not Nixon who really opened China?

# Julius Erving

James Naismith may have written the rules for basketball, but Julius "Dr. J" Erving was the Moses who brought them down from the mountain to the people for them to learn how to advance and play the game. Because it basically was with Erving that the NBA emerged from the darkness of conservative play, perhaps with some exceptions when Bob Cousy had the ball or when Elgin Baylor was hanging around with it. But it was the Doctor who provided the remedy for the ill health of the game at a time when rival leagues were battling, players were suing, and the fans weren't that interested. Until Erving pulled back the curtain and the greatest sports show began. Erving was hardly the first who dunked a basketball, but then came this kid with the beach-ball hair and a ballet of flight ending with a basketball thundering through the netting. Bill Russell brought the game into the air, though primarily on defense, and Elgin would seem to fly, or be suspended like an osprey before Connie Hawkins with the long, swooping presence that Erving inherited.

Erving with the Virginia Squires of the ABA wasn't seen. But everyone heard the stories. Erving didn't disappoint, even if his reign didn't match that of the great winners of the era with that one '83 title. Erving really was one of the first, along with Maravich and to an extent before them Cousy and Elgin, who turned basketball from a game to an experience and art form. They created visual masterpieces with their basketball artistry. If he only had a reliable jump shot. Some of Erving's highlight plays still make the greatest ever in NBA history. Like his swooping reverse baseline scoop with Kareem charging in the 1980 Finals, his "Rock the baby" dunk from announcer Chick Hearn over Michael Cooper in 1983, his hammer over Bill Walton in the 1977 Finals, and his free-throw-line flight in the inaugural 1976 dunk contest that Michael Jordan honored for the 1988 All-Star contest in Chicago. Erving was with the Nets during the merger, but his rights were sold to the Philadelphia 76ers to pay off the Nets' indemnity to the Knicks for invading their NBA territory. The Knicks at the time preferred the about $5 million indemnity instead of Erving, perhaps not the best basketball decision. In fantasy what-ifs, Erving was briefly teammates with Tiny Archibald on the Nets during the transaction with the 76ers and, in one signing ruled illegal, with the Atlanta Hawks when they had Pete Maravich.

Erving came from humble basketball roots, little known on Long Island, New York, and then going to play at the University of Massachusetts, a small basketball program. But talk began to circulate. Erving met Bill Russell at a seminar, and Russell said he'd been hearing about this Erving guy, but *The Boston Globe* kept misspelling Erving's name as "Irving," and Russell said he thought it was a Jewish kid from New York. It was the hands. And the stretch. With his long strides on the fast break, Erving would reach out, his giant hands above the square on the backboard by the time he'd begin his downward cycle. Erving was twice ABA champion and three straight times ABA MVP, with an NBA MVP added in 1981. He was ABA scoring champion three times and twelve times all-ABA or all-NBA. Combining points, Erving is all-time close behind Wilt. When Erving retired after the 1986–87 season with a season-long thank-you tour from fans, he handed off the symbolic torch of grandeur for Michael Jordan to carry forward into the next century for Kobe, LeBron, and beyond.

**PJ:** There was a story about Art Heyman rebuffing Erving and him not going to the Knicks because of that. Never heard that. The story I heard when I got to the NBA was about Artie with the Knicks playing cards on the bus all the time. They're driving to Philadelphia and Harry "the Horse" Gallatin was the coach, and they were coming back playing cards on the bus, and Gallatin came back to them and said to deal him in. Artie said no. "You didn't let me play in your game, I'm not letting you play in my game." But guys were intrigued by the ABA. Right off the bat some of the guys on the Knicks team went over to Jersey to see them play.

**SAM:** So did I. We loved the expansion leagues. The new leagues were cheap. So off we'd go to Teaneck, New Jersey, that first season to see the Americans, who became the Nets. The NBA, to drive them out, locked up all the arenas, and the ABA was playing in the Teaneck Armory. Then they move to Commack and some old airport hangar, which had no heat and you'd be wearing your winter coat—players, too, on the bench—watching the game. Concrete under the hardwood like where Michael first practiced at Angel Guardian gym when he was drafted by the Bulls.

**PJ:** We would go to Jersey to see Pittsburgh. We were intrigued by the ABA. How's it going to look? I went to watch a game of the Oakland Oaks when we were on the road and talked to Rick Barry about it.

**SAM:** The Pipers were a legendary team. That's where Connie Hawkins went when he first was banned from the NBA. Heyman was there, Ira "the Large" Harge, Barry Leibowitz from LIU, who gave all us little Jewish kids hope we could play. Let me tell you my Erving story. Magic probably was the most personable, approachable, and available star to media, but there was no one like Doc. So I set up this interview with him with the 76ers around '85. No cell phones, you've got to find a pay phone away from home. It's for 2:00 p.m., and sure enough my phone rings. It's Doc. I'm asking him questions, but it's loud in the background. Where is he? He says he got stuck in traffic and it got to be two and he knew he had to do an interview, so he pulls off the side of the road and is on one of these emergency phones they used to have off the interstates, standing by the side of the road because he promised 2:00 p.m. C'mon, who does that? And this is the Doctor.

**PJ:** They were trying to emulate the NBA at first and playing the game as it was, but they had the three-point line. In '71 there was almost going to be a merger, but the players' association, because the ABA was promoting increased salaries, killed it. I remember going to Washington, DC, and going into the committee room and supporting Bradley and Havlicek, who went to testify.

**SAM:** That was some amazing stuff that I wrote about in my *Hard Labor* book, Rick testifying against the NBA players, saying they made enough money and should have the merger. But that was because he wanted to be back in the NBA and the courts kept honoring the contracts he signed with the ABA. The notion was they were an inch or two short at every position and, until Artis, no big man. So in some sense it was the forerunner of the NBA of the 2000s, with small ball and high scoring and no post play or big men who really matter. So maybe finally honor the ABA stats like baseball has done with the Negro Leagues?

**PJ:** No ABA stats. They used to do strange stuff in those games. I heard McGinnis used to put the ball off the backboard, catch it, and put it up off the backboard again for an extra rebound. It was kind of like carnival stuff they were doing. They played the same team six times in a row. At one point when they were folding, all sorts of stuff was going on, with no one to play. But they did have Moses, McGinnis, David Thompson, Julius.

# Bob McAdoo

B ob McAdoo just was at the wrong place at the wrong time too many times, which was why he was one of the two big snubs for the top-fifty players in 1996, along with Dominique Wilkins. It all was resolved favorably for both for the top seventy-five. McAdoo was worthy, a player reminiscent of both LeBron James and Kevin Durant, a six-nine center who could run the floor and shoot like a guard. McAdoo playing center took advantage of the mismatches and dragged big men out to the perimeter against his jump shot, which was remarkable in the pre-three-point-shot era. McAdoo was averaging more than 30 points and 12 rebounds per game while winning three consecutive scoring titles following his rookie season—the youngest player to average more than 30 and 15—and in those three seasons combined shooting more than 50 percent from the field, and not on layups and dunks. Lakers coach Jerry West, an all-time great shooter himself, marveled at McAdoo's shooting ability. But the stoic McAdoo started in Buffalo, where no one noticed him. With Coach Jack Ramsay, who peddled a fast-breaking style when he was in Philadelphia, it looked like it was going to be a Magic/Kareem–type fast-breaking high-wire act with McAdoo and the deft Ernie DiGregorio, who set the rookie-assists record with 25 in a game that year. Ernie D got hurt and McAdoo bargained his way to the New York Knicks, where the coach and fans longed for the teamwork fives of the early 1970s. Bill Walton remarked he'd never seen a better shooter for a big man.

Portland actually had a chance to draft McAdoo in 1972. It was the first of Portland's draft oopses. It was because of a snowy weekend in Chicago in January 1972. Streaking UCLA was snowed in, and though they defeated LaRue Martin's Loyola team, Martin had 19 and 18 to Walton's 18 and 16. A few days before, Martin had 33 and 22 against Marquette star Jim Chones. A Trail Blazers executive was watching. The NBA-ABA signing wars were at a boil then, and the NBA was warning teams to skip McAdoo, a hardship expatriate after one season at North Carolina. ABA Virginia had drafted McAdoo number 1. So Portland went for center Martin, a lovely, soft-spoken man who became a big executive with UPS in Chicago. Buffalo with the number 2 pick selected and signed McAdoo, who became Rookie of the Year and soon the league's most dangerous scorer and shooter. But then there was the Knicks' experience when McAdoo came in as the expected savior and went out booed, and into his next team booed. That was to Boston during the famed ownership franchise trade when McAdoo was acquired by the owner without Auerbach's consent and was so unwanted that Auerbach threatened to leave. McAdoo, the league MVP in 1975, was booed on arrival in Boston, dumped to a Detroit team that was at the bottom of the standings, and actually soon cut. McAdoo bounced to an equally bad Nets team, his reputation growing as a selfish scorer disliked by teammates and fans. Losing produces unhappy reputations—which wasn't really the gentle but proud McAdoo. But your record also is your reputation. It wasn't until Mitch Kupchak suffered a severe knee injury and the Lakers decided to take a chance on McAdoo as a reserve that the sky brightened. McAdoo, just thirty years old, wasn't ready to play part time, but after sitting out a half season with the Nets, he embraced the trade to the Lakers and became an integral part of two championship teams. Then, still anxious to prove he was an elite player, McAdoo went to play in Europe, which wasn't uncommon for NBA players in that era. McAdoo was a five-time NBA All-Star and both NBA and EuroLeague MVP. He later reunited with his Lakers coach Pat Riley as an assistant coach and was part of three Miami championship teams.

**PJ:** When the Knicks traded him to Boston, Dave Cowens was coaching the team, and Dave was like, I'm not coaching this guy. He had lined up against him in the '74 playoffs, '76, sometime when Bob was still with Buffalo and Buffalo was a pretty good young team with Jack Ramsay. You remember Bob Kauffman? He went to Detroit and he ended up coaching there. I was like, How'd this guy get to be a coach? Pretty good athlete, effective player, but his career ended quickly and he was coaching. Why?

**SAM:** Sure, Bob Kauffman, Bulls guy for a season. He had this breakout season in Buffalo, like a 20/10 season, and made a few All-Star teams. Played two seasons with McAdoo there. Tough six-eight guy. Had an interesting career. Goes to the Pistons as GM and then coach and is fired because he tries to hire Cotton or Al Bianchi as coach and owner Bill Davidson falls for local mouth Dick Vitale, who didn't exactly shine in the NBA.

**PJ:** I was with the Nets in '78 and I went to the game to scout. Sometimes Red would say, "Go scout this team and I'll buy you dinner." I'm not the greatest scout. I would just be like, "This guy goes right every time he shoots." Then when I went to the Bulls, I had to get into scouting. I remember once sitting next to Rudy Tomjanovich at a game in Houston and Bill Fitch was the coach. He had Sampson and Olajuwon.

I asked Rudy, "Is your aspiration to be a head coach?" "Oh, no, I could never do that. I could never be a head coach." Then Carroll Dawson had an accident. Golfing accident—lost his eyesight. Rudy just got vaulted into that position; they kind of threw him in there, and he was successful. Then I was in Australia and I got a call. "Rudy, he can't coach anymore." I'm like, "What are you talking about? The guy just got hired as coach on a five-year contract. He's making the kind of money I was making with the Lakers. How'd that happen?" "It's too difficult for him. He's too upset. So this is what's gonna happen. You're gonna come back." "Well, no I'm not. I just got off here in Australia. I'll consider it at the end of the year." And then I'm back to coaching. Rudy'd had cancer, he smoked, he used to have a twenty-four-ounce Coke with him all the time—he'd come to practice caffeinated. I always liked Rudy as a person and as a player when we played him in the playoffs in '75. They beat us two out of three in that limited playoffs. Rudy had been the USA coach at the Olympics in 2000. Larry Brown replaced him at some point, and Larry got the 2004 team. I was surprised Mitch didn't know all he was going through. Like someone said, the hardest thing basketball teams do is hire a coach.

**SAM:** I have to say with McAdoo, though, there was a lot of negative stuff because of all the bad teams he'd played on, and he began to be linked to Sidney Wicks, who also had a tough stay in Boston around that time. But I remember the story of McAdoo standing up for women in the locker room when it was just becoming an issue.

**PJ:** We had a woman that covered us. She was a daughter of a famous journalist. She was still friendly with me, but she said I stood naked right in front of her. I said, "No, I had a towel." I said, "You must have been peeking."

**SAM:** That was Jane Gross, who died not long ago. Milton Gross from the *New York Post* was her dad, one of my favorite New York sports tabloid columnists, who befriended Oscar and who basically was one of the few media guys Oscar would talk to.

**PJ:** She broke the barrier, and I think the *Times* then had another woman, Robin Herman, who came in.

**SAM:** I didn't really know Jane, since I was a political writer in DC then. I wrangled myself a credential to cover the '77 World Series for one of our newspapers when Reggie hit those three home runs. I'm subliminally starting to think sports. Then I'm assigned a seat between Roger Angell, the *New Yorker* baseball poet, and Jane, and like a tennis match I'm listening to these baseball stories all night. Sports sounded like fun and not just the journalism toy store. That probably was the day of my career change to sports.

# George Gervin

George Gervin was to basketball what Miles Davis, John Coltrane, and Charlie Parker were to jazz: an original, and great with a solo. He was "the Iceman" because he was so cool playing the game, never seeming to sweat, a fluid grace with a languorous motion, his finger roll and the scoreboard clicking. Like Wilt in Hershey, he was part of one of the greatest scoring games that no one ever saw. It was April 9, 1978, the day of John Havlicek's emotional retirement ceremony in the Boston Garden. That was the national TV game and the TV story, and almost unnoticed was the league scoring race. David Thompson raced into the lead before Gervin's San Antonio Spurs played that day. Thompson, Michael Jordan's hero growing up and one of the greatest ever what-if and what-ever-happened-to guys because of drugs, scored 73 points to take the league scoring lead. Gervin began his game later that afternoon missing five of his first six shots, and his coach, Doug Moe, also an ABA expatriate, instructed his team: "They got Thompson seventy-three? OK, nobody but Ice shoots." Gervin scored a record 33 second-quarter points and was easily on the way to 63 and the lead when he sat out much of the second half in a meaningless last game of the season. Gervin won the scoring title by a tenth of a point. Must have been a Spurs thing, as David Robinson on the last day of the season in 1994 scored 71 points to edge out Shaquille O'Neal for the scoring title after Shaq had 32 points earlier that day. Shaq remembered and often took it out on Robinson, verbally as well as physically in later years.

Gervin's Spurs never got a title, but they were often close, one of the most forgotten elite teams of the late seventies and early eighties, the ABA team that best survived the cost of buying their way into the NBA in the supposed merger. They had a high-powered offensive core with the scoring-oriented Moe as coach. They had Gervin, eventually Artis Gilmore, Larry Kenon, unheralded James Silas, Billy Paultz, and then high-scoring Mike Mitchell. They blew a 3–1 conference finals lead to the Bullets when the most forgotten clutch player ever, Bobby Dandridge, made the winner. Then in 1981–82, the Spurs were moved to the Western Conference and the Lakers roadblock was too much for everyone. Gervin eventually ended his NBA career with a season in Chicago when Michael Jordan was injured most of the year, and then played briefly in Italy. It had been a bumpy road for Gervin, kicked out of little Eastern Michigan University in a fight that looked like it might end his pro career. He was playing in the CBA minor leagues for the Pontiac Chaparrals when Johnny Kerr, then working for the Virginia Squires, found him and eventually paired him with Julius Erving in the greatest two-man game also that no one ever saw, shuttling among three rural cites in Virginia. After the cash-poor Squires sold off Erving, they did similarly with Gervin to the then-ABA Spurs.

**PJ:** George was one of those unique players who came out of the ABA, like Thompson, who could get wherever they wanted to get on the court. Gervin was an interior guard, basically, but his length could get by you at six seven, six eight, great hand coordination with the ball. In basketball, certain people can develop a game that is unique because of their body types, and he is one. Bernard King was another. There wasn't anybody with Bernard's kind of quickness on the block. Not extreme size but extreme agility and elevation. Bernard came back after his injuries and had a 40-point game against us; still highly effective.

**SAM:** I remember that King game, right at the start of the '90–'91 championship season none of us believed you had a chance for, and starting 0–3. That was one of those losses. Bernard gets 44 and becomes an All-Star that season after missing two years with his ACL, and six years since his last All-Star game. But he only lasted another season. I remember Ice mostly for that season Michael missed with the broken foot and the crazy minutes restrictions. Seeing the great ones like that well past does dull the legacy some.

**PJ:** That was the year I came in to see Stan, wearing my hat with the feather, the dark tan from Puerto Rico, and it looked like maybe I wasn't ever going to be coaching.

**SAM:** To Krause's credit, he stuck with you; he was loyal that way. Bringing in Gervin was the other side of Krause. The famous minutes restriction story: So third game in Oakland Michael breaks his foot. Michael goes home to North Carolina, presumably for rehab, but instead starts playing pickup basketball, unbeknownst to the Bulls. So he's ready to play and the Bulls' doctors say, Well, there's a 10 percent chance if he cracks it again he's done. The Bulls don't want him to play, but Michael believes it's to tank for a draft pick. So they're on a conference call with the doctors and Reinsdorf tells Michael about the odds. They didn't know then how Michael liked to gamble. So Reinsdorf gives him a scenario: Say you have a headache and have a pillbox with ten pills and one is cyanide. Would you risk it? Last Word Michael says it depends on how bad the headache is. So they come up with the increasing per-game minutes plan that suddenly when the season ends they scrap, and Michael gets 63 in the playoffs.

**PJ:** Gervin played some in those playoffs.

**SAM:** I felt badly for George. I was so excited to see him play. I was in Virginia after basic training for my advanced training, which was tractor-trailer driving. George wasn't with the Squires yet, but I began to follow them and would go to see them when I was back in New York and seeing the Nets. George got caught up in the drugs, which were endemic on the Bulls at the time. George's signing probably also was the genesis of Michael's feud with Krause. Rod Higgins is basically Jordan's only friend on the team with all the guys going in drug rehab Jordan's rookie season. Michael buys a Ping-Pong table to practice because Rod's always beating him. So Krause signs Gervin as a free agent and has to cut someone. Right, Rod Higgins. Though when I think of Gervin, I also think about the HemisFair Arena and the Baseline Bums in San Antonio. Meanest hecklers in the league.

**PJ:** What about Robin Ficker? I remember Barkley paid for him to come to the Finals in Phoenix in '93 to yell at us. In San Antonio they used to throw guacamole on us when we were walking off.

**SAM:** Leon the Barber in Detroit was most everyone's favorite; he'd sit behind your bench and had everyone laughing. It would be "McAcant, McAwont, McAdon't." Got on the home team all the time, too. That's gone in the NBA. I remember when *The Jordan Rules* came out, and it's around Christmas and you're in DC, and Ficker is right behind your huddle reading passages of *The Jordan Rules*. It was the only time I saw Michael laughing about the book. In Phoenix, Ficker was waving the Esquinas gambling book at Michael. He wasn't laughing then. Of course, he did get about 50 a game, and you won those first two in Phoenix. The NBA kicked Ficker out not long after that. The Baseline Bums sat just by the visitors' exit in the old arena and would throw crap at you guys when you'd walk off. I remember them taunting Kareem about his house fire. Ugly stuff. It was a different league.

# Bill Walton

Bill Walton was basketball's Halley's Comet, a bright light streaking across the NBA skies briefly but spectacularly for all to see and marvel at. For a season and a half, perhaps no one ever did it better or more impressively, blocking shots and rebounding like the best centers, scoring like the best forwards, passing the ball like the best guards while taking his team on a memorable run to an NBA championship and then one of the best half seasons in NBA history, an almost unbeatable, hoops-perfection 50–10 start to the following season—dynasty, anyone?—when catastrophe struck, another of his many foot and leg injuries. Walton, a lover of the game as much as of life itself, came back in the playoffs. But that compounded the injuries with a broken foot, and he would never play for the Portland Trail Blazers again. But with the towering spirit that defined both his game and his humanity, Walton returned to basketball for one more shining moment with the 1986 champion Boston Celtics. It was perhaps most appropriate, because that Boston team was the epitome of teamwork and unselfish play, the tenets of Bill's life on and off the basketball floor. He blended perfectly in the great Celtics sixth-man tradition of Frank Ramsey, John Havlicek, and Kevin McHale, winning the league's Sixth Man of the Year award and playing the most games in a season in his career.

This was a San Diego beach kid who lived for the indoors and the basketball court. From his undefeated high school team through 88 consecutive wins with UCLA, Walton's team won an amazing 142 straight games. Can anyone match that? Typical Bill Walton, he blamed himself for the loss after number 88 despite having scored 24 points. Few made teammates better than he did, because Bill was capable of so much and did less so others could prosper, as evidenced by his 1973 NCAA title game, which was the best game ever in an NCAA tournament, 44 points on 21 of 22 shooting. Walton did what was necessary, averaging 18.5 points and 19 rebounds in the 1977 Finals. In the clinching two-point Game 7 win, Walton had 20 points, 23 rebounds, 7 assists, and 8 blocks, the closest anyone's ever come to a quadruple-double in the playoffs, let alone in a pressure-filled final game. Perhaps even more impressive was the way Walton sacrificed and bonded a team of mostly role players—Maurice Lucas, Lionel Hollins, Johnny Davis, and Bobby Gross—against a Hall of Fame core of Julius Erving, George McGinnis, Doug Collins, Darryl Dawkins, and World B. Free. Walk the walk and talk the talk, though ironically Walton could barely speak. He was outspoken in a controversial collegiate career off the court, arrested in an antiwar demonstration, delivering a letter to President Richard Nixon asking him to resign. But he'd had a severe stutter since childhood, resulting in an off-the-court hesitation to speak. Working with legendary New York sports announcer Marty Glickman, Walton conquered his stutter as he did anything in basketball when healthy, becoming an Emmy Award–winning broadcaster. His Hall of Fame acceptance speech was record length. He was a dedicated Deadhead, touring with the Grateful Dead religiously, attending more than eight hundred concerts. Walton was Finals MVP in 1977 and so dominant in 1978 that he was league MVP despite playing just fifty-eight games. In those two prime years, he was first team all-NBA and all-defense and led the league in rebounds and blocks in '77. He had some forty operations during his lifetime. Bill was fond, no matter the circumstances, of saying he was the luckiest man in the world. No one loved the game and life more. We were the luckiest fans to have seen him play. Those who knew him well were even more fortunate.

**PJ:** I knew Bill when he was a rookie in Portland. He blocked my shot the first time we played. He knew what I was going to do. He was already ahead of it. He was a rebel that Wooden wouldn't let be a rebel. Wooden was like, You can do that if you want, but you're not gonna be on our team.

**SAM:** That was hilarious the way Bill told that story. Wooden required haircuts the first day to properly represent the university, and Bill was what we called a hippie then. Bill loved Wooden, but he explains they're the champions, and what's the big deal with this facial hair and a little over the ears? Wooden agrees Bill is right and he can't make him cut his hair, but says they appreciate what Bill has done for the team and they are going to miss him. Bill pedals right to the barber shop and a half hour later looks like he's a seventh grader again. As we all know, Wooden remained Bill's idol. Bill had the Pyramid of Success in his wallet and posted on his refrigerator. I was visiting there once, and all the boys are there and it's breakfast, and Bill is going over some of the main themes, and they're, "Yes, Bill, OK."

**PJ:** Bill got right into Portland, and Portland's a hotbed of rebellion anyway. I think he was involved in the kidnapping group that kidnapped Patty Hearst.

**SAM:** Unsurprising, given Bill's political views and activism, that he'd run into Jack Scott, who went to Oberlin with that experiment about making sports less about winning. I guess that didn't work. I worked with Bill on some writing projects and didn't get paid on one. The next time I'm in San Diego he says I'm staying with him, and for a week he's taking my son and me bicycling, the zoo, a chef for dinner every night, playing the Grateful Dead instruments in his band room. Bill runs into this guy, veteran down on his luck, so he's also staying there. Former teammates like Greg Lee coming by all day like it's a train station, telling me stories of Bill paying their kids' college tuition. Most generous player ever.

**PJ:** Greg Lee was his assist guy, the guard that played with him at UCLA that he always wanted to play with. I invited Bill to come out to the native reservation Pine Ridge and do a basketball camp with me out there. Came out after they won the championship. He told me about his career. He played basketball all the time. He had these funny feet; his arch was so high that it was an impediment. He said he played too many games, like sixty games in high school. Three games on Saturday, two on Sunday after church. Then they go to these abandoned air force bases and they'd have these seventy-team tournaments. By the time he went to college, he'd played thousands of games.

**SAM:** Bill always was about winning the game and taking it seriously. There was this book called *The Perfect Team* of a player at each position, and I was asked to write the chapter for Bill. So we get together to talk about his career, and I never, not once, could get him to talk about the wins. He'd go into detail about the Notre Dame loss. Portland Game 6 when he's got almost a quadruple-double? Nah, he wanted to talk about Maurice Lucas. I've found this with the really, really great ones—it separates them from just the great. The players who separate from the Hall of Famers are shocked to lose because they never expect to lose. That's how you really know who the best of the best are. That was Bill.

**PJ:** I asked him, Do you think you guys can repeat with Portland? That's the thing we always regretted as the Knicks. But everything fell apart for them when Bill got hurt. Jack actually was not really a big favorite of his. I thought Jack did a terrific job. But Bill had Wooden and everything compared back towards Wooden. He was a special player because of his mental acuity. He was just prescient. He saw the game. He saw how the game had to react to make it work. Good passer, had this little bank hook shot or whatever. Had this little squat jump shot. Wasn't a great offensive player but always gave a lot of credit to Maurice Lucas: "That's what saved our team."

**SAM:** Though, of course, it was Bill, always Bill; might have been the best ever if not for . . .

# Moses Malone

M oses Malone checks in behind the two greatest rebounders ever, Wilt Chamberlain and Bill Russell, for players who played in both the NBA and the ABA, comfortably fifth in rebounding among all NBA players. Moses could get the ball, and even today when a player retrieves his own miss, it's referred to as a Moses Malone. Moses was *strong*, if not the most athletic player. He just worked his way in there, pushed you back with his butt to gain position, and chased and chased and chased the ball. Perhaps not a giant at six ten and probably 260 in his prime, after weighing in at barely over 200 pounds when he came to the ABA from high school, the first modern-era basketball player to do so. But his footsteps were loud; you could hear him coming. Maybe like the giant, "Fee-fi-fo-fum," the old fairy-tale opening line. Maybe changed to "I smell the bones of a Lakersman, I'll grind his bones." As Moses did in perhaps what he's most known for in that 1983 Philadelphia 76ers championship season, his "Fo', fo', fo'" prediction of three series sweeps, which was how "four, four, four" came out in his Virginia drawl. It was four in the Finals over the Lakers, though five earlier against the Bucks, 12–1. Just what a giant would do.

Moses was a giant of the era from the combination of the leagues in 1976 and into the late 1980s. He moved around a lot, which was unusual for someone so influential: He was the only player to have 20/10 seasons with four different teams. Taciturn and reserved, Moses was nevertheless popular with team-mates. Charles Barkley credited Moses with making him an All-Star by getting him to lose perhaps forty pounds as a rookie to keep up with the NBA game. Moses similarly helped lead the 76ers and Julius Erving to the NBA Promised Land in 1983. In one of the great underdog seasons ever, he carried a sub-.500 1981 Houston Rockets to a Finals loss to Larry Bird's new machine with Kevin McHale and Robert Parish. In a four-season stretch in Houston, Malone aver-aged a combined 27.4 points and 15.4 rebounds. And then Malone went to Phila-delphia and finished it off in 1983 when he also received the third of his league MVP awards. He played at least eighty games in eleven seasons, including eighty-three in his rookie ABA season.

The poor kid from rural Petersburg, Virginia, was taking the usual collegiate route to the University of Maryland when he decided to take the money and run, first to the ABA Utah Stars, who went out of business, and then to the Spirits of St. Louis, who were not invited into the NBA in 1976. Moses then began what seemed like his forty years in the NBA desert when the NBA team that drafted him, New Orleans, let his rights go for a draft pick, and then he was selected in the dispersal draft by Portland, which had Bill Walton, so they traded him to Buffalo, which wasn't much interested after all and moved him on to Houston. Where Malone was an All-Star in all his five seasons before arranging a trade to get a better deal with the 76ers, and four more All-Star appearances, before he was back on the road to the Bullets, Hawks, Bucks, Philly, and a brief stopover as David Robinson's backup in San Antonio just before Tim Duncan arrived. It was a somewhat unusual journey for such a celebrated and accomplished player, but it perhaps also resembled just who Malone was as a player: some-one who just put his head down and went where the ball was, and kept going back at it no matter the obstacles or roadblocks. Malone was all-NBA eight times and all-defense twice. He also was an ABA All-Star and led the NBA in rebounding six times, including five consecutive years, and is still the NBA's all-time leader in offensive rebounds.

**PJ:** Those last few ABA seasons we played preseason games against them for the leagues to make some money. They really needed it and took it more seriously. We played the Colonels in an exhibition game, and I think we lost to them somewhere in Kentucky. Played Indiana, the New York Nets. The games were mostly in ABA towns. I think we lost to the Utah Stars. They also had a power forward that was really good, Willie Wise. They had that guard who set a record for number of games played. Broadcaster for Utah for years.

**SAM:** Ron Boone. He was one of those legends no one knew because so few saw the ABA. By the time of the merger/buy-in (because it really wasn't a merger with all the money the ABA teams had to pay to get in), he wasn't the same guy. Broke Johnny Kerr's consecutive-games record. Played more than a thousand straight.

**PJ:** My parents drove down to watch that game from Deer Lodge, Montana, which is like four hundred, five hundred miles, a long trip. It was the only game my parents ever saw me play as a professional. They had no interest.

**SAM:** I guess that fit with the sheltered life you always talked about growing up.

**PJ:** People talk about leadership. I really don't know where it came from, but I've always been that way since I was a kid. My older brother Charles could sing, play the piano, things a minister's son had to do. He was called Reimer, for his dad's name, and was tremendously teased. "Is that a girl's name? Are you a poet?"

**SAM:** So bullying even in *Lonesome Dove*?

**PJ:** I remember stories like this growing up: My brother Joe has this belt, and my older brother says he'd like to have a belt like that. So my brother says he'd sell it for five dollars, and my older brother realizes, "That's my belt and he sold me my belt." That's the kind of conniving he would do, freer with money and into girls and cars. My older brother was into the classics and arts. Joe was into science and mathematics and became a therapist. There was that friction always between them. That's the transactional, transformational analogy I use. I went to grad school in psychology, two summers Upward Bound. One of the things I learned proposing theories was how transformational and transactional groups grew. My inclusiveness of everybody involved is more gestalt in how to get everyone involved.

**SAM:** Reminds me of Bobby Knight and the story he'd tell about Jordan at the '84 Olympics. Halftime of that game Jordan's got like 20 points and a triple-double and the U.S. is up about 30, so Knight decides he'll get on Jordan to get everyone's attention about not letting up. So he yells at Jordan that everyone is sacrificing and screening and Jordan's scoring. Jordan pauses and says to Knight, Didn't Knight say how Jordan is the quickest he's seen? Well, he's just setting the screens so fast Knight can't see. That was Michael, quick with the line, the last word, the quip.

**PJ:** I was fortunate to have brothers who always looked after me: Let's play baseball, pitch to me. Then Joe would take me with him out on dates, we'd go bowling. We couldn't go to the movies or dances; too carnal, too worldly. Pickup games they'd always include me, and all of a sudden I was pretty skilled. So Dad comes home and they're fighting again, and Dad is taking them to the basement for a licking with a razor strap; spare the rod, spoil the child. I'd sit on the stairs crying, "Dad, don't hurt 'em." Joe never cried. We had to change clothes when we'd come home from school. There were work clothes for school, jeans for play. My brother instead would pull his jeans on over his slacks and get reprimanded for that. One time my brother must have done something wrong, a wisecrack or something unbeholden. My dad is bent on punishing my brother Joe for whatever he did. Joe took off running because he knew he was going to get it. They did two laps around church before my dad finally caught him. The congregation was just driving out. "Was that the minister I saw running around the church?" My mother when she described me once to a writer said, "He was the oil in our family. He greased all the rough edges." I think paying attention to people and finding common ground, speaking to their interests, it's always been that way ever since I was a kid. Back home it was the two brothers who fought all the time. I was kind of like the guy in between them, like, "Why are you guys having this argument? Come on, we'll do something fun."

# Robert Parish / James Worthy

Talk about hiding in plain sight at seven one and about 250 pounds, but the nickname said it all. Cedric Maxwell referred to center Robert Parish as "Chief," the nickname drawn from the 1970s Jack Nicholson movie *One Flew Over the Cuckoo's Nest* and the stoic Native American character who looked menacing but said little and just blended in, like Robert Parish did during one of the great runs in NBA history on one of the greatest teams. The talk mostly was about Larry Bird and Kevin McHale. Like another vital third wheel, James Worthy, perhaps more noticeable with his athletic grace reminiscent of an eagle in flight, Parish—and Chris Bosh to an extent later—also was the third guy when everyone mostly saw two. Guys who had to leave their egos at the door. The team was able to count on Parish being there, running the court, putting up a little jumper when Bird or McHale or Danny Ainge or Dennis Johnson or even briefly Bill Walton wasn't doing anything. Robert Parish just came to play. If putting on your hard hat isn't too cliché, that's what he did: He heard the whistle, went to work, clocked out and went home, and came back again. After four seasons with a Golden State Warriors team in decline after their 1975 championship, Parish, perhaps due to his demeanor, was viewed as disconnected and disinterested, a player who supposedly was lazy and didn't care for the game. There was perhaps some stereotyping as well, his having come from a small

Louisiana college, Centenary. But then Red Auerbach did it again, recovering from poor-ownership hijinks to flip a number 1 draft pick of Joe Barry Carroll for Parish and a number 3 pick Boston used for McHale. And a dynasty was on the way. Making seven consecutive All-Star games starting in his first season in Boston, Parish played at least eighty games in five of those seasons and not fewer than seventy-eight. He never averaged 20 points in a season, but he did tally about 10 rebounds every year. Parish is eighth all-time in NBA rebounding. The only time he really became famous was in the 1987 Eastern Conference Finals against the Detroit Pistons. Earlier in the series Bill Laimbeer hit Larry Bird with a clothesline tackle, and in Game 5, Parish, to everyone's surprise, especially Laimbeer's, hauled off and fired several punches at Laimbeer and knocked him down. Nothing was called: The officials said they didn't see it. Everyone hated Laimbeer. That was the game when Bird made the famous inbounds steal of the Isiah Thomas pass to save the game and give Boston a 3–2 lead. Parish was suspended for Game 6, but with Bird scoring 37, the Celtics won Game 7 to advance to the Finals after Adrian Dantley and Vinnie Johnson knocked each other out chasing a loose ball. Parish said about the commentary after the punch, "I never realized how popular I was." Parish was an All-Star nine times and all-NBA twice. He played twenty-one seasons and finished his career with his fourth championship as a third-string center for the 1997 champion Chicago Bulls.

James Worthy was an All-Star seven times and split those six Boston/LA eighties titles with Parish. Worthy changed the NBA, though perhaps not like Wilt or Mikan with the lane size. The Lakers, after winning the title in 1982, nevertheless had the number 1 overall draft pick from another of the many peculiar Cleveland Cavaliers trades by owner Ted Stepien. The Lakers chose Worthy number 1 over Dominique Wilkins. Thereafter the NBA changed the draft rules to institute the so-called Stepien rule, not allowing the trade of consecutive number 1 draft picks. Worthy had a career scoring average of only 17.6. But Big Game James had 28 points in Game 7 in the "exorcising the ghosts" game in Boston Garden for a Lakers championship back in Boston in 1985 and was Finals MVP in 1988 with a triple-double in Game 7 with 36 points, 16 rebounds, and 10 assists. Worthy also had the famous steal to wrap up the 1982 NCAA title for North Carolina after Michael Jordan's winning shot, his first "the Shot" but not his last.

**PJ:** Motivated by Fitch, Robert got his mind into the game, which they said he wouldn't in Golden State.

**SAM:** Krause got crap over the years for some of his draft stuff; Motta always pointed out how he talked him out of drafting Tiny Archibald. But Krause was pushing the Bulls in the seventies for Parish. I remember reading at the time Krause saying a body like that comes along once a century. Parish went eighth, right after Scott May's IU teammate Quinn Buckner.

**PJ:** James was quick, quick dunker, great post moves. That also was Nellie at that time with what he called point forwards.

**SAM:** Remember the Bulls' Mickey Johnson? Little Aurora College outside Chicago, skinny six-ten forward was really the first point forward. Played that way once they ran Motta out. Actually ended up in Golden State, but before Nellie got there.

**PJ:** I mixed him up with the guy in Denver who won all the scoring championships who should have been on that seventy-five list, Alex

English. I guess no one spoke up for him. He's a kid who waited for me after a game in New York.

**SAM:** He played for Frank McGuire at South Carolina, who had that famous New York pipeline of players to the Carolinas. When I think back to Worthy and what-ifs, it's that supposed trade after the Lakers lost in '86 to the Rockets. Buss and Don Carter were negotiating directly and agreed to Worthy for the number 7 pick in that draft, which became Roy Tarpley, and Mark Aguirre because Magic wanted his buddy Mark. Anyway, Jerry West finally hears about the Worthy deal and blows up and threatens to quit, and the deal is rescinded.

**PJ:** Jerry threatened to quit a lot.

# Larry Bird

Larry Bird is associated with some of the greatest plays in NBA history, like the famous 1987 playoff steal from Isiah Thomas. If he had Marv Albert as the announcer, Bird might have been credited with the first great switch-hands layup, his lefty delivery of his own miss in the 1981 Finals after retrieving his own shot on the right baseline. There are so many remarkable stories: Here was this shy, rural kid who was overwhelmed being at Bloomington and Indiana University, so he quit and returned home to what he figured would be his life picking up trash on a garbage truck. Bird's informality was legend: When he finally began to grow a friendship with rival Magic Johnson, Johnson came home with him one time and noticed one of Bird's MVP trophies lying in the back of Bird's mother's pickup. Kevin McHale set a Celtics record, breaking Bird's 53 with 56 points against the Pistons in 1985, and pulled himself out late in the game so as not to pile on. Bird was incensed. "Kevin took himself out of the game," Bird said. "I couldn't believe that, especially against the Pistons. We didn't get along with them, so why not go for seventy, you know?" Nine days later Bird put up 60 against the Hawks and rival Dominique Wilkins. Bird's shots were so spectacular and creative that Hawks players were falling all over themselves on the bench cheering them. Coach Mike Fratello ended up fining several of his players as a result. Like Michael Jordan when he shot that free throw with his eyes closed to show up Dikembe Mutombo, the Celtics were so dominant in the 1985–86 season that Bill Walton said at the end of a road trip in Portland Bird announced to the team he was handling the ball only left-handed, and he basically did and got a triple-double with 47 points, scored the basket to send the game into overtime, and made the winner in overtime with three seconds left.

Yet great as he was—and it's something you hear only rarely and only among the truly elite—Bird, when asked about his play, would say, "My problem is I always remember the big misses and bad plays and shots I should have taken and didn't. I have a tendency to remember the losses more than the good times." If you want to know what separates Jordan and Kobe and Magic and LeBron and Bird and West and Kareem and Russell and Elgin from those not in the mythical top ten, it's that they expected to make every shot. And when they didn't, they were surprised. The Celtics probably have had more championship rebirths than any NBA franchise. Bird was responsible for the 1980s after Red Auerbach faked out everyone, picking him in 1978. And then came Bird's famous decade-long duel with Magic and the Lakers that began in the 1979 NCAA title game and that came to define buddy rivalries like Ali and Frazier, Palmer and Nicklaus, Wilt and Russell, Connors and McEnroe, and Tiger and Phil. It begat the modern era of NBA basketball. Larry led three title teams; along with Wilt and Russell, he was the only player ever to win three straight MVPs; he played in twelve All-Star games in thirteen years; he got on three all-defense teams; he won three straight three-point shooting championships; and he twice reached the elite benchmark of 50/40/90 shooting percentages for field goals, threes, and free throws. And then he added Coach of the Year and Executive of the Year awards. And to think they weren't sure in 1978 when he fell to sixth in the draft if he'd be all that.

**PJ:** I only played against Bird twice, in my last season, his rookie year. I remember one day later when I was coaching for the Bulls, we were playing the Celtics and before the game Bird comes out in warm-ups and asked the coaches who's guarding him. When we told him, he said we need to put someone better on him, he'll get 30 too easy that way.

**SAM:** That was the great Bird paradox, the shy country kid who was the merciless assassin. Ballbuster ego without the ego. I love the story the great NBA PR guy Brian McIntyre tells about that Dream Team. They're making all these guys earn all those fancy hotel stays in Monaco and Barcelona by signing basketballs USA Basketball can sell, and everyone is bitching about having to sign so many, Michael too, and Larry comes in and asks Brian how long everyone spent on it and he says, trying to reassure Larry, maybe fifteen, twenty, twenty-five minutes tops. Larry whips through them in eight or nine minutes, puts his marker down, and declares, "Won another," and walks out. Like that famous 1988 All-Star three-point shooting contest when Larry walks in and asks, "Who's finishing second?" Never takes off his warm-up and, needing the last shot to win, lets it go and starts walking off with the ball in the air and his number-one finger raised. C'mon, seriously? I loved the story that he walked in and saw Leon Wood practicing and when he got in the locker room said to Leon that it looked like he's got a hitch in his shot, and Leon rushed out to shoot more. He was out in the first round.

**PJ:** The guy who's a broadcaster now, Cornbread, he was the one who said by the time training camp was over, he knew Larry was going to succeed in the NBA. They still had Cowens, but Dave was at the end.

**SAM:** The Pacers really should have gotten Michael, because they traded their future 1984 draft pick to Portland for center Tom Owens because there basically was no TV then and they needed ticket sales and thus wins after James Edwards left as a free agent. Which is why they couldn't afford to take Bird, who was staying in college another year. So Bird goes to number 6 in the 1978 draft. They always needed players right away to stay in business. And Bird had this image: quit-IU, beer-drinking, softball guy. Portland has number 1 and doesn't give him a thought and takes Mychal Thompson. Gate sales were everything then. Indiana took Rick Robey at number 3 in 1978, believing it would help them remain more competitive. They also felt they couldn't afford Bird. The rule then was if you didn't sign the guy for a year, he'd go back in the draft. Bird seemed to like softball and working the garbage truck too much, they feared. Who knew what he'd do? Bird was playing golf the day of the '78 draft and never knew he was taken. When he was told, he asked if that meant he'd lost his college eligibility. He promised to stay and get a degree.

**PJ:** I remember when I was trying to gain some support for Bill Fitch for the Hall of Fame and had talked with Larry, but he and Bill weren't getting along at the end. Parish did always admit to the fact that if not for Bill pushing him, he never would have been in the Hall of Fame. He motivated Robert. He was very much behind him, but Bill did leave on bad terms by Celtics standards.

**SAM:** By that time, the Celtics were kind of on automatic. They got swept by the Bucks in the '83 playoffs, and Bill was out for K.C. Enough of Bill's marine drill sergeant stuff. And then they did go to the Finals the next four years at the apex of the Magic/Bird era and won two titles. K.C. was low-key, and they needed that after Bill.

**PJ:** Remember when K.C. famously got in trouble for being too low-key in the huddle coaching Washington during a TV time-out in the 1975 Finals? The press made a big fuss about it. K.C. let Bickerstaff diagram the play, and people said it looked like he had taken over. After that coaches didn't want the assistants doing much.

**SAM:** I remember watching that. I was working in Fort Wayne then, and we'd drive up weekends to see the Bulls. It was that time-out. K.C. is kneeling but not saying anything, and Bernie is scribbling away. It made it look like K.C. wasn't in charge. And then the Bullets after sixty wins were swept by the Warriors, who won forty-eight or forty-nine. K.C. always said he believed in being calm and not being a screamer in the huddle. It became known to coaches as the K.C. Jones Syndrome.

**PJ:** It's also why coaches didn't want those cameras in the huddle.

**SAM:** Those brutal end-of-quarter interviews you also see now in football and baseball. I'll let you know the first time there's something interesting said. I know you don't like those rankings, but if there's a regular guy / superstar GOAT it has to be Larry. Here's my story. I don't know Larry, but it's that magical '86 season or maybe the next one, and I set up an interview with the Celts, and they tell me to meet him after practice at the Multiplex. I get up there and wait, and now they're walking to the bus. I introduce myself and explain. Larry says no one told him and I can come at three, as he's always shooting early. But I say it's an in-depth piece and others will be there. There's a pause and I volunteer, "How about I give you a ride back to the hotel and we can talk?" He says OK. But I'm poor then and have a small Toyota sports car. He squeezes in and we're talking, and it becomes pretty clear I'm lost. They're staying at a Marriott near O'Hare, but anyone who knows the area knows there are no cloverleafs off the interstate there and you have to backtrack off city streets. It was not an area I knew well. Finally, he says to me, "We're lost, aren't we?" I'm mortified. I'd interviewed famous types, but this still was Larry Bird. We're driving around and he says, "You know, if I miss the game, Red is going to kill me." Finally I find the hotel, and as he's getting out he says, "Got enough? Want to come in?" I'm too flummoxed. Years later I got to know Larry well and asked him, "So why did you get in the car with me that day?" "Old story," he says. "Hoosier looking for a ride." I once played golf with Larry. We finish and instead of the clubhouse we go to the maintenance shed, where we drink beers for the next hour or so with the maintenance guys and the caddies. That's Larry.

# Magic Johnson

Everyone knows it means philosophy when you mention Confucius, knowledge with Plato or Socrates, soccer with Pelé, and basketball with Magic. Magic Johnson may not be in the all-time debate that usually involves Michael Jordan, Kareem Abdul-Jabbar, Wilt Chamberlain, Bill Russell, and lately LeBron James. But Magic's style, showmanship, and skill that produced the Showtime basketball of the 1980s Los Angeles Lakers seems to both transcend and encompass the game from the defining fast-break dynasty of Russell and the 1960s Celtics through Jordan's gravity-defying air attacks with the Chicago Bulls to the modern-era highlight scoring. Johnson had the championships, the awards, and the celebrity, and from the 1979 NCAA championship with Larry Bird to Johnson's magical performance in the 1980 NBA Finals replacing an injured Abdul-Jabbar, Johnson helped accelerate what is generally regarded as the modern NBA era that led to the exploits of Jordan, Shaq and Kobe, Tim Duncan, and Steph Curry. That Johnson did so in Hollywood, the worldwide symbol for glamour and make-believe, made it even more appropriate because it helped guide the NBA into an era of performance and entertainment that transcended most everything in sports and spread the NBA game worldwide to gain an audience that rivaled soccer in some respects. Johnson helped do that with a radiant smile and personality and a welcoming and appealing game, a remarkable alchemy that defied science with its appealing humanity.

Magic never wanted to be Hollywood, but like the old post–World War I song about how you were gonna keep them down on the farm after they saw gay Paree, Magic embraced Hollywood, and it loved him back. He almost went to the Chicago Bulls in the 1979 coin flip between the teams with the worst re-cords, the Lakers having the selection from the compensation in the 1976 Gail Goodrich free agency. The league stepped in later with the Ted Stepien draft-pick rule, and enough with giving up all these draft picks, the then–New Orleans Jazz effectively building the Lakers of the eighties. The number 1 pick in the draft used to be determined by a drawing between the worst team of each conference. The Bulls were there in 1979 and called heads. It was tails. Magic said in later years he would have gone back to school if the Bulls won the flip; that's not true. His agent George Andrews, who would negotiate Johnson's ceiling-breaking $25 million contract a few years later, said Johnson had be-friended artist Gilmore and wanted to play with a big center, either Kareem or Gilmore, but actually preferred Gilmore to the remote Abdul-Jabbar because Magic wanted to stay closer to his Michigan home. Even during those rookie negotiations, Johnson still was telling Lakers owner Jerry Buss he was going to return to Michigan to play for the Pistons and best friend Isiah Thomas as soon as he could. It hadn't been easy for Johnson growing up, bused across the city to high school and eventually adapting to the white world of his classmates. De-spite invites from every major university, he chose to remain at Michigan State.

Johnson's two collegiate seasons were performance art culminating in the most watched NCAA finale, against Larry Bird, which they carried into the greatest rivalry decade in NBA history. Magic was Showtime and subbing for the injured Abdul-Jabbar in the clinching game of the 1980 Finals, which re-mains one of the most historic games in NBA history and Magic's introduction as one of the stars of stars. Magic carried the Lakers to the title with 42 points and 15 rebounds. Then he proceeded to conquests and controversy, the shocking first-round elimination in 1981 that eventually led to the coaching him-or-me that got Johnson labeled a spoiled brat and booed nationwide, Pat Riley thus taking over as coach, Norm Nixon traded so Magic could complete his bag of tricks and become the point guard before the "Tragic Johnson" episode in 1984 when Johnson's errors in multiple games, lazy turnovers, dribbling out the clock trailing, and missed free throws led to the Celtics' victory. It was redemption for Magic in 1985 in Boston Garden, Magic's famous baby sky hook to win in 1987, and then, to close out their rivalry, a win in 1988 over old buddy Isiah.

Then came Magic's everyone-knows-where-they-were moment, like the Kennedy assassination or 9/11, when Johnson, after the 1991 Finals loss to Jordan and the Bulls, announced he was retiring from the NBA because he had HIV, and everyone believed it was a death sentence. Johnson worked for AIDS awareness at a time when the country wasn't ready to accept it, and he helped make the terror seem less so. He came back to play for the 1992 Dream Team, to star in the 1992 All-Star game with an MVP performance and a dramatic three-pointer as the last shot, after some players said because of the HIV fears they didn't want to be on the court with him. But Magic informed and relaxed a nation and the world, and he even came back to the NBA briefly as a coach and player, leading a team of touring former NBA players, playing overseas, and remaining a worldwide figure with partnerships in sports teams and a vast commercial and business empire. Which even transcended his basketball: five championships, three times league and Finals MVP, twelve times an All-Star, nine times NBA first team. Magic led the NBA in assists four times and in steals twice, and as a six-nine point guard forced everyone to try to find one for themselves. But like with Steph Curry, you can't, because there was just one.

**PJ:** You could tell with Bird that there was something really special about this guy because of where he took a little old school, Indiana State, and his shooting. You really couldn't tell about Magic. I'd been in the elevator with the Michigan State team when they were freshmen. They were playing in Indianapolis. Their whole team got on, and Magic was there as a kid and I saw him; he was skinny. So then Magic comes in and he can't shut up, Mr. Congeniality. I watched his first Lakers game; they played in San Diego. Kareem hits a hook shot to win and he jumps on his back. I'm thinking this guy really wants to be in the spotlight, wants to be a star.

**SAM:** I'll admit I also wasn't impressed at first. When I was in DC as a political reporter, I'd do some sports freelance for some of our clients. I covered the 1977 Capital Classic in Landover where the Bullets played; it was the forerunner of the McDonald's high school game. It was all about Magic at the 1977 game, but he didn't do much, and Gene Banks was the big star with a huge game. I'm thinking this kid can't shoot. Going to be like Happy Hairston or Satch Sanders, good role player. I stayed with journalism instead of scouting.

**PJ:** Here's my next memory of Magic. He injured his knee his second season. There was a comeback. There are twenty camera people on the floor when he came out to be introduced as starter. It's just crazy; the media is all over this guy. They're really enthusiastic about him.

**SAM:** The most media-friendly guy maybe ever. Players were so accommodating then, but no one like Magic. Magic talks about in high school how he scored so much, and one day the parents all are complaining that their kids never get to do anything, and it's the light bulb for Magic: Pass the ball and let everyone eat. OK, now it's into '87 or '88 at the Finals, and another Magic and Larry and nothing is bigger, the culmination of this decade of the greatest games. Back then the players used to sit at their locker before games and talk to reporters. Not all the players; certainly not Bird or Kareem. So Magic is sitting there for an hour answering everyone, and there's a big circle around him with all the heavyweights, *LA Times*, *Sports Illustrated*, *New York Times*, *Chicago Tribune*. So way in the back Magic spots Dean Howe from *The Flint Journal*, who covered him in high school. "Dean Howe!" Magic shouts. Tells him to come up, and now he's introducing Dean to all the heavy hitters. "This is Dean Howe, wrote this about me in high school, remember that game, Dean?" Guys who wouldn't give him a second look are shaking his hand because Magic's introducing him. Dean is absolutely beaming. That was Magic. Greatest assists.

# Kevin McHale

In some respects, Kevin McHale and Larry Bird were like Shaq and Kobe. For Bird and Bryant, basketball was life, and for Shaq and Kevin, basketball was just a part of life, a great part, a fun part, but maybe not the most important thing to distract from the real enjoyment of life. Though when it got serious, Kevin McHale could be as serious as a clothesline tackle. Which McHale made famous on the way to the Boston Celtics' 1984 championship with his hard foul—as it was called then—and a pair of free throws for Kurt Rambis and game on. The Celtics would win the game in overtime. Kevin McHale could keep the locker room light, the press conferences bright, but could still be his best in the harsh light of competition, with seven All-Star appearances and six times all-defense with the elite Big Three of the 1980s with Larry Bird and Robert Parish. Many select the 1986 Celtics team as the greatest of all time. And though like Kobe Bryant with Shaq, Larry Bird would sometimes say McHale didn't take the game seriously enough. In McHale's best statistical season, 1986–87, when he averaged a career high 26.1 points and still shot more than 60 percent overall, McHale played the entire playoffs on a broken foot, refusing to sit out in hopes of leading the Celtics to a repeat. Injuries from that and a subsequent surgery chipped away at McHale's effectiveness, and within two years he was back to playing off the bench, as he did early in his career in the Celtics' sixth-man tradition, and was out of the game by 1993. But McHale's joie de vivre should never obscure his accomplishments and competitiveness. Bill Walton said the long-armed, coat hanger–shouldered McHale was the best post player he ever saw after Kareem Abdul-Jabbar. McHale had a nice midrange jump shot to set up a potpourri of post moves with drop steps, step backs, up and unders, and hook shots that were some of the most baffling in the game. At six ten and ex-ceptionally long armed, many of McHale's shots were almost as indefensible as Kareem's sky hook. It looked so easy sometimes, the way McHale scored, that he admitted it could appear he was coasting. But that was his style, and playing through a literal broken foot for a month was evidence enough. Bird had to work so hard, and to Kevin it just came naturally.

McHale, playfully called Herman Munster by Mychal Thompson for McHale's sharp and angular features, came to the Celtics out of the hardscrabble iron ranges of Minnesota in the Red Auerbach prestidigitation that eventually cre-ated that immortal Big Three. McHale came off the bench behind Cedric Max-well for several seasons, winning consecutive Sixth Man of the Year awards and being named an All-Star despite not being an NBA starter. McHale produced some big plays at big times, like the defensive block on Andrew Toney to save the 1981 conference finals on the way to the title, and 21 and 9 in those 1987 playoffs on the broken foot. In 1983, McHale flirted with a free-agency escape to the Knicks. Auerbach responded by sending offer sheets for three of the Knicks' players. When the Knicks matched, they were out of free agency and McHale got his deal back with the Celtics. Boston fans were angry, though they got over it quickly because McHale was one of those people who never lost sight of what was fun in life. McHale eventually went on to be an executive and coach for his home-state Minnesota Timberwolves, coached the Houston Rockets, and be-came a popular national NBA broadcaster who also had some well-reviewed acting roles in the TV series *Cheers*. Talk about a guy who deserved the cheers.

**PJ:** I loved him as a player, a really talented post player. He'd give you this fake reverse pivot where he'd come up underneath—exciting move, but he'd travel. Shuffled his feet so quickly they'd miss it. Hibbing, Minnesota, the Iron Range, tough people.

**SAM:** That also was you without the offensive game. The coat-hanger shoulders and torso—you and McHale. Great Boston team, and great fun, too. Loved the stories you'd hear, especially after they pushed out your guy Fitch. Though Fitch was funny. Just in a marine way. Fitch told the story of when McHale got a broken nose and the doctor said they used liquid cocaine. McHale said better watch out or everyone would be coming in with a broken nose. Larry was always giving Bill shit about not bringing that 1965 jump shot in here. So K.C. is coaching, and in the huddle K.C. is drawing things up and Bird just goes, "The heck with it. Give me the ball and get out of the way." K.C. says, "Shut up, Larry. I'm coach. OK? Now, throw the ball to Kevin. Kevin, you give it to Larry, and everyone get out of the way." Anyway, first day they sign Walton and practice is over, and they're in the locker room gathered around and everyone's meeting Bill. So McHale says, "OK, Bill, now you can tell the truth. Did you have Patty Hearst in your basement?" Bill was always sensitive about that one. But there was no hiding on that Celtics team.

# Isiah Thomas

There's probably no one in the history of the NBA who represents the concept of cognitive dissonance more than Isiah Thomas, possibly experiencing as many heroic acts on the basketball court as he's participated in excesses, outrages, and blunders to overshadow them. There was his 16 points in ninety-four seconds in the final game of a 1984 playoff series to force overtime, his 25 points in a quarter in the 1988 Finals on a badly sprained ankle to nearly deliver his Pistons their first NBA championship. Then there was his mistimed pass in the 1987 conference finals that Larry Bird intercepted in one of the most frequently re-aired NBA plays. There was his leadership in dragging the notorious Bad Boys to consecutive NBA championships. Then there was leading the Pistons in their sour walk-off before time had even expired at the end of Game 4 of the Bulls' sweep of them in the 1991 Eastern Conference Finals. Thomas was left off the 1992 Dream Team, essentially a fashion show of the NBA's greatest figures, because of the league-wide disdain for him. Thomas ostensibly was defending rambling and emotional rookie teammate Dennis Rodman at the close of that dramatic 1987 playoff series with Boston and agreed with Rodman that Larry Bird wouldn't have been so celebrated if he were Black. The NBA forced Thomas to make a formal apology to Bird at the Finals. Thomas probably did more for his native city of Chicago than any professional athlete, investing in impoverished communities, setting up a basketball league for at-risk youth, and marching with religious leaders against gun violence. Yet Thomas often is reviled by Chicago fans for the way he played against revered Chicago Bull Michael Jordan, who retains no connection to Chicago. Thomas was blamed in the supposed freeze-out of Jordan at Jordan's first All-Star game, setting in place a storied rivalry between the two and their teams.

Thomas survived and emerged a star from his hellscape of the West Side of Chicago, where he grew up with army tanks patrolling the streets after the rioting of the late 1960s and got his meals from the Black Panthers serving his neighborhood, the youngest of nine children, who had several siblings die from substance abuse and AIDS. Thomas's mother, Mary, famously in a TV movie about the family that was produced by NBA Hall of Famer Chet Walker, had to take out a rifle to hold off neighborhood gangs that were trying to recruit Isiah. Which maybe is how someone listed generously at six one succeeded at such a level in the big man's world of professional basketball. Isiah was a prodigy, earning money for his family in heavily-wagered-upon basketball games as an adolescent. To avoid the gangs, he attended high school a ninety-minute ride away in Chicago's western suburbs. And then won a championship at Indiana University for Bobby Knight with his extraordinary individual play, a departure for a Knight team.

Thomas, with speed, a smooth handle, a reliable shot, a savvy court sense, and a fearless attitude, joined a Pistons offensive machine that was part of the NBA's highest-scoring game and scored 47 points. But watching the players who won, like close friend Magic Johnson as well as Larry Bird, Thomas reasoned it was less about his production than his teammates'. With Jack McCloskey remaking the team with defensive players, the Pistons terrorized the NBA and won consecutive championships in 1989 and 1990 with Thomas's scoring average dropping below 19 per game. Detroit's Bad Boys became a marketing bonanza, until the violence began to spiral out of control. The Pistons eventually tumbled out of contention, and Thomas left the game at thirty-two after an Achilles injury in 1994. A plan to transition into Pistons management fell apart, sending Thomas on a journey through the Toronto Raptors as vice president, the Continental Basketball Association as owner, the Indiana Pacers as coach, the Knicks as president, and numerous business interests, along with TV basketball analysis. Few in NBA history have done as much and been discussed as ambivalently. Thomas was a Finals MVP, twice All-Star game MVP as one of the best showmen in All-Star games history, an All-Star twelve times, league assists leader, and top ten of all time in league assists.

**PJ:** I liked Isiah. I saw him right away his rookie year. I went in the locker room when I was with the Nets, wished him well, and said, "It's going to be interesting watching you in this league," after his college career. He was friendly, another guy like Magic who liked the camera. We've always had a good relationship, even though I had to get on him in New York.

**SAM:** No residual from those ugly games against the Pistons all those years? Isiah even got Bill Cartwright to throw a punch. I'd never seen that. He could be really annoying.

**PJ:** Isiah was really good about all those series. I met him when he was working with the Knicks as team president and he wanted to hire me after I came back from my sabbatical. I spent a day with him at a place in Beverly Hills. It broke down over the players he wanted. His choices were the Chicago center who had been robbed at gunpoint with his family in his own house, Eddy Curry. The other guy he was going to go after and spend $27 million on was this center from Seattle, Jerome James. I said, This guy's a loser. He looks good because he's playing for a contract. We couldn't agree on personnel, and then it came down to protocol. He was all about "These guys have to wear jackets and ties." I said, That doesn't make any sense. I don't have my coaching staff dress in uniforms. We come to practice; they practice in what's comfortable for them. I saw he was going to be rigid like that. It wasn't for me. He got Larry Brown and had an experience with Larry.

**SAM:** I know Isiah wasn't popular, but the famous walkout really also was like the freeze-out, more urban legend.

**PJ:** It was Laimbeer, Rodman, and Isiah. Those three for sure. They just kept walking.

**SAM:** You probably didn't know how Michael killed them in the media before Game 4: The Pistons are undeserving champions because they were so dirty; they are bad for basketball. Michael got into their heads. You're supposed to respect champions. Not them. But that's what rivalries are about, and why there are none now. So Game 4, the sweep. Four minutes left and both teams pull their starters. Pistons players are hugging and the crowd is giving them a long standing ovation, and no one looks angry. Chuck and Isiah seem to be joking. Scott Hastings is taking every shot, and the last one is with 24 seconds left, and now the Bulls get the ball to dribble out that last 24 seconds, as we see in every game now. But remember the Palace. The exits for both teams were at one end, by the visitors' bench. So with about 10 seconds left, the Pistons players start walking slowly toward that exit. Maybe they'll even stop at your bench, but they seem to be waiting. Then there's a time-out with 7.9 seconds left for no reason. Time-out why? Now they are caught, and so they keep walking. Did you guys call it? Michael? It becomes the bad-sportsmanship walkout of all time. Gotcha? So bye-bye, Dream Team.

**PJ:** The famous Magic All-Star game in '92 in Orlando. I was getting on the bus with the players, and Isiah pigeonholed me and asked if I could get Michael to agree to do something. It was a players' union thing. He was the union president, but he wouldn't go talk to him personally. I said he had to or it didn't happen. Don't think he did.

**SAM:** There used to be all sorts of summer games and tournaments and events back then. Magic Johnson had a famous summer game that was sort of the gathering place after the Stokes game faded. Initially, Michael wouldn't go because of the freeze-out stuff. But then he and Magic reconciled and this pay-per-view thing came up for a Michael-versus-Magic one-on-one called *King of the Court* in 1990. But then it gets rejected because the players' association had to agree. Isiah, yes, was president then. The league didn't like the idea either, but the players' association put the kibosh on it. Michael's response was Isiah was just jealous, but if he were in it, no one would have watched.

**PJ:** Magic was close with Isiah but not with Michael until about then, and he dropped Isiah. You always kind of sensed Magic sensed the tea leaves and wind blowing and that kind of thing. That was the Dream Team time. I think Chuck knew it probably was the right thing to insist upon not having Isiah on the team. They bounced it off, brought it to Michael. Michael was like, "I'm not gonna deal with it." He's the kind of guy that he doesn't want to be on either side. He didn't want to declare. But they knew without having to get confirmation from Michael that it was the best thing.

# Dominique Wilkins

Dominique Wilkins was a lot closer to Michael Jordan than Harold Miner. Not that Miner, the two-time Slam Dunk Contest champion, was very close despite the "Baby Jordan" nickname. Wilkins had the slam-dunking chops, the shot that was pretty good but not quite good enough, and the in-game theatrics, minus the tongue flying out, and definitely not the shoes. Marketing does matter, and having a Hall of Fame running mate like Jordan did in Scottie Pippen. Wilkins's best teammate in his prime was Doc Rivers. Wilkins also had the bad luck to come along and elevate his team when the Eastern Conference was probably the most competitive in league history with the Boston Celtics and Philadelphia 76ers both brimming with Hall of Famers, a powerful Milwaukee Bucks team winning close to sixty games a season, a Detroit Pistons team on the rise to multiple championships, and then those Baby Bulls. After failing to crack fifty wins in sixteen of the previous seventeen seasons, Wilkins led the Atlanta Hawks to four consecutive seasons winning at least fifty games and to a then-franchise-most fifty-seven. Wilkins won the league scoring title and twice averaged more than 30 per game. He was top seven in scoring for seven consecutive seasons and first or runner-up three straight years, ten straight seasons averaging more than 25 per game.

Wilkins's Atlanta Hawks never got past the second round of the playoffs, even with what many called the greatest shoot-out in league history, the fourth-quarter battle between Wilkins and Larry Bird in the 1988 Eastern Conference Semifinals, when Wilkins had 47 points and 16 in the fourth but was beaten by a basket by Bird's 20 in the fourth quarter. Legendary referee Jake O'Donnell, the only official to work both Major League and NBA All-Star games, labeled that game and Jordan's 63 points against Boston in the 1986 playoffs the two most memorable games he officiated. But when your team lacks the so-called necessary supporting cast, which was a high bar in that era, and when your team doesn't have the miracle playoff moments, like Jordan did with his winning shot against Cleveland in the 1989 playoffs, you don't get in that elevated conversation. Wilkins never played with a Hall of Famer in Atlanta until the additions of Moses Malone, Mo Cheeks, and Sidney Moncrief in their last seasons. So often was Wilkins left out of the conversation that the biggest and most mysterious snubs were when Dominique and Bob McAdoo were left out of the NBA's top-fifty vote in 1996. They were both added to the top-seventy-five list. But Dominique Wilkins was in Michael Jordan's class for in-game acrobatic dunking, high scoring, and excitement matched by few in NBA history.

Playing the prime of his career in football- and race car–centric Atlanta, it was difficult for even the spectacular high-flying six-eight Wilkins to get as much notice, especially with a team that barely creased the national TV consciousness. But Nique was something to see with his powerful flying-windmill dunks. He won two slam-dunk championships and most agreed he should have had a third. But Jordan was such a sentimental favorite for the 1988 game in Chicago. Wilkins also was an underrated shooter. Thirteen of his 16 points, including a three-pointer, in that famous face-off with Bird came on jump shots. Wilkins was an All-Star nine consecutive seasons, and curiously with his team in first place and an All-Star he was traded that season to the Clippers at the trade deadline in February. The belief was the Hawks couldn't afford to pay Wilkins with his contract expiring. Wilkins then became a journeyman, playing for the Celtics, in Greece, for the Spurs, in Italy, and then back to the NBA to finish his career with Orlando in 1999. He was all-NBA seven times and an All-Star and cup winner in both Greece and Italy.

**PJ:** He was the guy who really challenged Michael.

**SAM:** The big names back then were Bird and Magic, and the big games the Celtics and Pistons, but the Michael/Dominique games were the ones I think the fans looked forward to most. I know I did. You could sit back and enjoy the show, the best basketball had. Sure, the Lakers and Magic were Showtime and the Celtics wore you down with their relentless half-court execution and Bird's innovations. But Michael and Dominique meant a show, two of the greatest in-game dunkers ever. That was another thing. You could circle it on the schedule and you could count on it, unlike these days. They never missed games. Michael missed one game after his broken foot in the next five years, and Dominique his first nine seasons from his start in '82 never missed more than four games and played at least eighty in six of those seasons. Both believed in the show and seemed to feel an obligation to perform. Like in the '86–'87 season, one game Dominique goes for 57 against the Bulls, Michael 41. The Hawks are blowing out the Bulls and Dominique sits the last eight minutes. Later that season, Dominique puts 54 on the champion Celts. Michael remembers, of course. Goes into Atlanta after actually going into the Hawks' locker room before the game to warn them. Michael scores 61. And so from there, the next few years in the Stadium it was the game of the season. Mostly forgotten, but great, great stuff.

# Clyde Drexler

Clyde Drexler as the running buddy of collegiate teammate Hakeem Olaju-won finally did get a championship with Houston. But he still was another player who never quite got out of the shadow of Michael Jordan. Supposedly Drexler was the reason the Portland Trail Blazers passed on Jordan in the 1984 draft for center Sam Bowie. The six-seven greyhound Clyde the Glide was Jor-danesque, as the theory went at the time, a high-flying athlete, a transition bullet train without much of a jump shot. Like MJ at UNC. So Jordan remembers, and here comes the famous 1992 shrug, six three-pointers that set the table for the Bulls' 1992 championship win over the Trail Blazers, who were supposed to be that season's team of destiny. It seemed that whatever Clyde did, Michael did it higher, faster, and better. Drexler dunked more with angry power than entertaining élan. He embraced the three, though he didn't shoot it well, which was the fundamental issue with his University of Houston collegiate finals upset loss to North Carolina State, one of the biggest upsets ever. But he did play for the best collegiate-nickname team ever, Phi Slama Jama. Drexler was an All-Star ten times and all-NBA five times, with a five-year scoring run into the early 1990s averaging about 25 per game. He also was one of the best rebounding guards.

**PJ:** Clyde would put his head down and start driving down the court and he was pretty unstoppable. He was a bull, taking that ball and running the length of the court, head down, dribbling like a battering ram. Michael had fun with him. Because Portland was a team that passed on him. The whole thing about Portland and their base and Nike. Everything just pointed to a perfect thing, and this one guy that was a challenge to him was Clyde Drexler.

**SAM:** Bunch of next Michaels like Clyde was supposed to be before Michael. Ron Harper before the knee surgery. Grant Hill. Vince Carter ran away from it more than anyone, the dunker from North Carolina. About passing over Michael in the '84 draft, Hakeem in his book claimed, though it was debunked by the Houston and Portland GMs, that the Trail Blazers offered Houston their number 2 pick for Ralph Sampson. Of course, Portland would have wanted Sampson, then Rookie of the Year, over Bowie. But everyone was going for two bigs then. No way Houston even listens.

**PJ:** Michael came back from an All-Star game and he had this story about Clyde coming to practice with two left shoes. Michael was like, "How could that happen?" I suppose it could happen if you're in a rush, but for Michael, you know, shoes . . . That's really important.

**SAM:** That actually was the famous Dream Team story when Clyde shows up at practice with two left sneakers, and Michael already is taunting him about the Finals and his six threes from "the Shrug" game, Game 1. I think Clyde claimed he got dressed in the dark and didn't see what he put in his bag. So Barkley's yelling that Clyde has two left feet.

**PJ:** Portland might have won in '92 if the league hadn't changed the rules for the Finals; at least that's what Rick Adelman has always said.

He's still mad at me about that. They have this brutal conference finals, and Buck Williams and Karl Malone are throwing each other all over the place, pushing, shoving, on the floor. They literally threw each other down. The announcers made a big deal of it. So we start the Finals and Darell Garretson comes in and says that the conference finals were an embarrassment, the alligators-in-the-lane thing Johnny Bach talked about. He says the physicality of the last series is not going to be tolerated. Which is a good deal for us, because we were worried about Buck dominating Horace. Buck was one of the monsters of the game; people don't know how good the guy was. He's not in the top seventy-five except in my mind's eye.

# Charles Barkley

Charles Barkley was named to eleven NBA All-Star teams and was voted all-NBA eleven times. He was an All-Star game MVP and league MVP. His jersey number was retired by two franchises and he has two Olympic gold medals. And then he really became popular and famous. One of the most unusual NBA stories has been the rocky road of Charles Barkley from NBA rogue to beloved public teddy bear. Charles Barkley is incongruous in American sports, and this is the secret: In an unapologetic world built on pride and ego for success, Barkley is unique because when the joke is on him, he'll laugh harder than anyone else. It's just not part of the DNA of these elite athletes who overcome challenges every stage of their lives. There's really never been anyone in professional sports willing to be the target of the prank and who welcomes it with such an endearing insouciance. Barkley was one of the premier talents of his era, a six-six dirigible of a man capable of doing the things both the six-foot and the seven-foot guys did, and often better than both. With an appealing immaturity that has enabled him to grow more popular despite the arrests and the outrages. His teams never won the ultimate game, but perhaps no one has succeeded more than Charles Barkley.

**PJ:** It always was something when we were in Philadelphia. Michael was always trying to hide his laugh. It's twenty minutes before the game, and our guys were shooting and now getting ready to get back on the court, and Charles is just coming in to put on his uniform and sneakers. "Charles, get in the locker room and get yourself ready for the game." "Nah, I'm all right, Coach."

**SAM:** Barkley admitted it was a rough introduction for him to the NBA from Auburn and little Leeds, Alabama. He'd had these incredible run-ins with Bobby Knight, who cut him from the 1984 Olympic team when he obviously was the second-best player after Jordan. Jordan said Barkley would be making fun of Knight, even challenging Knight to take it outside or quit yelling at him. Then-GM Pat Williams was having a ball with Barkley at maybe 295 pounds, made up all sorts of nicknames like "the Round Mound of Rebound." It was remarkable to see the way Barkley could take a rebound, usually away from even Moses Malone, and remind you of a runaway locomotive steaming full court and dunking the ball and hanging there. For the record, Knight had to have his guy Steve Alford on that '84 Olympic team, and you couldn't skip Patrick Ewing or Chris Mullin and Sam Perkins. But it also was Vern Fleming, Jeff Turner, and Leon Wood. Like the great 1960 Olympic team you always said you wished see play with Oscar, West, Bellamy, and Jerry Lucas. Also Jay Arnette, Allen Kelley, and Lester Lane. Lenny Wilkens always told me being left off that team was his greatest basketball disappointment, and not only because he was unable to represent the country. Lenny believed he was left off because it would have been too many Black players.

**PJ:** Michael talked about that Olympic tryout. It comes down to sixteen and they're sitting there, Michael trying to stifle a laugh, and Charles is doing a stand-up about Knight's wing-tip shoes—only old men wear those, oh, right, you're an old man, normal Charles Barkley humor. But also that self-deprecating type of thing.

**SAM:** The famous Jordan at number 3 in 1984. Billy Cunningham is coaching the 76ers, North Carolina guy, Dean Smith has been telling Billy the 76ers have to draft Jordan. Others say it now, but then only the 76ers would have taken Jordan over Olajuwon. The 76ers were offering the Bulls all sorts of stuff for the Bulls' number 3 pick. It was no secret the Bulls were losing games at the close of that season trying to get the pick for Olajuwon, though the Rockets were doing even better. The Bulls had drafted a bunch of guards in previous seasons, Reggie Theus, Quintin Dailey, Ronnie Lester. They needed size, and Sam Perkins was considered a prize. We thought they might take him. Like in '08 the Bulls needed scoring. It wasn't so slam dunk as everyone says now. Hey, I'd have taken Rose over Michael Beasley. The 76ers had picks numbers 5 and 10 and said if the Bulls wanted another shooting guard, how about All-Star Andrew Toney, then probably the league's best two-way shooting guard? The Bulls needed depth and talent, and we weren't sure about Rod Thorn's drafting acumen. He knew basketball but not so much the draft. But he got that one right. My favorite story that training camp was the first practice. Rod's back at the office after practice was called off early. He calls to find out why. Bulls assistant Bill Blair says Jordan just stole the ball from everyone and was dunking over everyone and they couldn't have a game. "Well, you finally didn't fuck up a draft," Blair told him.

**PJ:** Charles sure commands a lot of attention in the basketball world now. Even more than when he played.

**SAM:** We've all got stories. The *Trib* sends me out to interview him, but Barkley is fighting with the media already about his late hours and his weight, and I remember Pat Williams telling me he and Billy Cunningham are watching preseason scrimmage and Billy says, "This kid is going to be the death of me." Billy quit after Charles's rookie season. So Charles blows me off multiple times, but I'm just as stubborn and hang in there, and we finally have lunch and he goes, "Guess you're not such an asshole after all." There's never been a more fanfriendly player. I've seen him walk around giving out hundred-dollar bills. He talks to everyone. And listens. And has a moral code—even if there's been arrests, and he spit on a kid, and there was the famous Nike "I'm not a role model" thing, and him saying how he was misquoted in his autobiography, and the time he threw the guy through the window at Major Goolsby's in Milwaukee. Barkley was so welcoming he got the taciturn John Stockton to make a joke. Before the Dream Team practices Barkley was telling everyone not to run if Stockton has the ball because he'll only throw it to Malone. Stockton cracks back that it's true, but it's because he'd catch it and Barkley wouldn't. No one has heard John Stockton say anything funny before or since. Barkley suffered a career-ending injury in 1999, but he limped back onto the court for a last moment to go out on his terms with a layup of a putback and retired to become one of the greatest, if not the most knowledgeable, sports analysts in TV history. As Mrs. Seinfeld said in the TV show, "How could anyone not like him?"

# Michael Jordan

David Stern loved to tell the story about when he began courting the world. He was in China in the late 1980s, and the door to China for the NBA is opening a crack. They were interested in one thing in China about the NBA, Stern related. They wanted to see the Red Oxen. Which is what they called the Bulls, because of Michael Jordan and the flight and excitement he came to represent and embody. Statistics make sports fun and interesting and are the foundation for fantasies, fantasy leagues, and the modern podcast world. But there never has been anything like the worldwide embrace of a basketball player. Maybe Pelé or Ali, but no one really reached everywhere like Michael Jordan. Dennis Rodman's flirtation with North Korea began because Kim Jong Un's father was such a Bulls fan he'd try to contact the team for memorabilia. Watch some Law & Order episodes and see a Bulls hat on the bookshelf. Phil tells this story of one of the owners of the Bulls on a trip to the Himalayas, and he's lost his passport trying to go to France. He shows his Bulls identification and offers tickets for a game if the agent is in the U.S. He's waved through.

Sports is about the winners and losers, but also about the memories. And no one has produced as many as Michael Jordan. There was the 63 points in the 1986 playoffs against maybe the best team ever, the 1986 Celtics. "The Shot" in the 1989 playoffs against the Cavaliers to save that series in a win-or-go-home moment. The All-Star free-throw-line dunk contest winner in '88. The switch-hands layup in the 1991 Finals, a spectacular play. The eyes-closed free throw in 1991 just to show he could. "The Shrug" and 35 first-half points and six threes in Game 1 of the 1992 Finals. The 1993 Finals with games of 31, 42, 44, 55, 41, and 33 and every fourth-quarter point in the comeback before Paxson's three. Retiring to shock the world in 1993 to play Minor League Baseball. I'm back. Returning in 1995, a worldwide story, and the double-nickel 55 points in Madison Square Garden. The 1997 playoff flu game with 38 points after the Game 1 winner in that series. When Mutombo said Jordan never dunked over him to the 1997 playoffs then Jordan did. Like some years before when Jordan dunked on John Stockton and the Jazz owner chided him to pick on someone his size, so Jordan then dunked on seven-footer Mel Turpin. Then the sequence of the '98 Finals steal from Karl Malone and then full court and the jumper over Bryon Russell to silence the Jazz fans, the incredible scene of the arena going quiet—because they knew—when Jordan was just lining up to shoot and avoid the Game 7. And even when Jordan couldn't stay away and returned to play for the Washington Wizards in 2001, Coach Doug Collins, not realizing Jordan's all-time consecutive streak of double-figure-scoring games at 866, took out Jordan when he had 6 points. The next game Jordan scored 51 to show he still was Michael Jordan. There's never been another and likely never will be.

**PJ:** I end up driving over and Boston is playing Chicago. My CBA team was out of the playoffs. We went over as a family. Jimmy Rodgers got me tickets. Chicago is going to play Boston in the playoffs. We sat in the family section against the Celtics and we watched Michael Jordan. My son, Ben, he'd seen Michael in the Olympics and came then and told me, "You gotta watch this guy play." He was five years old. I'd taken him down to Puerto Rico when I was coaching there. They came to the games with me, sat on the bench. We ended up one game getting in a fracas, and the kids ended up off the bench standing right next to the court. My assistant was like, "Get your kids out of there. This is dangerous." He pulls up his pant leg and he's got a gun in his holster. I was like, "OK, I'm in deeper down here than I thought." I kept them off the bench after that. It was pretty ratty stuff going on there.

**SAM:** Which was what prepared you perfectly for the zoo that became the Bulls, right?

**PJ:** I'm not sure Michael was ever uncoachable; he was defiant. That was one thing pointed out in *The Last Dance*. Our practices were more difficult than our games. Michael brought that intensity to practice, to everything he did. We're on a road trip and he's at the top of his game the fourth night in five. Unbounded energy. Those were the stories that started coming out at the Dream Team of playing cards and he wouldn't let those guys go to bed and then he'd practice and kick the shit out of them and then go play golf, and then do it all over again.

**SAM:** We always said he was like a hummingbird, manta ray, a shark, definitely a shark, just never stopped moving.

**PJ:** Michael was a better practice player than Kobe, but for us Shaq distorted everything. I'd have to take Shaq out and we'd play this game we called "fireman's game," which was a four-on-four. I liked the players to feel they were competing. They need that. You've got to have fun with it. Everyone else would be lagging, dragging. Jerry would always say, "We can't keep a two-guard because Michael destroys these guys." A backup guard who did pretty well in New Jersey, Dennis Hopson, would have been a good backup for us.

**SAM:** The Hopson backstory was that, as part of the NBA labor deal, that year a player could sacrifice some salary for his team to add a player; Magic had done it. So Jordan gives back $100,000 and he believes they'll use it for his idol, Walter Davis, who is on the outs in Phoenix. But Krause goes and gets Hopson, and that was it for him with Michael. Gentle guy, Hopson, and Michael just ran him off the team in practices like he did with Rodney McCray in '93. I forget who he wanted then.

**PJ:** That game we first saw Michael in Boston, Ben hung out in the corridor hoping to get Michael's signature. He came out and wouldn't sign—had tweaked his hamstring was the report and didn't play the second half. But he was very kind. June said he smelled good. Ben was a little heartbroken. You could see he wanted to get close to the basket, was uncomfortable shooting shots, but so competitive. I watched him his first year and they'd be down 20 and he'd take over every fourth quarter, all kinds of plays, attacked the hoop, short bank shot. You could see he was all about winning. There was no stopping this guy.

**SAM:** Like those promises when Michael gets on the bus to the airport for Phoenix after the Game 5 "Save the City" loss and says, "Good morning, world champions." Like the last shot in Utah in '98.

**PJ:** I said Jerry Sloan will not call a time-out. Jerry didn't like teams to get set up. I said, "They'll come back downcourt and run a Hornacek screen for Malone, and Michael, you can double back on Malone and see if you can steal the ball." Michael fights through, knocks it out of his hands, and everyone got back and set it up and this time Michael didn't go to the basket. Though the game before I made a mistake. I should have called the last shot for Toni; he was eleven of thirteen. But we were so used to Michael making the last shot. Toni probably would have had an easier shot. We benched Dennis at some point in the play-offs because they started doubling off him.

**SAM:** I have a digression here; my apology to Mike. The thing I felt bad about was the line Michael used saying Republicans buy sneakers, too. It was a quip, a joke, to get me off his back when I was trying to make conversation about politics. It was Michael's get-the-last-word stuff, why I loved that Hall of Fame speech; that was him, slicing you up in fun. Anyway, he was joking and I put the line in one of the books I wrote about him, and it becomes red meat for the progressive extremists. Those were NBA apolitical times because teams were going out of business. So everyone agrees to a revolutionary salary cap to save maybe a hundred jobs, and even Kareem isn't politicking. No one's doing the activist thing they began doing ten years ago with the league prospering. It was just a joke, just Michael. Like we used to say as kids: Can't take a joke, you know what to do. Michael ever sign that autograph for your kid?

**PJ:** That had been my only connection with Michael. I'm an assistant now with Doug, and I'm saying how Red Holzman told me the significance of a great player is how much he makes everyone else on the team better; that's how you measure a good player. Doug says, "You've got to tell Michael that." I say, "Are you crazy? I've been here two weeks." Doug says he needs to hear that from someone who played on a championship team, a team like the Knicks. "Really?" "Yes, please do." So I did it. Other than that, I stayed away from Michael. Never asked for anything as he was pulled in so many different ways. I did mostly advance scouting, was not around the team that much as an assistant. Individually, I did work with Pippen the most. I could still play a little and played against him. We established a good relationship. Michael did say he was OK with the making others better. He said he could still lead the league in scoring. He said no one is going to average 30 points and there was nothing to doing that. He'd found his niche.

# Hakeem Olajuwon

Hakeem Olajuwon should have been setting up the metaphorical head-stones; he just killed guys. No one took out great centers better than Hakeem Olajuwon. The Rockets' big man, whose feet moved faster than probably anyone's but Fred Astaire's, took out Patrick Ewing and David Robinson when he led the Rockets to back-to-back championships in 1994 and 1995, the latter when Robinson was league MVP. That 1995 championship was when Olajuwon, with a late-season addition of aging former collegiate teammate Clyde Drexler, led the sixth-place Rockets, without home-court advantage in any series, to wins over the teams with the four best records in the league, teams that averaged a combined sixty wins. In that two-year run when Olajuwon averaged 30 points combined on the way to the titles, his Rockets beat teams led by Drexler, Barkley and Karl Malone twice each, Patrick Ewing, David Robinson, and Shaquille O'Neal, the latter swept. Anyone catch the license plate? Olajuwon was just too fast, both on offense and defense. He became the only player to win MVP, Finals MVP, and Defensive Player of the Year in the 1994 run. And this all came just about a decade after his "Twin Towers" combination with Ralph Sampson reached the heights of the NBA Finals with a so-called gentleman's sweep, four straight wins after an opening loss to the Magic/Worthy/Kareem

Lakers still in their prime, interrupting a run when the Lakers won three titles in four seasons, stopped only by Houston.

It was a long way up for the poor soccer-playing kid from Lagos, Nigeria, who uneasily ventured to another desert, Houston, Texas, to give basketball a try as he filled out to seven feet. Which was good for filling up the goal, as he did in soccer as a goalkeeper. But it turned out even better for basketball, where Olajuwon, schooled in summers by then–Rockets star Moses Malone, learned the subtleties of the NBA and with Drexler led their famous Phi Slama Jama dunk machine to consecutive NCAA finals, losing to the miracle North Carolina State and Jim Valvano and Patrick Ewing's overpowering Georgetown. With Michael Jordan looming, no one among NBA executives in the 1984 collegiate draft was distracted from pursuing Olajuwon, whose possibilities so captivated the NBA that the league instituted a draft lottery the following season because so many teams were intentionally losing games for a chance to get the number 1 draft pick and select Olajuwon, then known as Akeem. Jordan would go number 3 to the Chicago Bulls in that 1984 draft. And it seemed to make sense, as Olajuwon went to the Finals in his second NBA season. But teammate Ralph Sampson, the number 1 pick in the 1983 draft, was injured and soon traded. It resulted in a drift through the standings for Olajuwon's Rockets. Houston's slide in the standings, with four straight first-round playoff defeats and then missing the playoffs in 1992 even as Olajuwon was making all-NBA teams and leading the league in rebounding and blocks, led to a contract stalemate and Olajuwon's request to be traded. Offers poured in, but the Rockets held firm even as Olajuwon condemned ownership and management. The flexible, player-friendly Rudy Tomjanovich was hired as head coach. And Olajuwon, without the greatest core of teammates but with his blinding footwork and Dream Shake moves as irrepressible on the floor as Kareem's sky hook in the air, carried the Rockets to the 1994 title with a series-saving block against John Starks. Then came the famous domination of Robinson and on through Shaq and the loaded Orlando Magic the next season. Olajuwon became the NBA's all-time leader in blocks, though, of course, he'd be third if they counted blocks as official statistics when Wilt and Bill Russell played. Olajuwon was Finals MVP both years, twelve times all-NBA, nine times all-defense, and twice Defensive Player of the Year. He led the NBA twice in rebounding and three times in blocks and was MVP in 1994.

**PJ:** He had this lateral movement that was unbelievable. I can remember thinking, "This guy must be traveling. There must be something going on more than a normal pivot foot." He'd make a move and shoot his shot and would do an inside reverse pivot and shoot his shot around you, and then all of a sudden you'd say, "Where is he?" He used to try to steal the ball a lot in the backcourt because he was so agile, tremendous agility for a big guy. Shaq was athletic but more of a force, and he'd power straight ahead. Shaq didn't know what to do with Olajuwon and got swept in that playoffs with Orlando. The Rockets went on to have multiple sweeps. We barely avoided it.

**SAM:** You know, the biggest of the what-ifs was that Hakeem won his two titles when Jordan went on his baseball sabbatical. Could you have beaten them even with Michael? Those Rockets were the best team against the Bulls in that era, the only one with a winning record during the first three-peat years. I could see them knocking Michael out. Hakeem was like Michael in some ways. I remember reading about him when he first came to the Rockets, and he'd get doubled or tripled and teammates said to move the ball, and he'd say to throw it to him and he'd dunk on all of them.

**PJ:** I felt bad they didn't win an NCAA title on a fluke thing, fouled and fouled and fouled and missed. You saw Hakeem and what talent he had and the speed, the quickness, his noncompliant footwork that was kind of illegal. How's this guy getting away with this? Or was he just faster than the eye? He'd chase a ball down in the backcourt, so mobile at six ten, six eleven; he was imposing. Poor Ewing had to play against him when the Knicks finally got to the Finals. Hakeem was too quick for Bill, and Horace had trouble with Thorpe. He was too physical. Michael had a thing about him being in the middle there, and he rarely performed well against Houston. He didn't go to the basket as often with Hakeem. They were the only one to beat us like that.

# John Stockton

When they talk about power forwards in NBA history, the names of the showy ones usually are mentioned first, like Barkley, KG, Dirk, the Big E. And then they get around to the best one, Tim Duncan. Similarly, when they talk about the greatest facilitators, they talk about Magic and Oscar and Kidd and even LeBron, and the biggest thieves, Payton, Chris Paul, and often Pippen and Jordan. And then the guy who has so many more than the second guy it would take four more years playing to catch up. So maybe you can't make the case that John Stockton is the game's greatest guard, but you certainly could call him the Little Fundamental. Because quietly, efficiently, and professionally, the fundamentally exacting Stockton delivered the ball with precision and extracted it with aplomb in a reliable and lengthy career devoid of an NBA championship—which lowered his profile, though that part he never minded. In his nineteen years in the NBA, he played all eighty-two games a remarkable sixteen times, including twelve of his first thirteen seasons. Stockton, sticking to short shorts long after everyone went long, didn't score much, all the better to be noticed less. But in the classic view of the traditional point guard created to make others better, he certainly elevated his pick-and-roll teammate Karl Malone, with whom Stockton teamed for more than 1,500 games and a pair of disappointing NBA Finals losses to Michael Jordan and the nineties-dynasty Chicago Bulls.

Stockton and Malone couldn't match Jordan and Pippen, certainly not with a Rodman included. But it became two marvelous six-game series in which in Game 6 in 1998 Stockton's three-pointer with 41.6 seconds left put the Jazz ahead by three points before Jordan's miracle closing sequence won the series with the steal from Malone and the all-time silencer shot over Bryon Russell. And while Jordan had his "the Shot" against the Cleveland Cavaliers in the 1989 playoffs, in Salt Lake City Stockton's 1997 three-pointer against the Houston Rockets to put the Jazz in the Finals for the first time will always be their "the Shot."

There wasn't any flair to Stockton, just the finish. No behind the back or between the legs, no crossover, no hands under or on the side of the ball, even as large as his were. Just a straightforward bounce pass or chest pass; Tex Winter would be proud. Jerry Sloan was. If you were an NBA hotshot guard, you learned not to overlook this slightly built, six-one 175-pounder who came up in informal player votes as the dirtiest player after Dennis Rodman. Stockton might have been mistaken as a doppelgänger for the *Simpsons* character Milhouse, but you wouldn't want to look the other way. Few guards ever have screened with such ferocity, opponents complaining about Stockton's wandering knees, shoulders, and elbows. Who, me? Three times he had at least 25 assists in a game and once, in 1991, 28. He didn't attempt many but seven times shot more than 40 percent on threes with a career mark above 38 percent. His overall career field goal average was almost 52 percent. He led the NBA a record nine consecutive seasons in assists, almost 14 per game during five years in that stretch. All from little Gonzaga in Spokane, where as an unheralded number 16 selection in the 1984 draft he was dropped from the 1984 Olympic tryouts. He then played off the bench his first three years behind fleet Rickey Green. Once Stockton moved into the starting lineup, he was selected for nine consecutive All-Star teams. The Jazz's playoff futility during those early seasons, his career playoff mark being under .500, dimmed his accomplishments until the consecutive NBA Finals and a place on that unhappy list with Malone, Barkley, Iverson, Miller, and Ewing as the best to never win the big one. Stockton was all-NBA eleven times, all-defense five times, and twice steals leader, in addition to nine times assists champ. He appropriately shared MVP with Malone in the 1993 All-Star game in Salt Lake City.

**PJ:** I think John was better in the whole game than Isiah. He wasn't as prominent in scoring, but he was better in the whole game, defense, steals. When it became time, he would score, when forced to. If you remember John going at full pace down the court, you remember the power that he played with. You think about the fact that he dominated Steve Kerr. I couldn't even play Steve Kerr against him because that was no matchup for Stockton. It was like, You're putting this child out on the court here with me?

**SAM:** Kerr tells the story of when his father was helping him try to get a basketball scholarship because Steve in high school was with his father in Lebanon, where his dad, Malcolm, was later murdered by terrorists. Steve could shoot but wasn't fast, and no one had seen him anyway, but Gonzaga offered a look. "Hey, we've got this kid on the team you can play against." No problem, Kerr figures, white kid, kind of scrawny with these sunken eyes. John Stockton absolutely works over Kerr up and down the court; he can't get shots off, barely can get across half-court. "Thanks for coming, but no thanks." Steve called it his Spokane disaster until he got that last scholarship and favor from Lute Olson.

**PJ:** Steve had no idea who he was. He ended up going to Arizona by default. But literally, we've gotta hide this guy if we play Utah. But

Steve made that shot against Utah in the last moments of the first time we played them in '97. We did know what was gonna happen. We'd run that play before, and Michael scored on a last-second jump shot against Utah in the opening game of that series. That was a direct look. That shot's gonna be made.

**SAM:** Steve's explanation at the Grant Park rally was the best thing I ever heard at a championship celebration. Remember? Steve goes, "There's been some misconceptions about what really happened about that shot, and I wanted to clear it up. We called time-out with twenty-five seconds to go, went into the huddle, and Phil told Michael, 'Michael, I want you to take the last shot.' And Michael said, 'Phil, I don't feel real comfortable in these situations. So maybe we ought to go in another direction. Why don't we go to Steve?' I thought to myself, 'Well, I guess I've gotta bail Michael out again. I've been carrying him all year, so, you know, what's one more time?' The shot went in, and that's my story and I'm sticking to it." I've never been around an NBA player who understood the media better. I guess Stockton in his way, also. He was like Duncan in the respect that he mastered the art of saying nothing or making it so irrelevant and boring that everyone began to leave him alone, the locker room version of "It felt good."

# Patrick Ewing

Patrick Ewing was, like David Robinson, supposed to be Bill Russell. But when you don't have Cousy, Sharman, various Joneses, Heinsohn, and Havlicek, not to mention Satch Sanders, Frank Ramsey, and Don Nelson, well, then you become the offense as much as you can. David Robinson did and finally got his NBA championship when Tim Duncan showed up. Patrick Ewing had to carry on with John Starks, Anthony Mason, Charles Smith, Charles Oakley, Charlie Ward, and so many other fine players, but no one really who could allow Ewing to be the comfortable number two, or be the support for a fearsome number one. Don't let the ferocious look scare you. Patrick was a teddy bear, a bighearted big man hardened by the demands of New York basketball. Willis Reed was so much more celebrated, but so much less. Having Frazier, Barnett/Monroe, Bradley, and DeBusschere sure helped. Which is not to take anything away from them but to understand how much Patrick Ewing did and how much he sacrificed to get the Knicks as far as he did. They never won a championship during Ewing's fifteen-year run. But Ewing basically made the Knicks more relevant than at almost any time in the modern NBA era other than their brief 1970s magical period. He also ran up against the last great times of Bird's Celtics, Isiah's Bad Boys, who were badder than his, and Michael's run, which blotted out the championship sun for so many of the top seventy-five players, like

Barkley, Malone, Miller, and Stockton. Starks and Mason could look angry; it wasn't enough.

Ewing did have his moments, which came surprisingly more with the jump shot than anyone expected when New York celebrated with the number 1 selection in the first NBA draft lottery in 1985. Though almost immediately Ewing was away with knee surgery that haunted him his entire career and required multiple follow-ups. The enduring image of Ewing was knees wrapped and in a bucket of ice. And never mentioning it. Yet still having these defining performances, forcing a Game 7 against the Bulls in the 1992 conference semifinals, one of two seventh games Jordan and the Bulls would play in their six-championship run. Ewing's Knicks had the Bulls beaten in 1993 until Charles Smith couldn't finish a layup, and had the Rockets out in 1994 until John Starks couldn't make a shot. Ewing was on the way back to the Finals in 1995 until his floater rolled off the rim against Indiana, and perhaps in 1997 until a brutal brawl with the Miami Heat. Ewing was an All-Star eleven times and all-defense three times, and despite all those knee injuries he played at least eighty games in six consecutive seasons and at least seventy-six the next four, missing twenty games in a ten-year run when it took hours of rehab every day just to play. And being so close so often.

**PJ:** Willis would always say to me he couldn't believe Riley would not play Blackman, that Starks was, what, two for eighteen or something, and it's Game 7. How do you do that? Starks was a big favorite at the time and Oakley; they could do no wrong. That was their championship for that generation, though the year before Smith could not put that shot in. We escaped in '93; maybe '92 also.

**SAM:** That series in '93 with the Smith putback was when I realized something about Ewing, and more generally the difference in the "it" players and just the superstars. They won those first two in New York—you didn't have home court, Michael was being overwhelmed that season—with Starks's Game 2 dunk. So it's back to Chicago, and Ewing said the Knicks just had to win one. You never heard that from Michael. Down 2–0, he'd say they were winning the next four. The players who separated themselves expected to win every game and were shocked when they didn't. Ewing was much more normal than Michael, but the fans didn't want that. Nineteen ninety-two was the "X" series, when McDaniel was scaring the shit out of Pippen and Jordan came to his defense.

**PJ:** That's why I always told my teams in the early rounds you've got to sweep 'em. You can get mired up in a loss early in the playoffs and then it can take you down. You risk an injury or wearing guys out. That's what happened to us in '92. Pippen sprained an ankle and was seriously hobbled from games 2 to 5, and they're after Michael. Michael stood up for Scottie with X. But we had to go back for that seventh game. When I first started playing in the NBA, you couldn't double-team. You had to be close enough to your man. You could reach back and interrupt the dribble if you were still close enough. You were just taught this is how you played man-to-man defense, and that's how you played. Then Hubie Brown came in the league from the ABA and he was like, Why can't we double-team? Why can't we trap? Why can't we do this? Why is this not legal? He says we're not playing a zone, we're double-teaming the ball. And so we played man-to-man, full-court defense. But we didn't just outright zone and trap.

**SAM:** Hubie's the father of the double-team?

**PJ:** Hubie in '72, '73, sometime right around there, came from the Kentucky Colonels in the other league, and he went to Atlanta and he started using traps with his depleted team. He was into the second unit, playing eight-minute shifts, and some of the guys were trappers. They would go out and zone trap you.

**SAM:** All of a sudden someone asks why, and everyone goes, Why not? They always criticized Ewing for not being the big rebounder; same with Kareem and even Shaq, who should have been a 30/20 guy.

**PJ:** Sometimes guys are too tall, which sounds crazy. It's why Rodman was so good. Could track the ball better and pursue the ball to where it was going. One guy also was Bernard King; unbelievable, amazing lateral movement and ability to chase the ball off the rim, unbelievable before his injuries. Averaged close to 10 rebounds a game when he came in. Was he on that top-seventy-five list?

# Karl Malone

When you thought of one, you thought of the other, Batman and Robin, Bert and Ernie, Barbie and Ken, Tom and Jerry, bread and butter, salt and pepper, peanut butter and jelly, pick and roll; John Stockton and Karl Malone. The Stockton-to-Malone pick-and-roll for an astonishing eighteen consecutive seasons was one of the most enduring, reliable, and effective actions in NBA history. It never yielded a championship for either, but it enabled Stockton to establish all-time records for assists and steals that likely will never be rivaled, and Malone to rank third all-time in points, behind only historic legends of the game Kareem Abdul-Jabbar and LeBron James. Those two were not only both number 1 overall draft picks but also two of the most athletic and anticipated players in NBA history. Malone was a number 13 draft pick from a small Louisiana college, heavily muscled and lightly skilled, who just worked harder and played longer and more regularly. Ten seasons Malone played all eighty-two games. The majority of the games he missed were for suspensions, like his infamous takedown of Isiah Thomas, who had previously attempted to embarrass Stockton with a 44-point scoring output in Detroit as a message about who was more deserving of a spot on the 1992 Dream Team. As the Skipper said on *Gilligan's Island*, "No one messes with my little buddy." In the Pistons' next game in Utah, Karl violently took out Thomas, causing a gash worthy of forty stitches and an angry NBA giving Malone a one-game suspension; Isiah's buddy Bill Laimbeer carried the wounded and bleeding Thomas off the floor. Isiah couldn't catch a friendly audience. Malone did get the NBA to change some rules, however. As his play exceeded even his early expectations—he was a 48 percent free-throw shooter as a rookie who got himself up to almost 80 percent later in his career more by will than skill—Malone repeatedly agreed to contracts and then demanded renegotiations. It happened so often the NBA added a clause in one of the labor deals to prevent further contract modifications, which went on to impact Scottie Pippen in his later disagreements with the Bulls.

Malone had his share of controversies: He was a critic of Magic Johnson when Johnson came back to play again because of Malone's concerns about HIV. Malone also had personal issues from his early years. Malone bonded with state troopers, often referred to himself in the third person, carried boulders around for training, was always ready with a rifle in his pickup truck for some hunting, and scared the heck out of most of the top power forwards in the era, from Kevin Garnett to Rasheed Wallace. "Karl Malone flu" was a popular way to miss games in Salt Lake City. Pippen famously whispered to him that the "Mailman doesn't deliver on Sundays," a taunt about his nickname, in Game 1 of the 1997 Finals. Malone went on to miss two free throws and Jordan won that Game 1 with a jumper, on the way to winning the series. And in the 1998 Game 6 in Salt Lake City, Jordan also victimized Malone when he stole the ball from him and dribbled full court to score over Bryon Russell and end Utah's title hopes. Malone had a last bite of the title apple with Shaq and Kobe in the 2004 Finals. But he was injured in Game 3 and ineffective the rest of the series as the Lakers lost in five. Malone had grown up a wrestling fan, and in one of the more bizarre events in an NBA Finals and what was apparently their own cooked-up promotion, back during that famous Bulls-Jazz Game 6 in 1998, Dennis Rodman repeatedly tripped Malone and they collapsed on one another several times with everything but a pin and three-count. The six-nine Malone was twice an NBA Most Valuable Player, fourteen times all-NBA, four times all-defense, and at one point played eleven consecutive seasons averaging more than 25 points a season. For his career he averaged 25 points and 10 rebounds in almost 1,500 games, with a career-high game of 61 points. In 193 playoff games, he averaged 24.7 points and 10.7 rebounds.

**PJ:** Willis was good friends with Karl, close to Monroe, Louisiana. Willis says, "He calls me up and says, 'Come on, let's go hunting!' 'OK, where are we gonna go?'" His place. He's got like, I don't know, two thousand acres. It's all fenced off and he's got animals in there that he can go shoot. Karl says they'll go out in a go-kart, and then they'll get out of the go-kart to shoot 'em. His house was a taxidermist's dream house.

**SAM:** Sportsman, eh?

**PJ:** He was a run-ya-down, run-over-ya, go-through-ya guy. He was good at running the floor; he could run like a deer. When I got him, we had three kids, Kareem Rush, Luke Walton, and Brian Cook. Cook was a different kid, six nine from Illinois. We got in training camp. It was Kobe's crazy year; Kobe wasn't there. He was going to come later. He had to go to a pretrial hearing and whatever. We get to the University of Hawaii gym, fans on every corner. We have to practice in the morning because it's eighty-five degrees and humid. All of a sudden the practice stops and Karl just starts slapping this Cook across the face. "Come on, rookie!" Challenging him. Cook just stood there and took it and didn't do a damn thing about it. That was Karl, the intimidation factor.

**SAM:** That's the toughness that's been legislated out of the league.

**PJ:** Buss wanted to give it another shot. He knew Shaq was on his last year. That was his mentality: Get the best talent you can get. When Scottie was looking for a trade from Houston, Buss had to tell me we couldn't afford Scottie's contract. He said, "This is my only job; this is my income. We're already in the cap situation." Buss said, "We'll go after Payton and Malone." I was like, "I don't know, Gary's not a guy that can really do the things we need, but he's a great defensive player. Fish can't get over screens and Fox is limited in what he can do now." Malone could score. But I have this drill. We're early in training camp, and we do these drills. In the warm-up drill, we just do basic things—plant, pivot, stride step. Full court and I want you to jump up and do a 180. Karl couldn't do it. He couldn't turn his body 180 degrees going straight. He had no balance. He came back and said, "I can't do that. I can't even do it to my right side, let alone my left side." He knew what he could do and that was it.

**SAM:** Obviously that was the end for him, though he had some feelers after that season, Knicks, Spurs, but that Detroit series left a bad taste for a lot of guys.

**PJ:** Horace was one of those guys who used to miss him. He avoided playing his twin brother, too. I used to go around the locker room at the end of the season and say, "You played eighty-two games. Congratulations." Last game I coached the team I had six guys play eighty-two games that season. Karl was an iron man, no doubt about it. Malone intimidated Garnett. Garnett had no answer for him. Wallace was a loud talker, terrible anger, but a very talented player. But he didn't talk with Karl, didn't play a lot in Salt Lake.

# Dennis Rodman

He colored his hair, painted his nails, wore a wedding dress, pierced his ears, of course, but also his lips and nose, nipples, and tongue. Tattoos were scattered pretty much everywhere on his body, including on his neck and face, and many were too vulgar to mention. And few ever in the NBA kicked butt on the boards like Dennis Rodman. There have been many unique talents in NBA history, but there's never been anyone like Dennis Rodman. Likely, no one ever will be, or would want to be, bad as he wanted to be, as he said. Rodman was the premier defensive player/rebounder of his era, part of five championship teams with the Detroit Pistons and Chicago Bulls while also sparking rages and outrages galore, from assaults on officials and media in games to women off court, alleged diplomatic missions to see murderous dictators to studying from outrageous singer Madonna how to be even more outrageous. Police were sometimes called to Rodman's homes as many times in a year as he played basketball games. He threatened suicide and needed alcohol abuse treatment. Yet he also was an unrestrained pied piper for media, celebrities, fans, and teammates on postgame jaunts to bars and clubs and with his band buddies from Pearl Jam. He abandoned teams in the middle of crucial playoff series and even an NBA Finals and, with otherworldly defensive play, helped his teams to win some of those Finals. He acted in movies and appeared on reality shows and in numerous wrestling revues. Opposing fans reviled him; home fans revered him. He cried often about honors and friendships. He claimed to be the oldest of forty-seven children, though his aptly named father, Philander, said he sired only twenty-nine children with sixteen different women. He and Dennis were estranged for forty years.

Perhaps the greatest contradiction about Rodman was how shy he was and remains while acting out as bizarrely and outrageously as anyone ever has in professional sports. It was no secret around the Bulls, where Rodman was part of three championships after sabotaging the San Antonio Spurs' title hopes in 1994 and 1995, that Rodman was closest with the kids who mopped the sweat, the guys and gals who did the laundry, and the moonlighting cops who worked security. Michael Jordan said he rarely spoke to Rodman, and when he did, it would be the same as when he was addressing his kids when they were eight or nine, grabbing them by each temple and repeating, "Do you understand!" It was coach Phil Jackson who saved Rodman by replacing Chuck Daly as the surrogate father that Rodman always sought. Dennis was kicked out of his house after high school by his mother, who unfavorably compared Dennis to his more successful basketball-playing younger sisters. Imagine their surprise. Dennis went to work as a janitor in the Dallas Fort Worth airport and not long afterward was arrested for stealing fifteen watches during his overnight shift. He never took one for himself. He said he felt badly for his friends who couldn't afford a watch, so he stole and gave the watches to them. Which was classic Dennis, and it often backfired on him as alleged friends later took advantage of his generosity and stole millions of dollars from him. Then suddenly he had this growth spurt after high school of maybe eight inches to about six seven. Jealous of his sisters' success, he dedicated himself to basketball at Southeastern Oklahoma State.

In this draft era when a player's prospects were considered limited after twenty-one, Rodman at twenty-five was drafted in the second round by the Detroit Pistons. He fit into a valuable off-the-bench defensive role with fellow rookie John Salley for the nascent Bad Boys, who terrorized opponents into a pair of NBA titles in 1989 and 1990. Rodman's transgressions continued, luring in teammates to cover for the laconic-yet-bold Rodman. For all the unacceptable behavior, Rodman responded with historic defensive and rebounding play, unselfishness, and vulnerability. When the Bulls won the 1996 Finals, Seattle coach George Karl said Rodman was responsible for two of the Bulls' four wins. Rodman defended everyone from Karl Malone to Shaquille O'Neal during the Bulls' playoffs but also attempted to make the game a mockery by wrestling with Malone during a game to promote an off-season wrestling event between the two. Rodman was suspended for headbutting a referee during a game and kicking a sideline cameraman in the groin. And then he donated to help injured or ill police officers. You wanted to both scream at him and hug him. Rodman was only an All-Star twice, given his disinterest in offense and scoring. All-Star games were not for defense. He was twice Defensive Player of the Year, eight times all-defense, and seven consecutive seasons rebounding leader, with 18.7 in 1992 and 18.3 in 1993, and then he contemplated suicide. And then he teamed with Jordan, Pippen, and Phil Jackson in the greatest basketball show on earth or anywhere in the universe before eventually ending his playing career with the Lakers and back home in Dallas, before heading off to North Korea to see if he could stop the nuclear arms race.

**PJ:** When I came back from meeting Dennis at Jerry Krause's house, I met him over at our facility the next day, took him through it, showed him that room where I had all the Indian artifacts. It seemed to be a bond and we made the decision to make the deal. San Antonio was, "Here, take him off our hands; we'll take Will Perdue." Rodman was a gift for us.

**SAM:** It was right before camp, and I remember coming to see you at the Multiplex and asking you about who you wanted as a power forward. You never mentioned Rodman.

**PJ:** Well, Dennis was a small forward. "What do you mean 'power forward'?" They had John Salley playing power forward in Detroit. Dennis, he'd go in and play anything. Who could I defend? We even threw him on Shaq sometimes. I wanted Derrick Coleman; he was a very qualified player. We interviewed Jayson Williams. I called my teammate Butch Beard and said, "We're looking for a power forward. How about this kid you've got that is not fitting in there, who's maybe the best power forward I've ever seen, probably one of the best players I've ever seen, just isn't fulfilling his talent, Coleman?" Butch says, "You won't get him to do anything you want to do if you run the triangle offense." "Then how about Jayson Williams?" Funny guy, great sense of humor, shot and killed his chauffeur or whatever. Ugly, terrible thing. We could get Dennis Rodman for Will Perdue, but these other guys we can't. They're not giving up on them. We didn't even think of Rodman. He failed so miserably that he was laying on the floor in the playoffs. He couldn't fit in.

**SAM:** It was also the contracts. With Michael about to go into that big number, $30 million in one more year, and who knows with Scottie, they weren't taking on guaranteed deals. Dennis had a year left at maybe $2.5 million, so he goes nuts, you can cut him.

**PJ:** I was then able to speak to the team without Dennis there. There were no other free agents. I was telling them we're going to have to accommodate this guy who's a little bit of a loose cannon. Dennis was carrying a gun around in his car. Detroit knew they had to get rid of him when Chuck went to Orlando. I said, Rodman is misunderstood. We really had to take care of him. We had a therapist meet with him.

He went to fast-food joints in the mall. Had a therapist meet him at Denny's or Taco John's. Signed Jack Haley as mentor, handler. The question is, What does he bring with him? Does the talent outweigh the effect of his presence? We had to overcome that with Rodman: Will his effect be greater than his detraction? Teams make these calculations.

**SAM:** Dennis, the last time he was in Chicago for some wrestling thing, said you saved him.

**PJ:** That was nice of Dennis. Probably some truth in it. I think he's trying to get sober. What he did to himself is toxic. Jerry Buss told me when they were going to sign him, he was at Planet Hollywood in Vegas, and he sat with Dennis and talked rebounding. Dennis had seventeen kamikazes sitting with him. He was drinking them down like it was a beer. Dennis was a binger, Bamboo Club or something. I did an intervention with him. When we were in Philly we sent him with some teammates to Atlantic City; sometimes we'd have to put him on a plane back to Chicago. The Vegas thing in '98. Dennis just couldn't stand being in his room, not being at the party.

# Reggie Miller

Reggie Miller perhaps became more famous because of his interactions with star movie director Spike Lee at New York Knicks and Indiana Pacers games. Those games might also have made great movies for Lee. There was Miller's miracle 8 points in 8.9 seconds in the 1995 conference semifinals when he led the Pacers to the unlikely Game 1 victory and eventual series win; Miller being Miller, he called the Knicks chokers, just stuff you didn't do. Reggie did trash-talk. When you're a spindly kid who had steel braces on his legs until he was four or five and are way, way, way overshadowed in basketball by your big sister Cheryl, you develop that attitude to survive. Big shots and big moments no longer bother you. You survive to prove yourself. There were the 25 fourth-quarter points mixed in with taunts of Lee in the 1994 conference finals Game 5 that led to the first of two excruciating back-to-back Game 7 conference finals losses. And the push-off against Michael Jordan before the Game 4 winner in the 1998 conference finals, though again Miller's Pacers were denied the NBA Finals in yet another heartbreaking seventh-game loss. Miller rarely is mentioned among those stars who were denied a title in Jordan's era, like Charles Barkley, Patrick Ewing, and Karl Malone. Perhaps because Miller wasn't considered quite at their level, though when he retired he was the leading three-point shooter of all time. Miller did finally get to a Finals in 2000 against a powerful

Lakers team, which Kobe Bryant carried to a crucial Game 4 win and 3–1 lead after Shaquille O'Neal fouled out. It wasn't all theatrics with Miller, though he never shrank from the spotlight. In the 1993–94 season with Michael Jordan playing baseball, Miller made what seemed like a game-winning three with 0.8 left and then, Reggie-like, stopped to bow in each direction to the Bulls fans— the last season in the Chicago Stadium. Then Scottie Pippen was willing to make the inbounds pass to rookie Toni Kukoč, which he wouldn't do later in the playoffs. Kukoč made the walk-off winner, prompting Phil Jackson to wonder if Miller was bowing or showing his butt. All good fun for Reggie, though perhaps not when being the victim of Tayshaun Prince's famous chase-down block in the 2004 conference finals. So many so close. After all, when the six-seven, maybe 180-pound Miller was drafted by the Pacers at number 11 in 1987, he was booed because fans wanted hometown IU hero Steve Alford. No big deal being out-played so often by Cheryl, a women's basketball legend, and older brother Dar-rell, a Major League Baseball player. At UCLA, Miller constantly listened to taunts of "Cheryl, Cheryl." It was an era of great guards. So Miller was just all-league three times in his career. But coming from a military family, loyalty and dedication were hallmarks, and he refused chances to play elsewhere with con-tending teams to play eighteen years as an LA guy in Indiana and with the league sportsmanship award for his charitable work. Miller would stop at chil-dren's hospitals after practice regularly and asked the hospitals never to publi-cize his visits. Miller joined the exclusive 50/40/90 shooting club and played in five All-Star games while making more than 2,500 threes in his career.

**PJ:** They started to get some things going with Reggie and Chuck Per-son, though Dick Harter was the engineer of the defense, especially with those Pistons, the Jordan Rules. That's where they got the Bad

Boys image, the Kamikaze Kids at Oregon. He tried to carry it down to Charlotte, and we lost a game down there when they were an expansion team. Harter was big on taking a charge or holding your space.

**SAM:** Person reminds me of the story when Reggie was coming in. You're playing them in a preseason game in Cincinnati, and Chuck is telling Reggie to talk some shit to Michael, and so Reggie is right into it: "That all you got, bitch?" This and that. So of course Michael wakes up and scores six or seven straight on Reggie and yells at him, "Don't you ever talk shit to me again." Of course, Reggie does and actually gets Michael into a fight in '93 down in Indy. Never saw Michael get pissed like that, but Reggie gets kicked out. Hey, they came to see Michael. Michael did get suspended a game. Larry Brown, of course, gets them straightened out at the time until Bird replaced him for your last season with the Bulls.

**PJ:** Reggie was some competitor. No one stood up to Michael like he did, and at a time when nobody would stand up to Michael.

# Scottie Pippen

I f you were constructing the perfect basketball player, you'd probably make him six eight and about 225 pounds, long legs and arms with quick hands that could strike like a snake, the speed of a cheetah, the reactions of an acrobat, and the coordination and versatility of a gymnast. He'd be able to get the ball off the backboard against most anyone with his reactions, take the ball full court or pass ahead. If someone else rebounded, he could get out on the wing for an outlet pass and finish strong over even the biggest, most powerful centers, and with either hand. And then on defense he'd feel like an octopus to opponents, all arms everywhere disrupting movement and sight. If you looked around NBA history, you'd call him Scottie Pippen. Pippen might not quite fill up all the columns, since he wasn't the best shooter, though he had an uncanny ability to make clutch three-pointers and a reliable little left-side bank shot through his run in seven All-Star games and six NBA championships with Michael Jordan and the Chicago Bulls. Which became, at least in Pippen's view, something of a curse, if not also a paradox. Pippen ended up playing with the player generally regarded as the game's greatest, Michael Jordan. It resulted in multiple NBA championships and significant attention and opportunity, but also a view of Pippen as a sidekick, a Robin to Batman, the little-brother thing that also tormented Kobe Bryant during his primary years with Shaquille O'Neal. Bryant broke out of that with titles leading the Lakers with Pau Gasol. Pippen never had that opportunity, as a second back surgery after the Bulls' 1998 sixth championship left Pippen a much less athletic role player. If Pippen could be an opponent's nightmare, his brilliance often was overshadowed by his controversies. Which in an ironic way may also have indicated just how great he was. Lesser talents perhaps never would have survived refusing to play in a playoff game because a last shot wasn't designed for him, or condemning his team's management, or a notorious migraine headache in a crucial conference finals Game 7, and then even doubling down years later when he said he'd do everything exactly the same again.

But in a world of hardship stories and slam-dunk inspiration, few have matched the tale of Scottie Pippen, youngest in a family of twelve children in rural Arkansas, father and a brother paralyzed, just a small, skinny kid on a no-where high school team, a work/study grant student at a local college, University of Central Arkansas, who initially was an equipment manager as a freshman and a walk-on basketball player, suddenly sprouting to almost six eight after those point-guard days in high school. And he becomes a phenomenon. But he's at NAIA Central Arkansas, so who knows about it? Marty Blake had become a roving NBA college scout for all the teams and knew Krause from Blake's years as Atlanta Hawks general manager. Blake mentioned Pippen to Krause; NBA scouting was not so extensive in the mid-1980s. Krause dispatched assistant Billy McKinney to take a look, and McKinney couldn't believe what he was seeing. The Bulls attempted to get Pippen into hiding, but Pippen went to the pre-draft May Portsmouth Invitational, which was supposed to be for free agents and low-round picks. Pippen got noticed in the first round, but not that much. On draft day in June, *The New York Times* listed him as Scott Pippin. It was the David Robinson draft with a lot of speculation afterward. The Bulls had the number 8 and 10 selections, the latter of which they'd use for Horace Grant. He and Pippen were both backups as rookies. The Bulls were desperate for Pippen, now rising on teams' lists. The Bulls managed one trade to move up, but conditional. Seattle at number 5 wanted big man Armen Gilliam or swingman Reggie Williams. If either was available, no deal. Gilliam went number 2 to Phoenix and Williams number 4 to the Clippers. So the Bulls were able to swap number 8, a future second, and a pick swap for number 5, which they used for Pippen. And thus assured Krause's entry into the Basketball Hall of Fame and the Bulls' championship dynasty.

Pippen got his first start in the 1988 playoffs at the end of his rookie season. With the famed Dream Team in 1992, Coach Chuck Daly said Pippen was the second-best player on the team. Pippen became recognized as perhaps the game's greatest defensive wing player, ten times all-defense with eight times first team and a league steals leader. He is one of five players ever to lead his team in all five major statistical categories in one season, during Jordan's absence playing baseball. Phil Jackson said, "Scottie Pippen's defense is a one-man wrecking crew. He plays ninety-four feet at every position, both sides of the court." There has rarely been as much bitter with the sweet as with Scottie Pippen.

**PJ:** You'd have had to see him at the combine to understand what his value was as a player and how to use him. He and Muggsy were on the same team. I was still coaching in the CBA. I came up to watch. Went to the combine to make acquaintances. I wasn't a very good networker. There was a kid from Illinois, pretty good defender, pretty good athlete, playing with them. He wasn't NBA capable athletically.

**SAM:** Maybe Doug Altenberger? Played at Illinois.

**PJ:** The three of them were like, Let's just pressure these other guards. At the combine there's no system. It's basically a free-for-all and it'd be, like, 75–24, 75–40 for Pippen's team. A guy came to me during the year I was still coaching in the CBA. He said, "There's a guy from Wake Forest named Muggsy Bogues, and he's five four, five five, and he's gonna be an NBA player." I said, "I'll owe you a dinner if a guy who's five four can make it in the NBA." I owed him a dinner. Scottie was there, and when he went through his rookie year, I played against him one-on-one a lot. I told him, "Your shot's the issue. You have to learn how to use the backboard," and he became a good backboard shooter. We got to be friendly. I got a chance to coach the team a couple of times because Doug was thrown out. It's an amazing thing, and I credit Doug, that Doug handed me the game card. I said, "Brad Sellers, why don't you sit down and Scottie, you go in the game, and let's put some pressure on these teams that we're playing."

**SAM:** That's the enigma of Scottie. You're his personal coach and get him going in the NBA, and then all the stuff, the 1.8 seconds, and even though you were pissed then, you gave him cover with the team.

**PJ:** I like Scottie. I worked with him, talked to him a little bit about his game. I saw what he could do. I always had a good relationship with him. I had no qualms. My kids were more upset by his book. They know what that means. Once you use that word there's no way you take it back, because you can't retract it; it's going to be on the back page of something.

**SAM:** The confusing part was Michael always was crediting Scottie, like in his Hall of Fame speech, being his most important teammate, couldn't have done it without him.

**PJ:** One of the things about the relationship is that Michael, whatever their differences, trusted Scottie in the clutch, like in the flu game that was not a flu game, Michael was dehydrated and Scottie was supporting him the whole way through the game. "You score, I'll do all the other work. I've got you." Michael's upset about the fact that he lost a twenty-year relationship with this guy. He was hurt. Whoever was advising Scottie, to me, that's the issue. Who's he talking to behind the scenes? I'm not mad at Scottie. It's unfortunate. Bill Bradley sets up a Zoom with all his teammates. I don't see that happening with the Bulls, thirtieth anniversary, fiftieth anniversary. I had a couple of conversations with Michael about *The Last Dance* when they wanted to interview me. I called him up and said, "I don't want to do this *Last Dance*. It's going to make a lot of money for somebody, and I think people should get paid." He said, "I'm not getting anything for it." He just said, "If you don't want to do it, tell them." He said whatever he gets goes to his foundation and nothing to him personally. I called Scottie, left a message on his cell phone that I wasn't making any money either on it. I said, "I know how you feel, and I can't stand ESPN. They're going to make a lot of money on this."

**SAM:** I guess his book was a good time to vent, and Scottie is a proud, stubborn guy. I remember at an All-Star game after he retired, he was in one of those goofy contests they dreamed up with WNBA players and retired players. He said during the interviews that any coach would prefer him to Jordan because he made teammates better and his teammates liked him more. That's Scottie. I never could figure if he believed that stuff or just wanted to. But what I always admired about him, and what I felt made him the great player he was, was some of that crazy stuff he did and said. Because you have to be tough to recover from the things he did and said. My favorite was we're in Boston and he goes nuclear on Krause, wants out, team's a joke; this is before championships. We're back in Chicago the next day and the TV trucks are lined up at practice, dozens of media there. Before practice starts Scottie grabs me. "Hey, what's going on? Why is all the media here?" Well, I say, because of what you said. "What'd I say?" That was Scottie. I never knew anyone to compartmentalize and move on like him. I don't believe it was the zen, but that's an in-the-moment guy.

**PJ:** There were legitimate things Michael could do. He had good footwork, but like I told you, there were things he couldn't do. Most of them involved his left hand, left side. He never was able to develop his left hand the way Scottie had the ability to go left and dunk. I don't think I ever saw Michael dunk with his left hand. At the Multiplex Scottie's showing Michael how to do it. Said, "You have to have space. Guy jumps to try to prevent you from using the pick and you reverse pivot, go baseline dunk with your left hand." They helped one another.

**SAM:** Which was also why when George Karl called Michael in '94 when the Sonics were talking about that trade of Kemp for Pippen, Michael said, You'd be crazy not to. And even with Scottie's delayed surgery in '97 when Krause was trying again, Michael said he was ready to quit if Scottie was traded.

**PJ:** Reinsdorf asked me three times to come back and coach after '98. I said, "It's not fair to Jerry." He said, "Don't worry about Jerry, I can deal with that." I said, "Yeah, but it creates a situation, a mood that's not good." Scottie needed surgery again and then he suffered in Houston. He said, "We don't practice, the guys are lazy, Barkley won't practice, Olajuwon gets on the massage table and won't come out, everything is disjointed." He asked me to trade for him. He said, "Come and get me and get me out of here." But the Lakers couldn't.

# David Robinson

David Robinson was supposed to be the next Bill Russell, and maybe with his uncanny defensive instincts and reactions, and three inches taller than Russell, he could have been—with Cousy, Havlicek, Heinsohn, and Jones rather than Sean Elliott, Avery Johnson, and Vinny Del Negro. So as a result, the long, swift gazelle with the ball control of a guard and athletic chops of Dominique had to become Wilt Chamberlain. Robinson did a pretty good job of that, carrying the Spurs to a then-record thirty-five-game turnaround in his rookie season and leading the league in scoring with an average just below 30 per game in 1993–94, when he scored 71 points in the final regular-season game to nose out Shaquille O'Neal for the scoring championship. Robinson averaged 21 points and almost 11 rebounds per game for his career, also leading the league in various seasons in blocks and rebounds and winning league MVP in 1995. He hit the boards like Moses and was an Artis Gilmore but with grace and speed. The chiseled, regal, seven-one, 250-pound Robinson was a study in balletic grace and athletic form, streaking full court to flush a slam dunk or pull up with his deft left hand for a straight-on jumper. With such myriad skills it was not surprising he was one of four players ever to record a quadruple-double, along with Nate Thurmond, Alvin Robertson, and Hakeem Olajuwon. In that game with 34 points, Robinson had 10 each of assists, rebounds, and blocks. Like Russell, he wasn't a post player but possessed similar catlike reactions to the ball. In 1992, he averaged almost 5 blocks per game and in six of his first seven seasons played at least eighty games.

Robinson could never quite drag his Spurs over the finish line, the ultimate disappointment coming in the 1995 conference finals, when Robinson was MVP but Olajuwon and his deeper Houston Rockets with Clyde Drexler dominated the series. Despite Houston's talent advantage and the Spurs being undermined by Dennis Rodman's antics, Robinson accepted the blame and responsibility. Scion of a navy man and long in service to his country starting at the Naval Academy, Robinson understood better than most the patriotic concepts of loyalty, respect, honor, integrity, selfless service, courage, and duty. So he carried his underwhelming Spurs as far as anyone could until reinforcements showed up in the form of the best power forward in NBA history, Tim Duncan. Then that one-two punch delivered a knockout with two championships in five years. Robinson was one of the most civic-minded of players, who actually built and funded a school, and probably is the only professional player whose Wikipedia entry has his SAT score: 1320. He was also an accomplished musician. And then he handed the baton to the kids, Parker and Ginóbili, whom Duncan helped to fulfill the San Antonio dynasty desire with five championships in a sixteen-year run that established the Spurs as one of the elite franchises in NBA history. Which all started with the maestro David Robinson. Robinson was named to ten All-Star teams. He was all-NBA ten times, eight times all-defense, and Defensive Player of the Year. He won the NBA Sportsmanship Award and was also a national award winner for philanthropy.

**PJ:** I don't know anybody who could have become Bill Russell. What did Robinson miss, two years? Then he had to be in the reserves.

**SAM:** I think it was that he was six seven and they gave him a waiver to get in the academy, but then, yeah, he kept growing and he wanted to be a submariner or get a commission assigned or some such thing. But he was too tall for those hallways or the ships, so they agreed to two years and out instead of five, and he'd stay in the reserves.

**PJ:** Ewing wasn't as mobile as Robinson, but he was more a warrior. Did you ever hear this one? Jerry West was so frustrated by not winning titles he always used to say, "Why are we playing eighty-two games and then starting over to declare a champion? What do we play these eighty-two games for? We continue to diminish the regular season." But if you step back and look at that, the bulk of your income comes from these games. Jerry wanted something more to count.

**SAM:** He was right, in a sense, that the playoffs are more of a tournament, like that in-season thing they do now. Maybe give regular-season rings? Michael did say during the Dream Team summer, "David is not driven like me and other players." He did bring his saxophone to Barcelona and was playing when the others were gambling all night. Might even have had a keyboard with him.

**PJ:** The Spurs played down that year with Duncan in the draft. David probably could have come back. Musselman was adamant that David Robinson ended up hurting his back from sitting at his computer all the time, that's really how he hurt it. That was his claim. I don't know if it was true or sounded ridiculous, but I can see David being on his computer all the time. I did think Tim would have trouble moving to center when Robinson retired.

**SAM:** He didn't, because he and the Spurs were sensitive about that. By the way, David was known as a proficient computer hacker, too. The Spurs made everyone call Duncan a power forward. I was on the committee one year making the All-Star ballot. We listed Duncan as a center. The Spurs are furious. They call the league to object, "He's not a center!"

# Gary Payton

Talk about making an entrance. It didn't go exactly the way Gary Payton hoped, but his coming into the NBA in 1990 was like one of those James Bond movie openings or the start of *Raiders of the Lost Ark*; seriously, you've got to see this. The night before a preseason game, Payton, the number 2 selection in the 1990 NBA draft, tells Michael Jordan at a club that he's nothing and he's going to kick his ass. Jordan, predictably, jumps on Payton the next day to start the game, stealing the ball two or three times in a row, forcing coach George Karl to lift the rookie. But Gary Payton would make a name for himself beyond the bold trash-talking, a unique hoops polemicist who was one of the best defensive point guards ever, the first at that position to win Defensive Player of the Year, nine times all-defense first team, known as "the Glove" for his ability to cover an opponent, and a league steals leader with his long arms and pickpocket hands. Payton went on to team with Shawn "Reign Man" Kemp in one of the more memorable, if ultimately unsatisfying, duos, nicknamed "Sonic Boom" for Payton's thefts and fast breaks and Kemp's booming dunks. Though the rough edges that got them there also proved an obstacle with the highly emotional Payton, forever in combat with his coach, and the high-flying but moody Kemp. They had a famous first-round playoff meltdown as a number 1 seed after sixty-three wins, losing to number 8 Denver, Dikembe Mutombo famously collapsing with the ball to end the series. And then falling just short against Jordan's legendary seventy-two-win Bulls in 1996. Payton did finally get his championship in Miami in 2006, though as a bit player who, nevertheless, ended up making the big shot with nine seconds left in the Game 6 clincher, his only points of the game coming off the bench in the Dwyane Wade Finals show when Wade carried the Heat to four straight wins, averaging 34.7 points. Payton also was all-NBA and an All-Star nine times and among the top five of all time in technical fouls. He talked the talk, and he walked the walk, through seventeen NBA seasons, with an emphasis on the talk.

**PJ:** Wade got all those free throws in that Finals, like 20-some free throws a game.

**SAM:** It was a bad time for the NBA. Shaq is basically cooked in those first two games in Dallas, and we're prematurely writing him off for good. He did admit after that series he told Payton to let it be Wade, that their times had passed. Wouldn't do it with Kobe, though. Cuban then was killing the league and the refs, hiring former refs to write reports condemning the current refs, seeing a conspiracy in every game, fined constantly by the league. What comes around?

**PJ:** Cuban just screwed it up. Poor old little admiral had a championship waiting there for him. He waited too long to call a time-out. And then Gary Payton had a shot.

**SAM:** Dallas did unravel, but you know the way Cuban was then, talking to everyone like Jerry Jones, wanting to be the star of the team. But it did become laughable with Wade. He gets 46 free throws the last two games, 21 in Game 6 in a three-point win. There was no league conspiracy because there never is, but the refs see a guy who is naming names and wants guys fired, and, c'mon, human and all that. I remember Gary giving you a lot of trouble that season in '04. I remember writing, If only the Lakers had four future Hall of Famers instead of three, and Payton's yelling, "Who's this fuckin' Sam Smith?"

**PJ:** He had a hard time with the triangle offense. I thought he'd be great in the post because they ran it all the time in Seattle. It was difficult for him to exist because he didn't have a shot. He did endure.

# Shaquille O'Neal

**W**ilt Chamberlain used to lament to his frequent critics, "Nobody loves Goliath." But if anyone around the NBA got caught using a slingshot, it probably was the fun-loving Shaq. Four NBA championships, a Most Valuable Player award and a few in the Finals, and the unofficial title, certainly in his era, of most dominant. But few had more fun in life as a basketball star than Shaquille O'Neal. He celebrated his first Shaq-sized NBA contract by shutting down a water park for his friends. He'd travel the waterways on a Sea-Doo. He's an actor, a rapper, and an entrepreneur, and he made the most startling introduction at an All-Star game by dancing with the white-masked Jabbawockeez. He went bungee jumping off a tower in Portland. Who knew they had harnesses that strong? You definitely knew when Shaq, like Elvis, was in the building. The bigger-than-life big man, however, probably suffered the fate of many such giants, in that as much as they did because of their powers, everyone believed they could or should do more. Shaq's teams were swept in the playoff six times. He was such a poor free-throw shooter that a strategy was developed to highlight it, "Hack-a-Shaq," which came to represent attacking every poor free shooter, the way *gate* from *Watergate* represents every government scandal. But Shaq had his effect—if perhaps not like Mikan and Chamberlain given the size of the lane. Soon after his arrival in 1992, with rims being torn off back-boards, the NBA strengthened the stanchions and mechanisms to Shaq-proof them. So dominant was Shaq in the post that the NBA eventually went to its modified zone defense game, which led to the wide-open play of the Golden State shooting era and beyond. Shaq was more than a basketball giant. His foot-work was remarkable, light like a dancer's. He had a soft-touch shot, except from the free-throw line, and remarkable coordination to rival his power. Shaq's Orlando Magic looked like a dynasty with young Penny Hardaway. But Central Florida was not ready for a giant with giant salary wishes, and in 1996 the Lak-ers and Jerry West swooped in to nab Shaq as a free agent. West called it one of the greatest moments of his life. When Shaq did well, he decided to be the Big Aristotle, the Big Shamrock when he went to Boston to close his career, the Big Cactus in Phoenix, and just plain Superman. Probably no one was fouled more often and harder. But for Shaq it was like, Did someone drop a feather on me? The refs are human and figured if he's not reacting, then maybe they aren't hitting him. Not even Wilt shook off assaults like Shaq.

Shaq was a longtime friend of law enforcement and a reserve officer. He became one of the country's most visible commercial pitchmen and a regular on the popular TNT basketball show with Charles Barkley. With Kobe Bryant as wingman, their three consecutive championships from 2000 to 2002 were his-toric, with O'Neal putting up Finals numbers to match any in history: 38 and 17 in 2000, 33 and 16 in 2001, and 36 and 12 in 2002. Which led to the demand that he do it all the time, but Shaq just tended to rise to the occasion. That was one of the reasons for the epic feud that led to his split with Bryant. O'Neal went to Miami, where he won a title with Dwyane Wade, and then to Phoenix, Cleveland, and Boston as his basketball skills declined, but never his lust for life. He was an All-Star fifteen times and All-Star game MVP three times, once in tandem with Bryant when their differences subsided. O'Neal was all-NBA fourteen times and all-defense three times, twice a scoring champion, and ten times the field-goal-percentage leader.

**PJ:** First year I was in LA I met him as he was coming off the court. "What's the greatest thing Wilt did? Fifty points a game? Almost thirty rebounds a game? That's terrific, but that's not the greatest thing. You know what the greatest thing was? He played more than forty-eight minutes a game one season." He said, "Oh, he did that? I could do that." So I started playing him forty minutes a game that season. It lasted like five or six games, and then he sent Salley in to talk to me. That was his emissary, John Salley. "Coach, he's really tired, fatigued, and it's really hard on him." "Well, he can come to me and ask me about it, but I've been playing him forty minutes a game and I think he's getting in shape." I think he was probably in the best shape he was ever in. Shaq had that toe thing, and everything he did came off of two feet, and when he had the surgery, he lost the ability to vault off two feet; it became just weight and muscle. He couldn't get the elevation. He was an incredible athlete. My take was: I don't know how this guy's not gonna just dominate the game at his size and his speed. They got a championship out of him in Miami. But that's exactly what Buss said would happen: He'd win one more championship. Buss said, "I'm willing to allow that to happen because he's a really good player, but ultimately I think we'll be all right without him."

**SAM:** That was his decision at that All-Star game to pick Kobe over Shaq, and the eventual end for you, or at least sabbatical.

**PJ:** It was at the All-Star break. I was driving to practice, and Shaq called me up—the All-Star game was here in LA—and he was like,

"Did you see what Kobe said about you coaching next year? He didn't care who the coach was." I said, "Nah, I don't pay attention to that stuff." He said, "No, it was definitely something that was a slam about you." So anyway, I called Shaq, Fish, and Fox together, because then things started circulating about him. And the comeuppance was Dr. Buss had made a trip to Kobe's home during the All-Star break and told him that he was going to get rid of Shaq and he was going to sign him. He was going to be the chosen free agent that would stay. It became apparent because then Kobe was saying things like "We're going to have a new coach next year" and stuff like that. So these guys would come to me and say, "We have to corral him in or something, because he's just talking off, talking out of the blue about stuff." I was aware of it. So I said, "We'll just leave it be. We'll just see what we can do to get through this year and see what happens at the end." I had just gone in and told Mitch, "He's uncoachable. This guy, he's doing what he wants to do now. He's just disregarding the coaching. I think you should keep Shaq because Shaq's a willing guy, and Kobe's just resistant." That was kind of how that went down.

**SAM:** And off you went. It wasn't the popular move, because everyone figured they needed Shaq more to win, but Buss also understood basketball.

**PJ:** Dale Brown was his coach at LSU, and Dale tells me, "Phil, this guy just loves to be coached. He used to bring his speech from his English class to my office. 'Coach, can I give you my speech?' He just wants to please a coach; he's just really into that." He'd call me up and say, "Coach, did you hear what Kobe said?" "No, I wasn't paying attention." "How could this guy be that disloyal?" I explained he just was going through that time in his life. Everything was spitballed, the Colorado fiasco. Buss still hung with him. So Shaq started to lose it. We paid him $20 million, but he wanted $30 million. Buss figured

Shaq would win a championship first, but the Lakers would be OK with the younger guy.

**SAM:** So he knew more than just entertainment?

**PJ:** That trip back to LA after Shaq almost decapitated Brad Miller in Chicago. Shaq is laying out on cushions, and then he gets up and hands me a book report. I always asked them for reports. Kobe never gave me one. I'd given Shaq a Hermann Hesse book, *Siddhartha*. Shaq always said he was a philosopher. First year I gave him something by Nietzsche. He gives me the book report on *Siddhartha*: "He's a young prince and has a lot of advantages in life, goes on a quest and has a lot of money and women, just like me. He finds a spiritual path to elevate himself to become a leader just like me. —Shaq."

# Jason Kidd

Jason Kidd was the rarest of NBA players who could dominate a game scoring six points. There have been defensive specialists like Bill Russell and orchestrators like John Stockton. But few like Kidd with the triple-double package of points, rebounds, and assists and running a team in transition and the half-court and defending just as expertly. Kidd performed one of the greatest magic tricks ever in the NBA by making the New Jersey Nets appear. The forlorn poor relative invitee to the NBA in the 1976 combination with the ABA had missed the playoffs in fifteen of their twenty-five seasons going into the new millennium. They'd won one NBA playoff series in their history, the scratching-our-heads 1984 upset of the defending-champion Philadelphia 76ers. They were quickly out in six games in the next round and then didn't win a playoff game for seven years. After another seven-year miss of failing to win one playoff game, the twenty-six-win Nets traded Stephon Marbury for Jason Kidd, doubled their win total that first season, and went to consecutive NBA Finals. Kidd was gone in 2008, and after six consecutive playoffs appearances, the Nets made three in the next eleven years. He became one of the six players with at least one hundred triple-doubles, as of 2024. Kidd is in the top three in career assists and steals. None of which came without years of controversy that included a public breakup with his rookie star teammates Jamal Mashburn and Jim Jackson, allegedly forcing out coaches, a failed Backcourt 2000 with Penny Hardaway in Phoenix, an impaired-driving arrest, and reneging on a promise to sign with the San Antonio Spurs as a free agent after the two Nets Finals. Kidd was soon slowed by the dreaded microfracture surgery, no longer practiced on NBA players after basically ending the stardom eras of the careers of Chris Webber, Hardaway, Ron Harper, and Allan Houston. He averaged a triple-double in the 2007 playoffs, in which he played twelve games and led the Dallas Mavericks to the 2011 NBA championship over the first season of the LeBron James / Dwyane Wade / Chris Bosh Big Three. Kidd eventually went on to coaching, where his creativity led to Giannis Antetokounmpo's becoming a point forward and NBA force. Kidd, after some assistant work, returned as coach to the Mavericks team that had drafted him and led them to the 2024 NBA Finals. Kidd was an All-Star ten times, nine times all-defense, five times assists leader, and twice Sportsmanship Award winner.

**PJ:** I loved Jason Kidd's game. Jerry had those guys come in and practice on our court when they were in a regional, and I watched Jason Kidd play with that University of California team. Jimmy Cleamons ended up with him at Dallas. I always thought that of almost anyone Jason Kidd has the best idea of how to win a basketball game. He had the knowledge of how to do things, when to apply pressure and when to get a steal, how to change the game around when things were not going right, that inner knowledge the great guards have—I thought Jason was really good at that. But it still surprised me that we were unable to take advantage of him when he was with Dallas. We lost that 2011 playoff series after we'd beaten them the course of the year. They made the adjustments.

**SAM:** Jason Terry kicked your ass, as I recall. Got swept.

**PJ:** Pau was weak in that series and couldn't hold the post. They just pushed him out of there, and I went to the referees and said, "There is an arm bar and you cannot push a guy off the block." "Pau, you have to hold your block." Nowitzki liked to get him in the post. Jason knew how to throw the ball ahead, set up and run the offense, post up when things were needed, take advantage of the game. He didn't shoot it then, but if there was a problem in the game, he could shoot a three with remarkable accuracy; he was a real gamer.

**SAM:** Also fit that Western Conference style of play you talked about, if not triangle oriented.

**PJ:** It became more about passing movement—the West was always more wide open. More of a pattern in the East, a thoughtful game and a passing game, more zones. East way back had the YMCA gyms, the running tracks; you had to play a more controlled game. The East played a lot more zones and the West played more man-to-man, open game. Denver's always played like that because they think the altitude is an advantage, and Utah was run and run, the Stockton and Malone era. They were a mile-high city, too, but nobody really thinks about Utah being that high. Phoenix ran, Portland, San Antonio, Jason Kidd ran.

# Kevin Garnett

The best thing about Kevin Garnett might have been his loyalty. He was playing for maybe the most dysfunctional organization in the NBA in the coldest, dreariest place in the NBA. And his team made it past the first round of the playoffs once in his twelve seasons. Yet the Timberwolves just could not get Garnett to agree to a trade to join what seemed like a potential championship team with the Boston Celtics. Not that Garnett wasn't about winning, and he demonstrated how much he was in 2008 after the trade finally was consummated by getting Paul Pierce out of his cool stage and probably into the Hall of Fame. The wink in the NBA was that Kevin McHale had helped out his old Boston buddy and teammate Danny Ainge, the Celtics' general manager, with the prize final piece, Garnett. But Kevin Garnett wasn't about chasing a title. He was mostly about loyalty. The Timberwolves had committed to him and invested in him, and he, as he often said, signed up for the duration. What would players like Dean Garrett think? Who? That was a former Garnett teammate in Minnesota who generally averaged about a basket per game, but he stuck it out, and so should Kevin. It looked like a Shaq/Kobe pairing briefly when the Timberwolves acquired Stephon Marbury in a draft-day trade, ironically for future teammate Ray Allen. But Marbury forced a trade because he didn't feel he'd get enough shots playing with Garnett, the ultimate teammate.

Even in Minneapolis, Garnett changed the economics of the NBA with his then-massive $126 million, six-year contract extension in 1997, which often was blamed for the labor strife that led to the 1998–99 lockout. Garnett had that one big whiff of success in Minneapolis in 2004, going to the conference finals with Sam Cassell and Latrell Sprewell. Eventually Garnett did agree to a trade, joining Pierce and Allen and the "ubuntu" Boston battle cry meaning "humanity," occasionally translated as "I am because we are." And led by Garnett, the Celtics won the 2008 championship over Kobe's new Lakers with Pau Gasol. The Lakers got the next two titles, the latter revenge over Boston, and Garnett's knees began to feel the pain. He missed the next season's playoffs and never again came close to averaging 20 points, an occasional role player traded to Brooklyn and finishing back in Minneapolis because you *can* go home again. The ferocious seven-footer—another who preferred to be listed at six eleven for fear of being told to be a post player instead of the versatile big man he was—was selected for fifteen All-Star games, was all-defense twelve times, and Defensive Player of the Year. He was the league's leading rebounder four times. Perhaps no one banged their head on the basket stanchion more to prepare for games.

**PJ:** I went down to South Carolina and did some kind of a speaking engagement when I retired from the Bulls in '99. I'd do one each month. These grocers had me down there in one of those huge Piggly Wiggly conventions. I'm sitting at this table, and they say they had one of their kids go up there to Chicago to play. He's from Greenville, Kevin Garnett. He was caught in a terrible riot in the school. They enrolled him up in Chicago. I think that experience of having to leave his home base and go to Chicago and fit in was kind of like an adaptation crucible, the sort of thing that makes you adapt mentally and socially, and it changed him.

**SAM:** Those race riot things in the South were always suspicious, like the one with Iverson in the bowling alley. You figured these kids were being set up. He's charged with—get this—second-degree lynching. Supposedly he was not even involved, and eventually his record was cleared. But he comes to Chicago, Farragut Career Academy in Little Village on the West Side, and you have to survive there. He's Mr. Basketball and playing with this six-three highflier, Ronnie Fields, who is going to the NBA also but gets in a bad car accident and his NBA career is over. Kevin made it out.

**PJ:** His rookie year he was a player you saw potential in, but in between his rookie and his second year he really started to show. He had no game the first year, and I knew the coach, Flip Saunders. Flip and I would talk and I'd say, "He needs developing an inside game. He's just kind of a midrange player who's six eleven." I liked what Flip was doing with him, playing a zone, doing some nice things with his team. How's the kid to work with? Flip says, "He's good, he likes to work, he likes basketball, he wants to be a star." He was a different breed. I thought he was intimidating at a certain level, but when he got against a Shaq or a Malone or someone like that, it changed.

**SAM:** Kevin was skinny, and his reputation was he didn't like contact, which was why most believe he developed that fadeaway shot. He did like being the intimidator at 215 pounds. Not so much against Karl. He'd go after Kirk Hinrich all the time, but Kirk was a red ass and would be right in his face. Kevin was a heck of a versatile talent, but really didn't like to mix it up much. Liked to snarl and talk, but really not a fighter.

**PJ:** He had the bravado. The ultimate thing wasn't there. But he was enough for Boston to ride on. He had those young centers with him at that time. Perkins, who wanted to be intimidator. Wanted to be physical, too.

**SAM:** Flip said Garnett changed the culture there in Boston, and he was right about that. I remember Ray Allen saying that Pierce would tell him after a good game he could take a night off. Garnett gets there and it had been this fun-house environment with Pierce strutting around and taking all these crazy shots and Antoine Walker even longer ones—Pierce's famous explanation for why Walker shoots so many threes was because there are no fours—and Garnett comes in and the music goes off in the locker room. It gets overlooked, but that was a forty-two-game improvement with Garnett, Allen. The Celtics had lost eighteen in a row the previous season. Garnett shows up and I remember one of their coaches tells me they're in practice and Paul comes sauntering out in that sort of cool strut of his, and Garnett gets in his face and tells him to quit fucking around, was he going to take this seriously, and he was taking things seriously. Apparently no one had ever spoken to Pierce like that, and Pierce becomes a changed man. I'm convinced he's in the Hall of Fame because of that personality change. He was Sleepy Floyd or Purvis Short until then.

# Ray Allen

Ray Allen was a pioneer in the sense of being on the vanguard when the game was changing to feature the three-point shooter as both specialist and dominant player. Larry Bird, of course, was a premier three-point shooter, but he was more in the "greatest player" debate than just the greatest-shooter debate. There was an evolution from players like Dale Ellis to Reggie Miller to Allen and into the Steph Curry era and accompanying rules changes that flipped the game from postcentric to perimetercentric. The NBA—in one of the many influences from the ABA that saved its game—accepted the three-point shot in 1979. Teams initially used it as a last-minute, catch-up weapon. Pete Maravich, Lou Hudson, Hal Greer, and Bill Sharman could have been elite three-point shooters. But back then you got the same number of points for a layup. "Downtown" Freddie Brown with the Seattle SuperSonics had a sweet stroke. Allen's three-pointer with 5.2 seconds left to force overtime in Game 6 of the 2013 Finals and avoid elimination in the eventual Miami win is one of the historic NBA moments. Allen's opening line of his autobiography called 2013 "the shot of a lifetime." And Allen had an impressive NBA lifetime, championships with the Celtics and Heat, ten times an All-Star: elite if not among the most historic. He also might win best acting performance by an NBA player for his novice dramatic role in the Spike Lee movie *He Got Game* with Denzel Washington.

**PJ:** We came in to play New York just before the playoffs, and Jerry flew in with us to see the big college game, the Big East final, Connecticut and Georgetown and Allen and Allen, these two special guards. That's really when I first heard about Ray Allen. And then that draft thing that was kind of wacky when the Bucks wanted Allen but picked Marbury because they knew Minnesota wanted him with the next pick. Marbury was talented but kind of erratic. Ray was disciplined in his game. Right away you knew there was something different with his shooting.

The game was changing. The Houston Rockets, for example, long before Harden and Daryl Morey, used their guards to space out the floor, Kenny Smith and Sam Cassell—Olajuwon was able to take advantage of that, which gave us trouble. Horry was tall and came out of college as a shooter and could extend the floor. Houston was the first team that really was using the three-point shot as a weapon when Rick Barry went there, Calvin Murphy. Del Harris was coaching them at the time. Del was an innovative coach. Rick was maybe thirty-four or thirty-five but still a threat. Mike Dunleavy was the other guy, kind of a specialist. They weren't full-time players, but they came in and you had to pay attention to them.

**SAM:** That began to change with guys like Reggie and Ray, who were stars for their team. Your buddy George Karl was certain you should have been playing his Bucks in the 2001 Finals, and they probably would have given you a better series than the 76ers. George had a point. Remember that series? Scott Williams, your old enforcer for the early Bulls titles, gives Iverson an elbow in Game 6 and gets a flagrant 1. Between games Stu Jackson upgrades it to a flagrant 2 and suspends Williams, even though Iverson never even seemed hurt. The 76ers go on to win Game 7 and then Game 1 in LA, and then—oops—lose four straight to you guys as Kobe returns to Philly for the true gentleman's sweep. Ray claims he saw David Stern cheering for the 76ers. George said the league wanted the Iverson-versus-Kobe Finals. Another one of those conspiracies. The 76ers had nine fewer Ts, despite having Iverson, and shot 66 more free throws. I'm sure it was coincidence.

**PJ:** Like Bavetta in New York. The commissioner wasn't fond of me suggesting the Brooklyn-born Bavetta was assigned to that 1992 series to help the Knicks. But the three: Like everyone else then, we thought it was a risky shot, good if you needed to catch up and get back in a game when you were down. It took a while in terms of philosophy, and people practicing it enough to be proficient. Though the prevailing philosophy was always that penetration creates shots. That's what you did: put the ball in the hands of your big guy, people collapsed on him, and then you had jump shooters and it didn't matter if it was an eighteen-footer or twenty-two-footer; it was a good shot if you were open. Tex and I spoke about it a few times after this one game in Dallas where they made a three to win at the end. Tex said, "That's going to be the game, they'll start to coach the game that way." The problem was the baseline corner three: We always saw it as the jeopardy shot because you were out of the play and couldn't get back on defense.

**SAM:** That was one of Johnny Bach's seven elements of a good shot, as I recall, that your guards had to be in position to play defense.

**PJ:** It's why Doug was so resistant to the triangle: because the guard was in the corner. Doug played for a really great coach in Will Robinson. That corner was a place where the dead man went. Cazzie Russell would shoot that baseline jump shot and that would put him in jeopardy, because if it didn't go in he was late on defense. Doug had it drilled in his head that you have to be back, and so he was a denier of the triangle. But we teach guys how to get back because you're also in position to play pressure defense. That was one of the big adjustments I had to make coaching between the Bulls and the Lakers, the three-point shot. We used to coach that the whole thing was getting the guards back in tandem, two people between the ball and the basket. That's how you stop the ball. Then you can't do it because two people are in the corners. So you have to get your big guy back, post sprinter, stormer, whatever you want to call it, getting the same kind of effort on defense as on offense. Then the guard can go out on the perimeter and find the next viable scorer besides the ball carrier.

**SAM:** But you still go to the conference finals in '89 for the first time in fourteen years. Did you see Doug getting fired?

**PJ:** There are an awful lot of good coaches in the NBA who never get a second chance, a third chance. When I was on the Bulls staff, Jerry told me not to go for an interview with Minnesota. I had a relationship with the owner's son-in-law. Krause had his peculiarities, or whatever you want to call it. He could turn on someone really quickly. We were able to get along famously until your book came out. And then he had those page markers he kept showing me with the 186 mistakes he said he found in the book. But before that there was this expansion team, and Krause said, "They'd like to talk to you about coaching." Krause said, "You're not going there. That's where you get fired after two years and you're done. It doesn't matter how good a coach you are. You're getting fired and those losses are on your record." I always credited Jerry for that. I'd done some appearances with the Minnesota owner's son-in-law when I was in Albany, so we had a relationship and I thought I had the in. But the owner wanted Bill Musselman, who coached college there. He'd had that fracas with Ohio State. Good coach but was intense, wild. He came to fill a spot in Albany when I left.

**SAM:** You once told me you also were having some feelers from the Knicks at the time. Of course, you know that never lasts long. At least then it didn't.

**PJ:** I sat with Tex after that Cleveland series, and Tex was saying they wouldn't have the nerve to fire Doug after that. We all assume he's coming back. Then we go to Detroit and he makes Michael the point guard because that's the only way we can get the ball up court against Joe and Isiah, and we play really well. But Michael burns out at point guard. Then we're at the predraft player combine after the series and the Knicks send over an emissary, Dickie McGuire, to talk to me: Would I be willing to go to New York? Rick's going to Kentucky. My scouting role with the Bulls was to diagram the screen/rolls against Mark Jackson. Jackson couldn't play against screen/roll; that was my advice to Doug, and it worked. Then all hell's breaking loose in Chicago. Reinsdorf asks me: Would I rather go back to New York to coach the Knicks or coach the Chicago Bulls? I told him, I think the Knicks may be able to win a championship, but I think Chicago is a young enough team and can win multiple championships, and I'd rather be here. No one thinks Doug is out. But I don't think I was getting the New York job, anyway. They hired Stu Jackson. And I'd interviewed with the Bulls before, and then Jerry hires Doug and I'm thinking, "What the fuck happened here?" This is a guy with no coaching experience.

**SAM:** Doug was what they needed then, but he was too young and inexperienced for where they were. He has since admitted still resenting the fact that his playing career ended so prematurely. The rumor at the time was Michael ordered the firing, but Michael didn't do that kind of thing. I know Reinsdorf called Michael and said he was going to fire Doug. I heard Michael said Reinsdorf didn't have the balls to do it and hung up.

**PJ:** I didn't know if they'd do it or not after I met with Jerry Reinsdorf because of the momentum of press; the fans liked him, the press liked him, he was a smart coach. I did have an uphill battle those first two years. Until we won the championship. But we started off that season like 0–3, and there was this whole to-do.

**SAM:** That was me. I asked Michael about the triangle when camp started, and he said he'd give it three games.

**PJ:** He wasn't resistant, but he wasn't meant for that offense. We kind of had to gerrymander. Michael operated out of the post better than anyone I've ever seen coaching or playing. His elevation—he could shoot that turnaround jump shot against anyone, and he had that drop step he used until they eventually began calling traveling on him. But he was very slick and drop-stepped to his right shoulder. Then the next year we moved him down to forward and put Pippen at guard, and that made the whole difference. Pippen had a guard mentality. Pippen rebounded and could take the ball the length of the court; he was a wing runner. And then they were ready.

# Kobe Bryant

Kobe Bryant's story is perhaps the most universal imaginable, considering the triumph and tragedy, so many massive forces to overcome in succeeding at the most sublime levels, NBA titles, sporting acclaim, artistic excellence, and shame, scorn, and redemption. Bryant's story is his basketball legacy, but perhaps more enduring is the message of succeeding despite and because of the failures. Bryant became celebrated and castigated and emerged from everything only to meet the most tragic fate, passing away accompanied by his beloved daughter Gianna in a helicopter crash while he was doing the most prosaic of tasks, coaching an adolescent girls' basketball team, just being Daddy.

The son of NBA journeyman Joe, Bryant mostly was raised in isolation in Europe while his father chased his basketball dream. Kobe eventually returned to begin his quest in Philadelphia in high school with such arrogance he'd travel to the Philadelphia 76ers facility to challenge the 76ers players to shooting contests . . . at eleven years old. Kobe had no problem being himself. He broke into the NBA shooting multiple air balls to close out his first playoff series as a rookie after skipping college, and then in his first All-Star game ordered Karl Malone out of the post so he could post up Michael Jordan. When players throughout the NBA after 1998 feared even playing for the Bulls because of the inevitable comparisons to Michael Jordan, Bryant embraced them to the point of twice trying to get the Bulls to acquire him. No one but Wilt Chamberlain scored more points in an NBA game than Bryant's 81 in 2006. And in his final NBA game after returning from Achilles surgery, Bryant scored 60 points. He did attempt fifty shots, but that's not easy, either. A swift and graceful six-six athlete, Bryant played for five NBA championships, twice was Finals MVP, and was league MVP. He played in eighteen All-Star games and was All-Star MVP four times. He was all-NBA fifteen times, twelve times all-defense, twice a scoring champion, and once a dunk contest champion. He also won an Oscar for an animated short film.

**PJ:** When I came to the Lakers, I was surprised when I looked at film of Kobe shooting three or four air balls in an overtime game; Kobe was a rookie and Del gave him the ball, even though he had the other kid, the left-hander, Van Exel, who was really terrific. I couldn't believe Del put the ball in his hands like that.

**SAM:** Kobe credited Del, said that Del's faith in him drove him to practice more. I remember Jerry West commending him for the shot attempts, at least publicly, though I doubt that's what Jerry was saying as it was happening.

**PJ:** The competitive drive. One of the coaches I worked with, Davy Wohl, when he was an assistant with Rambis and I asked him about Kobe, said, "The thing about Kobe is you tell him a bar is eight feet high and no one ever jumped eight feet. And he'll go and try it again and again and again and again. There's nothing he won't attempt to do. Even though it never happened, it's going to happen." Kobe had a better left hand than Michael. He broke his right the first year I was there and couldn't play for six weeks and just worked on his left hand. Then he started doing it all the time and I'm asking my assistants, "Is he just showing off?" He got really good at it. Kobe had that kind of energy. Michael brought the same determination and dedication to the game, although Kobe used to tell me the only difference between him and Michael was the size of the hands. He couldn't do that thing where Michael showed the ball out front and pulled it back. Kobe was in touch with Michael a lot.

**SAM:** I had a lunch with Kobe when he was on his redemption tour after the assault charges in Colorado. He couldn't have been more charming and humble. I was asking him about Michael and all that trade stuff about coming to Chicago, and he laughed and said Michael had gone beyond basketball and was an urban legend, that people never thought he missed a shot. "How can I compete with that?" he said. Of course, I knew he didn't believe it.

**PJ:** It wasn't very good from the start with Shaq. They'd had that little slap fest during the lockout when they both showed up at the same gym, players practicing on their own. So they have this little thing and then Shaq says, Kobe will be my little brother, and Kobe says, I don't have big brothers, I have sisters. He was his own guy, no doubt about that. When I first gave him a book, he didn't want to read it, didn't want to give me any feedback. Guy wrote a hip-hop type thing, teenaged skateboarding I thought he'd like. But he's not giving me any credit for giving him a book. Then he eventually started reading them and I found out he was a big reader. Loved those fantasy books like Harry Potter, wizards. That's what he wrote when he wrote a book. He sent me a copy prepublication and inscribed it like this: "You and John Wooden have been my heroes as coaches. I'm practicing without a ball." Various things a wizard would do. He was so proud of that

Oscar based on the "Dear Basketball" poem he wrote. He said it meant more to him than the championships, like Reinsdorf with baseball.

**SAM:** So your relationship was strong? I always wondered how you fixed it after that breakup in '04; your book—yikes—the uncoachable Kobe, named your kidney stone after him, won't pass.

**PJ:** They wanted me to come back and coach. I said, "I have to talk to Kobe." So I talked to him and I said, "How're we going to do this? If I come back, how are we gonna do this?" He said, "Don't say anything personal about me. Let's just keep it between us, the two of us. Don't go through the press." I said, "OK." He asked me not to ever give up confidential stuff that we talked about. I said, I've been pretty open with reporters in my career, but yeah, going forth I can do that. I'd gotten asked that by Pete Carroll. I've done some consulting with coaches, mostly in the NFL, the Eagles, about personnel and relating with players, and Pete asked me that, how we went about coming to terms again, when he was having some issues with players in Seattle.

**SAM:** It was a tough start for you with Kobe, right? He did like Del. I do remember it supposedly was Shaq who told West he wanted you as coach.

**PJ:** With coaching you hope to have people who have a willingness to have an open mind. People who are resistant to coaching, that's one of the things you have to either see them bend or come into a viewpoint where they are submitting to the desires of the group or the whole, which is one reason Kobe and I had this interaction the first two years. There was what he wanted to do and what was best for the team. Eventually Kobe became a proponent. How do you get in the flow? What is the flow about? How do you capture this flow? That's why the samurai got a foothold in Japan. You can't plan for an opponent to be there. It's why samurai warriors were proponents of Zen. You can't look at swords. You can't preplan what comes in the next moment. You have to do what comes in the next moment. That why I always felt MJ and Kobe were different. We started talking of taking over a ball game: Don't try to take it over. There are too many obstacles in trying to take it over; just do what comes natural. If you stay in the system, what comes natural is just second nature. All these things mechanically you practiced to do, now the next thing happens and you are there and you do it, you exist in that present, the "chop wood, carry water" type thing. Like sitting on the toilet is the most important thing in that moment; those specific things.

**SAM:** I'm not that surprised that at nineteen Kobe figured you were nuts.

**PJ:** I always had the feeling with Michael that he would do what was best for the team. Though at times he'd feel he had to do what he needed for the team to win. Tex always used the old line about there being no *i* in *team*, and Michael's rejoinder would be "There is in *win*." So there's the balance between special players and the group. How far do you lean over, and how much does the talented player incorporate himself into the team? There's a lot of conflict along the way.

**SAM:** I sort of wrote a book about that.

**PJ:** We're playing San Antonio. We've got a game plan. We'd trap Duncan when he was on the left block. He had a hard time throwing out of the double with his right hand. So he now has to pass the ball with his left hand. Kobe starts double-teaming him from the corner. Stephen Jackson is over there in the corner, makes three three-pointers. After the third quarter I call time-out: "What're you doing? Why aren't you following the game plan?" "Oh, I know this guy. I played against this guy in high school; he won't continue to make three-pointers. He's a ratty personality." "Yeah, but Kobe, that's not the game plan." Michael took coaching. Kobe didn't. He finally did, and we finally got in a groove where he sounded like me a lot of times when he ended up talking in the press or whatever. It took a long time to get him there.

**SAM:** Though there were moments like Portland in 2000, their breakthrough.

**PJ:** That's after the third quarter. Rick Fox gives this big speech, gets into everyone. He's saying, "Are we gonna do this again? We're gonna fold? Go out without a fight? What's going on? Like we folded against San Antonio, against Utah?" They were weak-natured. Shaq, when he saw things going in one direction, it was like the kryptonite is on the table. He just wasn't around. Then Kobe comes down at a critical point in the game, it's close, and he gives that lob pass to Shaq. He recognizes he could have scored. Then in the championship round in Indiana, Shaq sprains his ankle. Kobe manages to be the difference in an overtime game, and Shaq recognizes Kobe's genius emerging and gives him a bear hug and picks him up. They'd been through all that defeat, swept in '97 and '98. It was either survival or defeat.

**SAM:** Kobe did come around in a remarkable way. But he also needed to be Kobe.

**PJ:** I recall John Salley coming to me and saying, We can't get him to go out; he just hangs back in his room, eats room service, watches videos, works out. So I ask Kobe, "What's the deal? You wanna be captain?" He says, "Yeah, I should be captain by now." I said, "You at least have to associate with them." He said they just talked about hubcaps, girls, getting laid, cars. Remember, hubcaps were big back then, the spinners.

**SAM:** He really came around on even Smush Parker, who I recall he went after hard. By the way, we never thought Kobe was coming to Chicago.

**PJ:** I told him the year before they traded Shaq, basically, You are going to find out how hard it is to win 50 percent of the games if he's not here. This is a tough league to win games; you have to be a good team to win 50 percent of your games. He said, "I'm a winner. I'm not ever going to be under .500 on the teams I play on."

**SAM:** Which tells you why he was so upset that summer.

**PJ:** Kobe was impossible to coach at that time; too much anger. He was mad at the world. He'd fallen off, the Colorado situation. He's on TV with his wife next to him to apologize to the world, had to go to counseling, got hauled over the coals, and was mad, mad, mad. Shaq got the league to turn on Kobe. Swore he'd kick the shit out of him; we had to separate the two of them. Brian Shaw had been with Shaq in Orlando, confronted Shaq a few times about it. Shaq also was beyond angry. Brian is like, "What are you talking about, Shaq? You got like eight rebounds last night. You should be getting eighteen." Buss's final present to Pat was trading him Shaq. I asked Buss about it and he said at the end for Pat he told Pat it was time for a new voice. Buss said, "Why don't you take a year off, get away and come back?" Pat went with Checketts and never said a negative word about Buss. So deciding to trade Shaq was a present to finish it off with Pat. I did begin to give Kobe leadership books, how to open up and be more of a leader, and he became the person who'd say, "Hey, let's go out tonight, guys." Here's a remarkable thing. So I come back that first year and we are in the Benson Hotel in Portland, one my favorite hotels, waiting to have breakfast, and Kobe comes in the side door and has ashes on his forehead; it's Ash Wednesday. He got up at eight and went to Mass. I gained a lot of respect for him; he was working on something with his wife. I told him I admired him for that.

I don't think he really disliked Smush. That time in the playoffs in 2006 against Phoenix when we went up 3–1 and lost the series, after Game 7 Smush started crying. There was so much pressure on him to play Nash full court, maintain the pressure. He couldn't shoot, but he kept the defense going. Kobe gave him a lot of love. After the game we did my normal Lord's Prayer circle, a chance to cool down. Smush broke down and cried and Kobe hugged him; he was right there for him. I have to give Kobe credit for that. Then there was this time there was this substitute for Jay Leno, and they invited the team after we won the championship, and Adam Morrison sat in the back, and the host said, "Who's that?" dismissively, and Kobe was right on him: "Everybody on this team contributes. Adam comes to practice, works really hard, practices, competes against us. He's had some injuries that limited his career that were not fair." It was a different Kobe from when I left in 2004.

**SAM:** Kobe had to know you always were closer with Shaq, big-man thing and all that.

**PJ:** I favored Shaq over Kobe. I wanted Kobe to play into the Shaq thing. He didn't want to deal with Shaq. He didn't have any resonance with his personality, didn't jibe with Shaq. At that All-Star game in '04, Buss told Kobe he was going to get rid of Shaq and it was going to be his team. I said to Shaq, "Let this kid take over," senior statesman and all that, and Shaq said, No way. But I did develop a close relationship with Kobe. I talked to him about being a father. After the birth of his youngest daughter, I said, "You've got to do some bank shooting, because you're not producing any boys. You need a bank shot." He liked that. I went down to see him in his office in Orange County just a week before he passed. It's amazing that he's gone; it's hard to think about it. He wanted me to come down to see what he was doing with this voice-over with ESPN. I went down there and asked him how he was getting back and forth to Westlake, an hour-and-a-half-to-two-hour drive, this big warehouse facility he was using for his girls' basketball team. He said he was using a helicopter, used it for games all the time living down in Orange County. He took helicopters to the game, and he'd take helicopters after we'd fly. We could get in at two in the morning and there would be a helicopter waiting for him. He wanted to move out of the LA area and be down away from people, less distraction so he could focus on the family.

# Allen Iverson

It's sometimes said one reason Michael Jordan edges out LeBron James in that tiresome "greatest" debate is that Jordan did more than elevate and change basketball; he changed society. Bald became fashionable for men, earrings too. Long shorts and sneakers made a statement, especially sneakers. Perhaps the same can be said about Allen Iverson, whose basketball brilliance was enough for a league MVP award, eleven All-Star games, and twice being an All-Star MVP, since no matter what everyone else did, he took those games seriously. He was all-NBA seven times, four times a scoring champion, and three times steals leader, and is still known for his infamous press conference when he mentioned the word *practice* twenty-two times and wondered why he was being indicted for practice flaws. It didn't seem unreasonable; after all, they were talking about practice and not a game.

Iverson in some respects was the Sugar Ray Robinson of hoop, the greatest ever pound for pound at really maybe five ten and 160. In high school he was the state's best in both football and basketball, playing offense and defense. At Georgetown, he was scoring leader and Defensive Player of the Year. He'd been victimized and basically falsely imprisoned over a brawl in high school, the sort of racial incident that caught up George Gervin and Kevin Garnett. And then Iverson went to the NBA with an uncanny football player's mentality in a Muggsy

Bogues body. It became a joke of sorts when the 76ers went to the NBA Finals against the Lakers and Iverson thwarted the projected Lakers sweep in Game 1 with 48 points. That Philadelphia team's strategy was for Iverson to shoot and Eric Snow, Ty Hill, Aaron McKie, and George Lynch to retrieve the ball so Iverson could shoot again. Rinse the opposition and repeat. If banging into six-eight, 250-pound men forty times a game wasn't enough, Iverson finished just about every night down the road in Atlantic City with an unending nightcap and energy and fearlessness to match the next game. If Michael Jordan brought style and corporate culture to the NBA, it was Iverson who introduced the NBA community to hip-hop and the style of its Black fan base whose generation admired Jordan but who wanted to be Iverson. There was the jewelry, the sleeve that became fashion like Jordan's shoe, the baggy pants, and the crossover that once undressed Jordan. You're talking practice? This guy had game.

**PJ:** The big thing about Iverson breaking down Michael was they decided, here's this number 1 pick in the draft, and it's OK to cuff the ball when you do a spin dribble. That came from the playgrounds into the game and it just kept expanding.

**SAM:** I think that was the point at the time, or at least what Iverson was making. The NBA wasn't exactly enamored of him at the start. Like the ABA modernizing the NBA game when it came in the late seventies with the so-called street ball, the dunks and the show; that also was Iverson in the next generation. I recall David not being thrilled.

**PJ:** The idea also that we didn't have to practice anymore, the whole bit with Larry Brown. Practicing is really important. I think the NFL has found out in their training camps that the first two weeks of football are like, "It's just training camp now," and everyone says they aren't ready and injuries happen.

**SAM:** I know it became fashionable to mock the Iverson practice rant; Iverson even made fun of himself in recent commercials. But it is now rare when NBA teams practice during the season. Union concessions, teams being cautious, agents waiting out the next deal. The irony is they rarely practice and there's so much less physicality. And guys get hurt more than ever. You need to practice to play to avoid injury, really. The NBA doesn't get it. I know, old man rant; here we go again. And at my place in Phoenix I have no lawn, which is an inconvenience.

**PJ:** George told me in Denver how nocturnal Iverson was, late nights, didn't like to practice, liked to drink expensive champagne. Like Rodman. It shortens your career.

**SAM:** Probably did, but here's a guy maybe a hundred pounds less than everyone, probably going to the rim as much as anyone, taking a beating. What an amazing competitor. It maybe reached its fruition at the 2007 All-Star game in Vegas. That was the hip-hop All-Star game and really the official beginning of the NBA accepting its audience.

**PJ:** I got along with David, but we had our discussions. One of the last things he ever said to me was he should have fined me more.

**SAM:** There was that famous NBA magazine cover around 2000 when Iverson's tattoos and earrings were airbrushed off. Don't think he had the cornrows yet. The league got the backlash and began to notice this guy's influence. The NBA still tried the informal Iverson-rule dress code about how players looked coming to the games and on the bench. That also evolved.

**PJ:** Kobe did call Stern out one time about that. At an All-Star game, Stern went into the locker room and talked to the players, said he's not putting up with this shit, that you guys can't be wearing these fifty-pound chains and prison clothes. Kobe went right back at him for the players. They did respect Kobe.

# Steve Nash / Chris Paul

Two other players are on that list, if often overlooked, of the best players not to win an NBA championship, Chris Paul and Steve Nash, the latter with more than a hundred playoff games without reaching the Finals. You just seem to discount them when mentioning Barkley, Ewing, and Malone. Paul is up there among the leaders in playoff games without a championship, too, though he snuck into the Finals a few years back with his fifth team, the Phoenix Suns. Nash and Paul have been elite at what they do: Both are among the all-time top five in assists, and Paul is second in steals, while Nash has rare back-to-back Most Valuable Player awards. Paul had a dozen All-Star game appearances and was all-NBA eleven times despite checking in at barely six feet and 175. Paul also was steals leader six times and assists leader five. Nash, at six three but not much heavier, the savvy soccer player from Canada, appeared in eight All-Star games, was all-NBA seven times, was five times assists leader, and has the all-time most 50/40/90 seasons, enabling him to make an all-time shooting case, if not at the Steph Curry distance. Nash shot 49 percent overall for his career, 43 percent on threes, and 90 percent on free throws.

Though they have different styles and reputations: The demanding Paul has a well-earned reputation for not playing well with others and has had ugly breakups with his Lob City Clippers and James Harden and the Houston

Rockets. Nash, by contrast, has maintained a lifelong friendship with former MVP-teammate Dirk Nowitzki even after Nowitzki's Mavericks declined to match Nash's free-agent offer from the Phoenix Suns. In Phoenix with Mike D'Antoni, Nash and the Suns shocked the NBA with a so-called five-out, fast-break offense that effectively changed the offensive landscape of the NBA and inspired the Golden State Warriors' run of four championships with Curry and later Kevin Durant. Nash and his Suns were denied by flukes, like the Robert Horry–generated fight in the 2007 playoffs that resulted in multiple Suns players being suspended. And then came almost a dissatisfaction with too much success: losses in the conference finals that led the Suns to acquire an aging Shaquille O'Neal, which destroyed their fragile offensive dynamic. Nash's Suns, like Nowitzki's Mavericks, also made fatal financial mistakes, Dallas its refusal to match Nash's offer sheet and Phoenix its refusal to keep Joe Johnson because of contract demands. Nash was originally drafted by the Suns, a little-known Canadian from small Santa Clara whose draft selection was met with derision because of his anonymity. Benched behind Kevin Johnson and Jason Kidd, Nash was shipped to Dallas and developed the elite pick-and-roll game with Nowitzki. But owner Mark Cuban didn't want to weigh down Dallas's already big payroll. So Nash went back to Phoenix and reinvented NBA offense with a contagious style that teammates said fostered unselfishness in everyone. Much like Curry in recent years, Nash was often considered the player other players would most like to have as a teammate. Paul was more of a ball-control point guard, finding the right player for the right shot, while Nash was more likely to push the ball to create fast-break tempo. Both brought their teams close but not close enough, often because of injuries, given their size.

**PJ:** Jason Kidd was my choice. Chris Paul couldn't hold a candle to Jason. Jason was big enough to do a lot of things Chris could not do.

Chris had to be the center of attention, a little bit of the Isiah Thomas kind of thing. I loved to pressure him. Take the ball away from him. He never liked to work to get the ball. Pressure him because then someone else has to come up and help get the ball.

**SAM:** We saw that strategy from you with the Bulls all the time, on Mark Price, Magic, Kevin Johnson.

**PJ:** My rationale was if we have agile enough defenders, we can throw people at the point guard and make him have to come to grips with pressure. It was interesting, at a reunion we had guys talking about how fatiguing it is for a guard facing pressure and having to bring the ball full court, haul the ball up court, and manage things. So much so when we played Phoenix that Kevin Johnson slapped B.J. Armstrong in the face during the course of the series. He couldn't put up with it anymore. B.J. didn't retaliate, but after the series was over, the pressure on B.J. to keep it up was so great he broke down and cried. He was on the court with that final five when Paxson got that shot.

**SAM:** B.J. was the only one who didn't touch the ball but the most dramatic as he collapsed in joy—and maybe exhaustion from the K.J. defense—as Paxson's shot was going in. Of course, you'd hardly know it from Paxson's cool Ohio reaction.

**PJ:** Price was too quick to trap, so we'd force him down the sideline, because that pick with Daugherty was too much for Bill to come out and deal with. So we just got on top and chased him from behind. That was also the ultimate thing against Detroit, to put Pippen on Laimbeer. Then when Isiah came off that screen from Laimbeer, Pippen is jumping out and challenging the dribbler. Force Laimbeer to put it on the floor. He didn't want to do that. You're coming at that right hand where he wants to shoot. Now what's he gonna do? Give the ball to Dumars. With Chris

Paul you could take advantage of him because you know he's going for the steal. He's not good on the pick. I did see some comment Barkley made that he was the best team leader at the point guard position; people do have high regard for him. He is a remarkable competitor.

**SAM:** Not a suffering-fools guy. Paul did come up clutch a lot, but hamstrings and all sorts of stuff—he always was getting hurt at bad times. Supposedly with that Clippers team he was really tough on Blake Griffin. I remember when Jimmy Butler was a free agent before going to Miami. He told a friend that Harden had called him and was begging him to sign with the Rockets. Jimmy said Harden told him Chris Paul never shuts up and he can't deal with it anymore. The other great thing with Paul was the referee feud with Scott Foster, though I recall Bill Spooner apparently hearing enough. Goes on one of these podcasts in a classic and says, "Chris Paul, in my thirty-two years in the league, was one of the biggest assholes I ever dealt with." They say, "Not Rasheed Wallace or da-da-da?" "Nope."

**PJ:** Don't know why they got enamored with Terry Porter in Phoenix. Steve wanted a defensive mindset. D'Antoni kind of got rid of himself is what he said. It was like almost ruining the franchise to bring Shaq in: "We can make a center work," D'Antoni told him. D'Antoni was about offense, not concerned about the scouting report, concerned about how his team was going to play the offensive game.

**SAM:** The modern NBA game?

**PJ:** I throw it more to Dallas when Nash and Nowitzki were there, the three-point shooting.

**SAM:** What happened in Phoenix was the classic old line: You listen to the people in the stands, you end up sitting with them. Steve is GM then because he'd known Sarver, who needed NBA help. Steve asks D'Antoni about coaching Shaq: Can he do it? Mike says he can. He knows in his heart it won't work. He feels that's what everyone wants, and he's a little pissed at Steve being there, because Mike had been GM and coach before.

**PJ:** Mike's had a great career. Probably in the Hall of Fame. People argue he's the guy who brought about the change in this game, but it was really Don Nelson when he had Nowitzki and Nash, before Nash left Dallas and went to Phoenix. Don was elevating big guys' outside shooting and three-point shooting and guards. Run TMC in Golden State or whatever that was.

**SAM:** I think of Nellie now like that TV commercial with the two guys drinking and watching cows push a ball, and the one guy asks who's winning, and the other guy says they are because they are doing nothing. Nellie in Maui, golfing and smoking dope with Willie Nelson. Nellie wins.

# Tim Duncan

It was Shaquille O'Neal who probably said it best about Tim Duncan when he called him "the Big Fundamental." Michael Jordan was the greatest, and we debate LeBron, Kareem, and Kobe, but when a coach or teacher explains basketball at a clinic, they're describing Tim Duncan. There's the textbook footwork, face-up shot, old-school bank, drop step, post up, square on defense, help and recover, everything a player needed to do to be a star and a star of a teammate. That was Tim Duncan, helped by four years in college at a time when he also would have been the number 1 selection after his sophomore (Joe Smith) and junior (Allen Iverson) years. The statistical credentials are as impeccable as any, five championships being the best player on the team and mostly with no one else from the top seventy-five, with David Robinson winding down his career, twice MVP, three times Finals MVP, and overlooked at least once for MVP because the media was getting bored selecting him, as with Jordan. All-Star MVP, fifteen times an All-Star and fifteen times all-NBA—that's right, did you even notice?—fifteen times all-defense. He played right in the midst of the excellence of Kobe, LeBron, Wade, Curry, Garnett, Nowitzki, Iverson, and Durant, never got much mention, and fittingly, when he retired, *The Wall Street Journal* said the greatest player was hiding in plain sight.

Duncan walked into the league in 1997 with an understated 21 points and 12 rebounds that first season and pretty much did the same for the next decade, every season. Never three bears–like, too big or too small or too noticeable, but just right. Never more than 26 points per game when he obviously could have challenged for the scoring title every season. Best not to be noticed. The Spurs had been around for a long time and were pretty good with Ice, Artis Gilmore, and a wild, fast-breaking group that included Larry "Dr. K" Kenon and some terrific guards the NBA didn't get to see in their prime, like James Silas, and they were close plenty. And then the Admiral sailed in. But they never got there until Duncan's second season, when he finally got David Robinson that first title with a bunch of guys they didn't always much want, like trying to cash in Tony Parker for Jason Kidd and never quite knowing what to make of Manu Ginóbili. With Duncan steering the ship, the Spurs added on a few more titles and could have had even more but for some of the most startling roadblocks, like Derek Fisher's you've-got-to-be-kidding shot in 2004. Efficiency doesn't produce celebration, just success. Don Nelson, who knew those things from being there, decided Duncan was like a combination of Bill Walton for the intelligence, McHale for the inside versatility, and Bird for the clutch play. Just that fans and media never thought of saying that out loud. Shaq said he could get to even the great ones, trash-talk and rattle them. Shaq said Duncan would look at him like he was bored. And then score.

**PJ:** I liked Duncan. I liked who he was. I used to yell at him all the time; he'd complain to the referees. I'd yell, "Get a whistle, get on a striped shirt, get in the locker room and get a shirt." Just to talk at him. He'd look at me like, Are you crazy, Phil? I didn't realize how good Duncan was when he came out of college. Tex at his summer league was talking a lot about how good he was. I said, What's his deal? He said, His skill level is above and beyond. He had a block that he preferred.

**SAM:** The left block, right? Always like to say it that way.

**PJ:** I never know what to call it. Do you call it when you're looking at the basket? Or do you call it when you have your back to the basket? I'd double-team him on that block because he couldn't throw the ball left-handed. He'd have to throw it out right-handed. Just get on his shoulder and bury his shoulder so he can't throw the ball out on a double-team. Limited free-throw-line shooter; got nervous about shooting free throws. Really improved in his overall game all the time, though. I thought his career was over a couple of years before it actually was. He was having knee issues. He played what, fifteen years?

**SAM:** Nineteen.

**PJ:** I screwed up Pop with him one time. In a series we were down 0–2 we came back and we swept them four games. Tony was killing us. Stephen Jackson was kind of erratic, kind of like, What day is it? Tony just couldn't deal with it and he was young, maybe second year, and Pop blew up, lost his temper on him at the bench. We didn't have to do it the rest of the series after that. Fish won that series on a ridiculous turnaround jump shot. That was one of the better playoff games I've ever experienced. I kept telling guys, "We're gonna beat this team tonight." And then Duncan hits that shot and I was like, "Holy cow."

**SAM:** That was such an amazing finish, the point four. I remember looking at Duncan, who gets the inbounds pass from Ginóbili with about four seconds left. This is right before the Fisher shot. Duncan's moving left, which he doesn't do, and fading away. Score is like 72–71, something ridiculous like that, as the NBA hadn't changed the rules yet. Shaq's right in his face, Kobe helping. Duncan shoots off one foot like Dirk. Duncan's eyes bulge when his shot goes in, like, C'mon, I made that? This is Tim Duncan: Steve Kerr told me this story about when he signed with the Spurs that summer after the Bulls' sixth title. It's preseason and Duncan is a star already, Rookie of the Year, he'd averaged 21 and 12, an All-Star. So preseason is in San Antonio and the rookies and free agents are staying at a motel. The team bus is unloading these extra guys back at the practice facility, and Duncan is getting off the bus with them. "Where are you going?" Kerr asks. The motel, Duncan says. No, Kerr says, the starters, the veterans, the stars, certainly don't have to. "You mean we're allowed to stay at our own houses?" Duncan asks him.

# Dirk Nowitzki

Dirk Nowitzki in his way cleared the path for his successors, finally removing the stigma from professional basketball players of European descent. Because he proved he could be tough, leading his team to the NBA championship in a Finals series with a torn tendon, the best player on his team and in the league, the first NBA superstar whose primary language was not English and who hadn't attended college in the U.S. And then came Pau and a parade of stars who became league luminaries and MVPs, like Giannis Antetokounmpo, Luka Dončić, and Nikola Jokić. Every MVP until Nowitzki in 2007 attended college in the U.S. And then from 2019 to 2024, an international player was MVP in five of six years, the exception being Joel Embiid, a native of Cameroon who played collegiate ball in the U.S. Nowitzki was playing professionally in Germany at sixteen, applied for the NBA draft at nineteen, and was selected number 9 by the Milwaukee Bucks and immediately swapped in a draft-day trade to the Dallas Mavericks in a series of deals that also brought Steve Nash to Dallas. Nowitzki and Nash soon went on to be one of the great pick-and-roll duos in NBA history. After an uncertain start, Nowitzki would collect his championship in a classic run of twenty-one seasons with the same team, the longest in NBA history. By his fourth season, Nowitzki became an All-Star for a run of eleven consecutive seasons of his fourteen appearances at the mid-season event. Nowitzki's fadeaway off one foot and remarkable accuracy enabled him to become one of nine

NBA players with a 50/40/90 shooting season. They were trademarks of his versatile game—he was a seven-footer whose shot could not be reached. Nowitzki had memorable moments, like his three-point play to send Game 7 of the 2006 semifinals against defending-champion San Antonio into overtime for an eventual Dallas win, and 50 points in the next round to assure a first trip to the NBA Finals. After a 2–0 lead in that series against Miami, the Mavericks lost the series. But in the next five seasons of averaging fifty-six wins, including sixty-seven in one season, Nowitzki brought the Mavericks back to the NBA Finals in the matchup with LeBron James's first team in Miami. Dallas won in six games as Nowitzki, playing through injury, averaged 26 points. Nowitzki was all-NBA twelve times, won an All-Star three-point contest, was regular-season and Finals MVP, and won FIBA World Cup and EuroBasket MVP awards.

**PJ:** One change in the game has been these individual trainers when they're thirteen, fourteen years of age now.

**SAM:** That reminds me of Dirk, who always had that trainer from Germany with him who he credited often, Holger Geschwindner. He was a national team player who spotted Dirk. Dirk went pro at sixteen—hard to imagine. That wasn't the American thing.

**PJ:** That wasn't even part of Michael's beginning. He always practiced on his own. Until he got his infamous trainer, there wasn't a whole lot of individual stuff going on. It was not in vogue, no sense that you had to have your own individual trainer.

**SAM:** Tim Grover. He did make up the fake poison-pizza story for *The Last Dance* about that flu game in '97. That was important for the *Last Dance* documentary.

**PJ:** Chip came in to me and said that Andrew Bynum had a trainer, a guy who was a chiropractor. I asked, Why do you think you need a personal trainer? He said Michael Jordan had one.

**SAM:** I told you that was why Mike was the GOAT. Nobody wanted to copy LeBron. You thought you could maybe be like Mike.

**PJ:** You wanna know how Michael Jordan got his trainer? This guy was in a workout with the wife of our doctor in Chicago, John Hefferon. He didn't know anything about basketball. He knew something about being a trainer. Michael said there was so much pressure by the Bulls to work with Al Vermeil. Is there anyone you can recommend? Hefferon said, My wife's got this trainer. And what a big thing it became for the NBA, and to think that's what sprung all these guys into becoming separate satellites out there. We want everyone to work out together? No. We work out on our own. But how many years for LeBron? Really unheard of. I remember when we were talking about players playing fifteen years, and you'd go like, "Fifteen years! Get a life. You still want to be doing this after you're like thirty-six years of age, hanging out with these crazy kids and flying around the country?"

**SAM:** Pay's gotten better.

# Paul Pierce

Paul Pierce could be the poster child for how NBA teams overthink the draft. He's six seven but a little heavy, like 235, so probably too slow for shooting guard, and is he athletic enough for three, what they now call the wing? Turns the ball over, and what about that handle? Not so great. He can score. Which is what Paul Pierce did, the Boston Celtics' second-leading all-time scorer behind John Havlicek. That 1998 draft, Pierce was tenth pick, well down from college teammate Raef LaFrentz, who was third after Michael Olowokandi and Mike Bibby. Pierce was from a rough neighborhood in Los Angeles and there were stories—he was stabbed eleven times in a Boston club before the 2000–01 season—and he played at his own pace, perhaps as John Wooden had advised to be quick but not to hurry. Pierce quickly shot down a lot of rumors, and opponents. He was Finals MVP in 2008, a ten-time All-Star and four times all-NBA. He joined Larry Bird as a Celtics three-point-shooting contest winner. Amazingly after that horrible stabbing, not only was Pierce ready for opening night, but he played all eighty-two games and led the Celtics in scoring at 25.3 per game. He averaged at least 25 per game in five of seven seasons from there. But the Celtics were a losing isolation team, and Pierce fell in with a dysfunctional USA team in the 2002 FIBA World Championships and got a lot of the blame for the unpleasant Ugly American sixth-place finish. Pierce came out of it an angry, often disconnected player as the Celtics had one of their poorer eras, with three losing seasons in five. Pierce seemed to have given up even on himself, until the Celtics acquired the manic Kevin Garnett, who pumped energy and life into not only the Celtics but also Pierce, who became a reliable defender and scorer and a motivated team presence and champion. The Celtics, with Garnett's leadership, Allen's shooting, and Pierce's clutch play, went on a run to rival some of their predecessors, averaging just under sixty wins in a four-year stretch before injuries overtook the aging players. Pierce played for the Nets, Wizards, and Clippers before retiring after nineteen seasons. He is considered, along with Bird, one of the greatest scorers in Boston Celtics history.

**PJ:** I'll never forget one of the last conversations I had with Willis. It was about that '08 series with the Celtics. He said Boston, they had all those guys and all the momentum. He said, "You just let them get pummeled. Your team was down by twenty-five at halftime or something, and you just let them out there to get shit-faced." He said, "You did it on purpose, didn't you?" I said I did. They weren't ready to win. We'd just gotten Pau Gasol and had taken off as a basketball team. San Antonio was the top team, but we replaced them at the end in first place. San Antonio has a crazy thing. At midnight their charter plane contract runs out, and if they get there late, no plane. They fly the next day. So they only had one day in between to recover, and we swept them or beat them in five in that series.

**SAM:** Pau was getting the shit beat out of him in that Finals, Perkins, Powe, Big Baby; I remember Chip telling me Pau went straight to the weights after that series. Kobe was dragging them as far as he could.

**PJ:** That started with Pierce with that wheelchair.

**SAM:** Caused the lame to walk, eh? Pierce, I read, admitted a few years ago he had to go to the bathroom and needed to sit in a chair because the, well, discharge was coming if he stood. Which I guess is why he dove back into that game with such energy. Which reminds me of another of those real stories. That was the time Michael punched out Kerr in the 1995 preseason. It had nothing to do with Steve showing Michael he could stand up to him. Michael did regret it, and I think he appreciated Kerr because Kerr made up a good story. That summer is a lockout. No games missed, as they settled late September. Kerr is the Bulls' player rep, and it's about the cap, and Kerr's on the side of expanding for the so-called middle class, more mid-level exception, and the agents ran things for the players and David Falk is lobbying for more at the top of the cap so his clients, like Michael, Ewing, etc., can get more. So he tells Michael that Kerr has been criticizing Michael as selfish, which he wasn't. So camp starts and Michael tells some players Kerr's not getting away with that. Michael takes the shot at Kerr. He is remorseful immediately and storms out. I didn't see, but I get home and get a call and get filled in. So I call Kerr to see if he'll comment. Do me a favor, he says. "I'm trying just to make this team. I get on the bad side of Michael, I'm gone." I also don't need to start a fight with him again writing about his sucker punch. So I let it go, and Steve gets going and tells it his way, and it becomes the legend of Killer Kerr.

# Carmelo Anthony

Carmelo Anthony was one of the most gifted scorers to ever play in the NBA, adept primarily in the midrange but powerful, with an ability to create inside and the strength and accuracy for long range. There's always this narrative about the main players who haven't been on championship teams. Usually it's about, as Michael liked to say, the supporting cast. And when you examined the likes of Patrick Ewing, Charles Barkley, Karl Malone, Allen Iverson, Dominique Wilkins, Vince Carter, Chris Webber, Reggie Miller, Chris Paul, Damian Lillard, and James Harden, there usually were team-wide talent elements lacking. But there also were other issues: often too much offense without defense, chaos-provoking narcissism, a "be the man" syndrome. Anthony may have been one of the most efficient and productive scorers for USA Basketball in Olympic competition—though perhaps because he seemed to understand there were more talented teammates and he could just play, instead of having to perform. Carmelo won a scoring title and made ten All-Star games, though his regular-season NBA teams lost thirteen of their sixteen NBA playoff series. He wasn't a loser. Just because your team doesn't win the final game doesn't mean you are a loser, despite our generally accepted binary win/loss sports world. But he could be difficult to play with despite the remarkable talent.

**PJ:** I remember watching that championship game between Syracuse and Kansas, and Carmelo actually wasn't the dominant guy. They had that little guard, McCarthy? McClellan? And Gerry McNamara and another guy who played in the NBA, Hakim Warrick, inside athletic player. Boeheim played zone, so you never knew, Can this guy defend? He could really score, and when George Karl took over that Nuggets team, he had Chauncey Billups, and Chauncey was able to throw thirty-foot passes to him when he'd leak out.

**SAM:** A lot of great players can't defend, but I heard that was a big part of why Detroit passed on him. But how do you keep your job picking Darko Miličić over the NCAA title winner and the tournament's Most Outstanding Player? And then get an extension? Joe Dumars never talked openly about it, but a big reason they supposedly let Rick Carlisle go was that Rick would not play Tayshaun Prince. Joe told me if they took Carmelo, that was Prince's spot, and could you imagine the team chemistry with Carmelo suddenly having to get his 25 points? He had the pure talent, but that Detroit team didn't need it. How's that go—too many cooks spoil the broth? You would know from the kitchen.

**PJ:** George came up to Montana one summer with his son, Coby, and he says, What do you think was my game plan when we went up against you in the conference finals?

**SAM:** You know, George was absolutely psyched out coaching against you. He opens his book by calling you his coaching nemesis. George wrote that you burn sage and incense and he burns brain cells, you want quickness and finesse and he wants contact and collisions. But he said he'd never criticize you because you always kicked his ass. George did say Carmelo was the best offensive player he ever coached but a user of people, addicted to the spotlight, unhappy when he had to share it with others, so talented that if he decided to, he could lead the league in rebounding, scoring, or assists. But when he was in the Olympics with Kobe or LeBron, he needed to impress them and stayed in a lane.

**PJ:** George told me that their game plan was, let's get the big guys and not worry so much about Kobe. Kobe's going to get his 30 points and we'll deal with that; shut everybody else down. Carmelo interjected, "No, I disagree with that. We've got to defend Kobe first. We've got to throw everything at Kobe, double-team Kobe and make it difficult for him." You know why? George asked. He said he wanted to be the top scorer. After being with Carmelo in New York, I knew. That season in New York I bring him into the office; he's going to sit out after the All-Star break. I tell him, "OK, we're not going anywhere. Let's give you ample opportunity to rehabilitate yourself and come back next year and get after it." We're two games under .500 going into the holiday season, and I was going to meet my family in Missoula and we're losing, eight, nine in a row and everything is going south, which was kind of the beginning of the end.

**SAM:** That was after Carmelo was courted by the Bulls. Thibs was pushing for Carmelo, desperate for someone to replace Derrick. He felt he could control Carmelo. I actually happened to be having lunch in Chicago the day Mike D'Antoni was going to quit. He told me that day Carmelo was giving the Knicks a "him or me" ultimatum. That was after Carmelo had sabotaged the Linsanity phenomenon. Mike said Carmelo told him he wanted the ball and to stop letting Lin run point.

**PJ:** Hornacek said Carmelo wanted the ball. I think the best thing I did in New York was get them out of that huge luxury tax spending thing they were involved in, getting salaries down to give them a chance. We got Porziņģis, which helped, but Ntilikina . . . The NBA game turned out not to be for him. I thought he'd be great in a two-guard system, six four, agile, but he never could shoot.

**SAM:** Did you regret going there?

**PJ:** I was reluctant. But it was, "Oh, go and meet Dolan." OK, I'll meet him. He's hired McKinsey, the search firm. Buttigieg was working there. I hired Derek, but the unfortunate thing was that Derek wasn't ready to coach. My fault. I thought, you know, he had two years kind of as like a player/coach kind of relationship in Oklahoma, smart guy, head of the players' association. I regret it simply because my relationship was going to change with Jeanie. I warned her: "I don't think our relationship can survive this. I'm not going to take this job." "No, don't worry about it, we're going to be fine." But she got pressure from the league because they worried about the idea of collusion that could happen between an owner and a president.

**SAM:** Life's about experiences, right?

**PJ:** With Carmelo it was "Let's fix your knee, get it going." We had a good thing going the next season through December, four or five over, January we lost eleven of twelve games, fell apart, and I realize something must be going on coaching-wise and replaced Derek. I think that actually was a relief for him to get out of that situation. Kurt was interim. We took our lumps. But it got them out of the penalty situation financially with the cap. Big kid Porziņģis was a good draft pick, but his brother was in the way all the time. I had this meeting with Jim Dolan. I said, I don't want Carmelo back on the team; we've got to find a way to trade him. I said, Let's sit with Leon Rose and explain we're not going to win a championship. Carmelo wants to win a championship; he wants to be on a team that has a chance, and he should be; he's a Hall of Famer. Carmelo, he's not a confrontational guy. But when he came out of the Rose meeting, he went to the press: "I don't know what's going on here" or something like that. He wasn't totally negative; it was "This is confusing." I had wanted to pick the Virginia coach, Tony Bennett. He said, My kid's still in high school, so I'm not doing that. He finally left Virginia because of the NIL craziness. Ntilikina hurt his knee in the EuroCup finals. Dolan said to me, "Are you going to get run out of town by the media?" I said, I know who the media is; that doesn't affect me. But Dolan felt it was too much. He said, "I don't want you to go through it. I know what it's like to deal with these people." I said, Unfortunately my relationship with Carmelo is kind of busted, and if he's going to be here, it's probably best that I go. Silver fined me $20,000 for saying Kobe wants to play another year or he can play another year, something innocent, but a tampering charge, which they like to do. I was never insinuating he'd come to New York.

**SAM:** Of course, who'd want to come to New York?

# LeBron James

You better be good if you start calling yourself the King and you have a mural of yourself as Jesus Christ painted on a building across from your arena. LeBron James came pretty close, at least in basketball terms. James went on to pass Kareem Abdul-Jabbar as the leading scorer in NBA history, playing longer than anyone, with impressive durability and determination. James took teams to eight consecutive NBA Finals, though he slips a bit in the eternal debate of "greatest ever" with Michael Jordan because once Jordan went, he always was holding the trophy. James went home a loser more often but rivaled Bill Russell in attendance. He was the rare prodigy, a child star whose fame only grew. His games were televised nationally in high school and he was on the cover of *Sports Illustrated* and other major magazines. And if not the closer like Jordan, Kobe, Kareem, and Bird, at least not early in his career, James impressed from his much-anticipated first game in Sacramento when he scored 25 points and quickly went on to immediate playoffs feats like 25 straight points against the mighty Pistons, who were in the midst of six straight conference finals runs, and a memorable chase-down block to win a championship, highlights on offense and defense. There was 45 and 15 in a fulfilling 2012 Game 6 in Boston that led to his first title with the Miami Heat. Then down 3–1 to the historic seventy-three-win Golden State Warriors, there's the comeback for the ages to bring a title back to his home state and Cleveland before he took off again, this time to Los Angeles to polish his off- and on-court résumés. The Lakers got a title in the 2020 pandemic-enclosed season and James sprouted to billionaire level with Hollywood business and movie successes.

He was like Mike in many ways, and trying to do more. LeBron joined Wes Unseld and David Robinson in funding schools and became a political activist and players' association leader. He also ran through coaches, David Blatt in Cleveland when the team was 30–11, and apparently only stopped by Pat Riley from cashiering Erik Spoelstra during dim times after James came to Miami following the ill-conceived ratings bonanza *The Decision* to determine the location of his 2010 free agency, which had a half dozen teams eagerly courting James. He virtually demanded to run your team. Everybody feared it, and everyone wanted him anyway. He guaranteed you success like no one else in his time. Four championships, four Finals MVPs, four regular-season MVPs, twenty-one times an All-Star by 2025, three times All-Star MVP, led the league in scoring and assists, though also changed teams three times. At least twenty times all-NBA and thirteen first team, also the most ever. Nobody has done what James did at such a high level for so long. He was one of the most physically gifted human beings to inhabit the planet, a rock-solid six nine and maybe 250 pounds with the speed of a Derrick Rose and the power of a Karl Malone. He was playing into his forties and with his son, another of his many firsts, as he established milestones virtually every time he scored, rebounded, or assisted. He almost was worthy of the biblical word and pictures.

**PJ:** I don't get into the rankings. It's an impossible thing. I recently saw Michael must have said something about Curry, because I listen to Colin Cowherd, and he was like, "Oh, yeah, these are the greatest, and this guy said this guy's in the top ten." Comparing people and what their effect is? Stephen Curry's in a league all by himself. What else do you do with that guy? He's not a point guard. Curry can't set up the team and run the offense. They start putting pressure on him. But bringing the ball up, he actually kind of figured out how to do it. I was impressed he made that adjustment. Wasn't looking so much for his own stuff but to generate the team offense.

**SAM:** I do get into the rankings; it's Michael, but I'm still living in Chicago and wrote three books on Michael, so we say that. I always have said, to break the tie, it's effect and impact on society, men welcoming being bald, the earrings, the sneakers. I did a little talk when the Jordan Brand people were in Chicago, and they gave me as payment—not reporting it—a pair of Air Jordans. I told them it was my first, and the kids there were horrified. You never had Air Jordans! This also is why Michael is a billionaire and I'm still writing Bulls game coverage. The Air Jordan comes out and it's, what, a hundred dollars? This is pre–*Jordan Rules* and he likes me giving him shit. I say he's nuts. No one's paying a hundred dollars for sneakers. Changed the world. That's what "greatest" is about.

**PJ:** So if I have to say, LeBron is not the greatest, maybe not in the top five players? Shaq didn't have him in his top five, and I saw he got berated for it. I don't know if he's in that group with Michael, Kareem, but people do say this generation has been marked with LeBron in ten Finals. So that's impressive. He is impressive.

**SAM:** The modern consensus is one or two. The so-called old-school guys would say he didn't win like Russell, didn't score or produce like Wilt or Elgin, wasn't as versatile as Oscar. So top ten? We'd get social media trouble for that.

**PJ:** Miami did lose twice of four times and probably was lucky with the one with the Ray Allen shot. Reminds me of the loss we had in Orlando the year Michael came back and had the ball taken away from him; if we'd have won that game, they would have folded. Swept them the next year. Shaq was done there, ripped the urinal off the wall. Michael went to the Finals six times and won six championships. And how many Game 7s in the Finals series did Michael have to go to? He never did. Take nothing away from either player, but it's still a fact that Michael went to the Finals six times and won six championships.

**SAM:** Hey, there's nothing wrong with second. Who would have more impact with players, LeBron or Kobe?

**PJ:** Kobe had an impact on all those guys. Kobe worked with Wade, LeBron, Carmelo on the Olympic team. "Get up at five in the morning, meet me downstairs thirty minutes." LeBron would come down, Wade. They would hang in there and do the work. But Kobe upstaged LeBron often, like on his draft day with his free agency. Michael was a better shooter. Michael always was embarrassed if he wasn't a 50 percent shooter. That was one of the goals. Win half the games on the road, shoot 50 percent from the field, 80 percent from the free-throw line. This is what our standards were. Talked about that with one of the writers I did a book with, Huge Deli Sandwich.

**SAM:** That was your Zen book with Hugh Delehanty. People have no idea about your constant name wordplay.

**PJ:** I once made him watch a tape of this game. Scottie had a good first half. I don't know who was guarding him, if it was Ehlo or Sanders or whoever. But he had a real run, and I don't think Michael scored in the third quarter. Everything dried up in the fourth quarter. Michael had to pick it up, so he just kept going to the basket and they kept throwing him down on the floor. I wanted him to see the nuts and bolts of what playoffs whittle down to sometimes. You're in the moment by the seat of your pants as a coach, hoping you have the right directive. Like the seventh game of the playoffs against the Boston Celtics in 2010 where it was just like, "Kobe, get in this system. You're like six of twenty-four, for god's sake. It's just not going your direction. Incorporate your teammates; it'll be OK." He finally did. We were down like 12 points in the fourth quarter. He still was looking for his game to show up so he could be the impetus to win. But he had to give up that notion. Pau got a three-point play and Artest a three-point shot. Hardly made a three-point shot the whole series. Things started naturally happening with his teammates when he played that way. A big playoff game against Cleveland comes to mind. They were a really good team, and nobody's given them the credit they deserved. Fourth quarter starts; Michael's gotta have his rest. All of a sudden Pip comes in dry. Michael comes in and he can't get going. He's been sitting back watching Scottie play. So he just made a decision—I gotta go to the basket. He gets knocked down like where three guys come at him, Daugherty, Nance, and Williams. He goes to the free-throw line and shoots his free throws. Now he's got his touch back and he can shoot the shot and he's able to carry us through the rest of the game. Nobody really caught the essence of what went on. Giving the game over to Scottie, allowing him to exploit what he could exploit. Not saying, I gotta stay sharp by keeping scoring, I'm gonna lose my feel for the game. He didn't allow that to happen. I see LeBron get fouled, get up, and complain somebody hit his hands. That's a difference. He's in the same category as Michael Jordan by sheer strength of his game. Not his mentality.

**SAM:** LeBron's six times all-defense, five times first team, by the way.

**PJ:** He gets steals. I remember the Tayshaun Prince rundown blocks in Indiana. That changed that whole series. Definitely got the athletic talent to do it, and when he's wanted to and needs to, he has been impressive. And it has been something doing it at his age. I've been surprised at that level of energy. He has been a remarkable player.

# Dwyane Wade

In another of the "greatest" debates that are so popular these days, there's Michael Jordan and Kobe Bryant for shooting guard, obviously, and then perhaps unexpected but also widespread agreement that next comes Dwyane Wade. Which certainly is surprising, since most doubted Wade would be the third-best shooting guard . . . in his NBA draft. For one thing, Wade, well, was a pretty poor shooter, which sort of is the definition of the position. You think in modern times of Ray Allen, Reggie Miller, Damian Lillard, or Steph Curry, since point guard has mostly melded with shooting guard. Or old-school times with George Gervin, Sam Jones, Jerry West, and Bill Sharman. But Dwyane Wade, even shooting 33 percent on threes in college, though with few attempts, and less than 30 percent in the NBA, nevertheless was one of the most efficient shooting guards of all time, thanks to a reliable midrange jump shot and such explosiveness, quickness, and finishing ability that he practically had to pay rent at the free-throw line. Combined with an uncanny knack for finishing not only against bigger and stronger players but also with unusual body control. And possessor of that ice water in his veins when it was time. Randy Pfund, the former Lakers coach who was a Miami Heat executive, admits to some bias. "You give me anybody in NBA history and I have to run the clock down and get the last shot of a game, I'm going with Dwyane Wade," he said. "He can get the shot and his timing was impeccable. I think the most time he ever left on a clock was his first playoff game winner on Baron Davis and left like a second on the clock." That was at the close of an exciting rookie season when Wade's winner carried Miami over the New Orleans Hornets. It was just a preview of some of the greatest playoff performances in league history, averaging 24 points in five Finals, including the 34.7 in the 2006 Finals, carrying an ancient Heat team, with Shaquille O'Neal, Gary Payton, Antoine Walker, and Jason Williams nearing the end of their careers, to an unexpected championship. Wade scored 12 points in the last six minutes of Game 3 after Miami lost the first two. Miami won the next four games for the first championship for Wade, before his famous combination with LeBron James and Chris Bosh in the historic 2010 free-agency. That produced the notorious black-hat Heatles, who won two titles and lost in two other Finals before James went back to Cleveland. It was mostly made possible after their defeat by the Dallas Mavericks in 2011 when Wade, who was all-NBA and a Miami hero and top celebrity, volunteered to play a supporting role to James to enhance James's skills and provide a more appropriate order of succession. Always willing to provide assists and averaging almost 7 his first seven years in the NBA, even while winning the scoring title and being among the scoring leaders every season, that assist was perhaps Wade's most influential. The result was consecutive NBA titles before a 2014 loss to the Spurs and the end of that era. Though celebrated for his individual athletic and two-way player prowess and among the all-time blocks leaders for guards, the six-four Wade played a reckless style the way he hurled his body at the rim and opponents, resulting in continuing injuries to his knees and other body parts. It all probably shortened Wade's career and certainly cost him dozens of games per season injured. But he was acknowledged by the NBA with thirteen All-Star appearances, the 2006 Finals MVP, all-NBA eight times, all-defense three times, and a league scoring championship.

Wade had a tough childhood in Chicago. His mother went to prison. He was passed around to relatives and eventually out of the danger of the city. But as a result he was also less noticed by recruiters, playing for a less prominent high school. He got to mid-level Marquette and was not even eligible initially, eventually climbing the draft boards with an eye-opening 29-point triple-double against powerful Kentucky that led Marquette to the Final Four for the first time in almost thirty years. Wade became a surprising number 5 in that LeBron James / Carmelo Anthony NBA draft. Wade did eventually go to play for the hometown Bulls but returned to Miami for a fond farewell. Wade also became an entertainment and media star to transcend even his basketball fame. He's married to actress Gabrielle Union. He became a minority owner in the Utah Jazz and the WNBA's Chicago Sky and a host of a network TV game show. He's been featured in *People* magazine and *GQ* for his clothes and personal appearance and in *Time* magazine as among the nation's most influential people.

**PJ:** Tex saw this kid and said he was going to be a really good player. We thought he'd be a six-three point guard. Pax went with Jerry Krause to watch him play, and he went like two for seventeen or something and, Jerry was, "No, we won't draft him. He can't shoot."

**SAM:** Everyone was sure he'd be there in '03 for the Bulls at number 7. So sure were the Bulls they barely scouted anyone else. Not that Kirk Hinrich was bad; he was a good, quick recovery when Miami took Wade.

**PJ:** No one figured on Wade in Miami because the guy they drafted that previous year, Caron Butler, they liked. So where would Wade play? Eventually came to the Lakers. I'd asked Michael, "How come you drafted Kwame Brown first?" Michael said he beat everybody when they came in for workouts. One of those big guys who played guard growing up and then grew a bunch of inches, so he could dribble the ball, but terrible hands. Kobe comes to the bench one game before we traded him. Kobe says, "You won't believe this. Kwame said, 'Please don't pass me the ball, I can't make any free throws at this time in the game.' 'You don't want the ball?' 'No, don't pass me the ball—I may drop it.'"

**SAM:** He was in the trade that got you Gasol. Funny thing about Wade how tough—dirty even?—he was behind that welcoming facade. It's the 2012 All-Star game in Orlando. Kobe starts cookin' right away, ball between his legs and crossover, and Wade is stumbling around and everyone starts laughing at him. Next possession—I'm right in front baseline, when they still gave us good seats—and Wade just punches Kobe in the nose, breaks his nose. Kobe shrugs it off like just a bloody nose, but Wade clearly did it intentionally. Like I remember he kicked Ramon Sessions in the nuts one time like Draymond Green does. One of the tougher guys hiding behind that beatific smile.

**PJ:** City kid; it comes out once in a while.

# Kevin Durant

Kevin Durant probably is not going to catch LeBron's scoring record the way LeBron still is producing at forty years old. But Durant sure looked like he was going to settle into second all-time ahead of Kareem Abdul-Jabbar. And mostly with jump shots, many more than both Kareem and LeBron. Steph Curry likely will carry the crown as the king of the shooters, but there probably has never been anyone whose shot has been as unchallengeable—other than Kareem's sky hook—than Durant's. Dirk had a whiff of it, but not quite with the range and versatility of Durant. Like some other players who didn't like being called seven-footers, Durant downplayed his height. He was tarnished publicly for jumping from the Oklahoma City Thunder to the Golden State Warriors, but the Warriors likely don't get those titles in 2017 and 2018 without Durant, who was Finals MVP both seasons. He also was a league MVP, twice All-Star MVP, and in the double figures and counting for All-Star games and all-NBA designations. He's been set back with some serious injuries, including the dreaded Achilles tear. But baller that he is, he returned where he left off. His graceful play included internationally, where he became the premier scorer in several Olympics for the U.S. He's led the league in scoring four times and twice, a decade apart, reached the vaunted shooting Valhalla of the 50/40/90 club. He joined Curry and Klay Thompson. How'd they keep them under 200 points per game?

**PJ:** He's in that other realm of scorers, a remarkable player who has a certain sense of the game. I don't think he's selfish. I think he just believes in himself and what he can do. He is a game changer. If he stays healthy and continues his career at some level, he's got to be right up there to get the scoring record, a guy who can post up, shoots from distance, gets to the basket, midrange, shoots threes, unselfish, knowledge of the game. Not a great defender, but not bad. His Oklahoma City team was really good. They ran stuff for Durant coming off single/double and post actions and should have won that 2012 series against Miami. That series was badly refereed. Even that last shot on his home court he's fouled on that inbound post-up situation and there was no call, down by one or two and everything goes in Miami's favor there. That was a tough one for Oklahoma City.

**SAM:** And off went Durant, like Howard Cosell calling, "Down goes Frazier." The story we all heard was Westbrook was so out of control running up the court a hundred miles an hour that Durant couldn't take it anymore.

**PJ:** It was the mistake the Lakers made with getting Westbrook. He's too fast. LeBron liked to take the ball the length of the court and run when there was an opportunity, but he's not for a speed team. This guy Westbrook gets going and you can't even turn around, and he's full court, like, in three seconds. That's not how LeBron wants to play. Not sure how he didn't see that.

**SAM:** Durant's journey reminds me of one of my favorite David Stern stories. The greatest story never told in the NBA is the smooth and suave David Stern and his explosive temper. Stern wants a new arena for Seattle and goes to the state capital to help Howard Schultz get money at least for an upgrade to KeyArena. So the Speaker of the House tells Stern they're not impressed with some big New York hotshot and you can sit down and shut up, and so Stern is like, That's the way you want to play it? So Stern recruits these oil guys in Oklahoma who helped host the All-Star game during Hurricane Katrina, and Stern sets up the sale of the Sonics, knowing they'll move the team. Sure, not great for the NBA going to the mini-mart in Oklahoma. But Seattle voters also pass an initiative restricting subsidies for sports teams. Stern has seen enough, and off go KD and the Sonics to Oklahoma City. David declared the NBA wouldn't return to Seattle as long as he was commissioner. You don't mess with the real king.

# Stephen Curry

There will always be a debate regarding Stephen Curry because he was the right person for the right time. But can we judge someone the best computer programmer ever when we never gave Leonardo, Ben Franklin, Edison, or Einstein a chance? The greatest is a debate we love to have in this era, and when it comes to shooting a basketball, the consensus, at least in the twenty-first century, is that it's Stephen Curry. To the point that Curry gets compared with the likes of George Mikan, Wilt, Kareem, and Julius Erving, players who changed the game. Everyone shoots the three-pointer because of Curry, and it's become perhaps the most vital part of any NBA team's arsenal because of Curry and the success of the Golden State Warriors, with five consecutive appearances in the NBA Finals, four championships in their 2010s dynasty era, and an all-time-best seventy-three-win season. Curry's partnership with fellow shooter Klay Thompson made their Splash Brothers a historic NBA moniker.

The slightly built six-two Curry, mostly ignored as a big-time collegian because of his size, mystified the NBA talent scouts because of the uncertainty of his position and whom he'd defend, a player the size of a point guard who plays shooting guard. Those so-called tweeners usually failed in the NBA. Curry seemed on the way to doing so with multiple ankle surgeries his first two years in the NBA, and he was nearly traded to the Milwaukee Bucks before recovering physically and changing the game artistically. Curry became the first unanimous league MVP and first to achieve the elite 50/40/90 shooting percentage (shots, three-point shots, free throws) while averaging more than 30 points. But again there were the contradictions, since with players like Mikan, Wilt, and Kareem, rules were changed to limit them. The NBA's evolving rules changes and not only the expansion of three-point shooting but also limitations on contact on the perimeter gave Curry room to shoot that guards before 2000 never had. But you take advantage of the good fortune that comes your way, and after all, no one else in the NBA has done so quite like Curry. There are too many shooting marks to recite, including becoming the best free-throw shooter ever, as Curry went into his mid-thirties and smashed all the three-point shooting records. More significant has been the range in which he's shot them, which separated him from the great shooters of other eras, though, of course, until 1979 there was no three-point shot in the NBA. Curry also owned what his coach Steve Kerr called the greatest hand-eye coordination of any basketball player and an unusual combination of playing arrogance and off-court humility. Curry is perhaps the greatest so-called trash actor who offends the fewest opponents, despite his celebratory antics, which include his shimmy dance, chest pounding, mimicking putting opponents to sleep, spreading his arms in flight, and forever manipulating his mouth guard. Curry's pregame ballhandling routine became almost worth the price of admission itself. At the time of those four titles, he had two MVPs, double figure All-Star game appearances and all-NBA teams, a couple of scoring titles, three-point contest titles, and multiple times leading the league in threes made and in steals.

**PJ:** I don't think that he's the best shooter ever. I don't get into that, but there have been great shooters. I think he's best distance shooter ever. It's the DNA. His dad was a great shooter. His brother. It's in his genes. I don't know how good a shooter their mom is.

**SAM:** Dell isn't often mentioned, but he had maybe the best shooting form in his era. He just couldn't handle the ball so was mostly a spot-up reserve. Curry's amazing; everyone agrees, and he's produced. But you can't tell me if it were worth an extra point, you wouldn't have had guys practicing it back then. Dolph Schayes made 90 percent of his free throws multiple times shooting two-hand sets. Bill Sharman, also a professional baseball player, so talk about hand-eye, usually shot 90 percent from the line. And this with all those hardships and never missing games. There always have been great shooters. Rick Barry, Maravich, Oscar, Jerry West, Gail Goodrich. Bob McAdoo was shooting three-point distance even though it was worth two. And if Dražen Petrović wasn't killed in that auto accident, he was just starting to become a star with the Nets. Reggie Miller told me he thought Dražen was the best shooter until Steph came along.

**PJ:** When Steph came out, I remember in college they were saying he was too small. Who knew what he was going to be? That was the year Kurt Rambis went to Minnesota. They had four draft picks in the first round. They picked four guards and didn't pick Steph Curry. Picked two guards ahead of Curry.

**SAM:** That probably ended whatever hopes I might have had—or any of us in the media—for being an NBA GM. My old newspaper colleague David Kahn was the beat writer for *The Oregonian* on the Trail Blazers when I got going with the NBA in the 1980s and worked his way to Timberwolves GM. I remember talking to David then: He was convinced Ricky Rubio was the twenty-first-century Bob Cousy. Then Jonny Flynn had a good NCAA tournament and he picked him number 6, right before Curry. I know the Knicks at number 8 were salivating for Curry. But Nellie was back with the Warriors, and if someone's going small with shooting, it's Nellie.

**PJ:** Nellie saw that was the direction basketball was going. A lot say Mike D'Antoni with what he did in Phoenix, but Nellie was the guy. Don always liked in practice three on three, four teams, and winners play winners and losers play losers and winners get a case of beer or some fine money. Running a lot of that stuff back in Dallas when Nash got there, that high-speed game. We thought Curry would be a good shooter. But everyone thought he'd be a specialty player. The other guard was the lead guard.

**SAM:** Monta Ellis, who actually was more popular then. I remember I used to write these what-if trade columns, and when I'd mention Ellis, I'd get the angriest reaction from the Bay Area.

**PJ:** Curry kept having foot injuries. He'd be out with an ankle. And then when he had this last ankle surgery, Mark Jackson had him to church and they prayed for him.

**SAM:** That was in the book about Curry by a Golden State writer. As the story went, there was a tradition of faith healing at Jackson's church. Curry had ankle surgeries his first two seasons, and there were plenty of doubts. Herb Kohl told me when they traded Bogut for Ellis, the Warriors weren't sure to give up Ellis or Curry. Anyway, Jackson calls up Curry in church, and they anointed his ankle with oil and prayed for healing. There was chanting and blessings, and the story in the book was that Curry began to jump around to show his ankle was better. I'm not a believer, but Curry basically never had problems again. Hey, who knows?

**PJ:** What Curry has done changed the game, because all these kids, they want to stand out thirty feet and shoot jumpers now. I mean, little kids. I'm not talking about NBA players. I'm talking about kids like my grandson; he's eight years old and he wants to be shooting three-pointers. "You're not strong enough, gotta get inside," I tell him.

# James Harden

J ames Harden in some sense came to define the new offensive era of basketball into the 2010s, the era of so-called small ball, less contact, and league MVPs who never played defense, like Steve Nash and Steph Curry. There were no-defense exceptions who snuck in, like Charles Barkley, but the MVP award once suggested an all-around game. Perhaps no one benefited more from coming along at the right time than James Harden, though the doors began to close on him late in his career. At six five, but not so athletic or quick twitch, Harden nevertheless began to produce some of the most productive offensive seasons in NBA history, moving into sentences that only the likes of Wilt and Michael occupied before. Harden moved into Wilt, Michael, and Kobe territory in 50-point games, triple-doubles with at least 50 points, consecutive games with 50, and more than thirty games straight with at least 30 points. He was also Wilt-like in the sense that it all led to even fewer championships than Wilt enjoyed. Signing on with the Morey/D'Antoni shoot-'em-up Rockets, it also led to Starksian playoff figures when Harden's Rockets missed twenty-seven consecutive threes and the Warriors went on to the NBA Finals. Hey, Coach, they all felt good leaving my hand.

It was all a surprise at first, when Harden was just a sixth man with the newly minted Oklahoma City Thunder, who were great with talent evaluation and not so much with what to do with it, when they let Harden go to the Rockets to retain Serge Ibaka. And so began Harden's historic offensive run with D'Antoni's principles from his "seven seconds or less" Phoenix Suns days and Daryl Morey's mad-scientist analytics three-ball game. It never achieved the ultimate, and then Harden became defensive, if never much on the court. He forced his way out of Houston and Brooklyn and Philadelphia with historic pouts. Though also with historic numbers, three times leading the league in scoring, twice in assists as a point guard, seven all-NBA teams, double-figures All-Star games, and as good a beard as Darnell Hillman had hair.

**PJ:** Amazing guy, really. He gamed the game. He learned how to get to the foul line. Led the league in foul shooting attempts how many years? Maybe three, four, five years in a row.

**SAM:** Those were the infamous rip-through times when he'd throw his arms through the defender.

**PJ:** He also does the flop move because he's a left-hander. That was like, How can you make that call? Well, we have to call it. I said it's not a basketball play. I ended up doing a little thing with the referee Bob Delaney. We were watching the defensive player, he said. These offensive players get away with everything, get away with throwing an arm out when they dribble the ball so it's like a stiff arm. LeBron's been doing that for years. When I was with New York, I brought it up. I said, It's the wrong attitude. You should be refereeing the game and not focusing on the defensive player. I used to referee practices all the time. As a head coach you almost have to referee practices.

**SAM:** Do a lot of coaches do that? I don't think any coaches do that now.

**PJ:** If you don't, your assistant coaches get maligned. They're the ones who are being yelled at. When you referee, you're watching the play. You're not watching a man. It's like Zen Buddhism; you have to have soft focus; that's what it's called. You have this soft focus, which is what they also teach you when you're doing whatever it is, surveillance. Because if you have hard focus, you don't see what's going on. I brought this up with Bob about how they allow these photographers to activate the light system. So when they take a photograph, the lights flash in the arena. I didn't notice this. I knew something was going on, that blink. So I'm watching a game film and Kobe gets a pass thrown to him by Fish. He's spun out, so he's got his back turned. Ball's up above the rim. Ball goes off part of his hand and off the backboard. I know this is something this kid can do. I saw in the second frame the whole shot blows up, all whited out. So I said, "Kobe, I want you to look at this." He looks and says, "No wonder I lost sight of the ball. When I came back to get the ball, you'd see the light flash blurred the vision out totally and I lost the ball in the process." That's the way the referees see it. Then I started noticing photographers are taking pictures of the game-winning shot. It's all washed out. I have a good friend, Andy Bernstein. Asked him, How's this happen? How'd you guys get away with doing this? They plug into a system that allows them to use the arena light. It gives them extra lights. But then the referees are at a disadvantage. Then the referees get shit from the players about not calling a foul when it's not their fault.

**SAM:** I better let the fans know. What did Delaney tell you?

**PJ:** All these shooters do now is they take two steps back. Bird started that. Naismith all the way through: You cannot pick up your pivot foot and put it back down. That's the definition of traveling. You need to find a pivot foot. If you pick this one up and don't shoot the ball and put it back down again, that's a travel. We're just ignoring all the rules. Same thing with our government; they're just aborting the constitution.

**SAM:** Knew we'd get there.

**PJ:** The rules have gone by the wayside. I said, That's when you lose the game. When you can't referee the game anymore and the play dominates how the games are played, you lose the concept of what your game's about. Now you see kids on courts, they don't know the rules of the game. You watch a guy at the three-point line, he will step back behind the three-point line, pick up both feet, and have a three-point shot. You can't do that. It's a travel as soon as you move that pivot foot and step back. You watch Steph Curry. He's got this thing, take two steps to get away from the defensive player to shoot his shot. Harden's the real guy that can get away with this. He's left-handed, so he needs these two steps. Left-handers shoot better going to their right, and right-handers better to their left, because it frees up their shooting arm.

**SAM:** LeBron, obviously, finally developed a somewhat reliable shot going deep to his left like Dončić.

**PJ:** Some guys learn to get squared up to shoot their shot. Reggie Miller was kind of like that. Even though he had kind of a bad, weird release. Bob said, We know but can't do anything about it. We're teaching skills that are useless. My group came in and Jimmy Walker was the first to cup and spin off the dribble; he carried the ball. Earl kept his hand on top of the ball, pronated the wrist. You remember the year all the NBA clubs complained about Michael picking up his foot on that baseline reverse he was doing? They were going to call him for traveling. But you let Iverson carry the ball like that? Delaney said, "If we call it on him, we'll have to call it on Michael." I said, "Please, please call it on Michael." These guys can figure it out. That's why they're special. You don't have to give them any access. Right away they gave Allen Iverson this liberty. To this day it's made these little guards capable of "OK, I'll put it over here. Well, no, I'll put it over here." Now you see Trae Young, then Ja Morant came in and stole his thunder. Morant doesn't have good judgment, either. But my grandsons are in awe of him. It's the game the kids want.

# Damian Lillard /
# Kawhi Leonard /
# Russell Westbrook /
# Anthony Davis

Damian Lillard, Anthony Davis, Kawhi Leonard, and Russell Westbrook. It's with players like them where the so-called Mount Rushmore process becomes difficult. What's lost when you debate whether a player qualifies for one of these top-fifty, top-seventy-five list discussions is that it's often taken as a criticism. They are Hall of Famers. That's the golden ticket to immortality. So don't be offended if you're not top seventy-five. Perhaps it should be a few dozen and end the discussion. But it is a discussion and debate, and it's also business. It's also a point in time. Nikola Jokić and Luka Dončić were left out of the top seventy-five, but by the time of the top one hundred, they should be in that top quarter. Probably Joel Embiid also. Likely by then Jayson Tatum and who knows how many others, like Shai Gilgeous-Alexander, Anthony Edwards, and, of course, the next greatest of them all, as we've been told, Victor Wembanyama. You can make a case for any of these four, and the majority of the voters did. Damian Lillard was an All-Star game MVP and, at least in shooting range, the only one truly close to Steph Curry, a regular All-Star but rarely a deep playoff visitor, eventually forcing his way out to a better team so a real star could try to help carry him to a championship season. Davis has all the All-Star and defensive credentials, but you always feel like he's been running away from it, frequently missing games, his biggest jukes seeming to be away from the spotlight. Westbrook has numbers basically only like Oscar, but who likens the two? It always seemed like Westbrook chased the stats, a player going at 78 rpm even when everyone else was told to go at 33 or 45. Dennis Rodman did make the list and does seem to qualify, and he is unique in NBA history. Maybe for too much outside basketball. But he also did inflate some of those rebounding numbers. Luc Longley mentioned how Dennis would ask him to box out on the free throws so he could get the rebound. Luc, good bloke that he was, proved anxious to please. Kawhi was right in the middle of a couple of championships but perhaps should be eliminated for basically introducing the pernicious concept of load management. What about someone never mentioned for anything, like Mark Aguirre? Mark was second in the league in scoring one season at a fraction below 30, started for a pair of championship teams, and had a six-year run cumulatively averaging almost 25 points. Like the guy he was traded for, Adrian Dantley, who averaged more than 30 points per season for four straight years, albeit with bad teams, a career scorer of almost 25 per game, half dozen All-Star games, but not a popular guy, at least not like Dame and AD and, OK, Russ wasn't everyone's favorite. Why are some in and others out? Dwight Howard was a popular debate. Perhaps no one more so than Alex English. He averaged more than 25 per game for eight consecutive seasons. How do you miss that? There was Pau Gasol with scoring, multiple championships, and performing as Kobe's Scottie Pippen. How about Vince Carter with eight All-Star games and playing more than twenty years? Kyrie Irving with the historic handle and some numbers as well, and back a bit with players who excelled in their eras with as many All-Star nods, like Bernard King, Bob Lanier, ballhandling pioneer and multiple champion Bob Davies, a great shooter like Lou Hudson with a seven-year run averaging 25 per game. Sweet Lou finally was enshrined in the Basketball Hall of Fame. Being omitted from a top-seventy-five list is no insult. They've got impressive company.

**PJ:** Anthony Davis? Everybody kind of marvels at his shooting ability. He is a good shooter; the rest of his game is limited. Doesn't want to be a center. They play him at center anyway. I saw him against the Knicks. He didn't want to take a shot down the stretch. Ball was in his hands, he was looking for people to pass to. Very talented player. I don't know what's been holding him back from really being a true dominating player. The other thing: He's always playing with superior talent. You look at these guys, they play with superior talent in colleges.

**SAM:** Obviously, it's a person-by-person thing. We hate to reference everything to Michael, but he comes to North Carolina as a freshman and they've got Coach Dean Smith, Worthy, Perkins, and Jimmy Black and Matt Doherty, the last two upperclassmen. You know Dean and all those college coaches were big on the upperclassmen. But here's freshman Michael coming to practices and keeping a list on the chalkboard of how many times he's dunked over Worthy and Perkins. Seriously, who is this guy? Being with the stars doesn't bother everyone.

**PJ:** You go to Kentucky to watch their team practice. You watch them in a little practice gym, and they've got pictures of all the guys that went to the pros on the wall. There's like twenty of them. Here we are, we're an elite school, elite team, elite players. And we don't ever have to do anything on our own. Somebody's gonna step up. Might not be me. That's kind of the attitude maybe you see with him. He got with LeBron, so you thought maybe this guy can develop into a leader. But then when LeBron was out, it didn't look like he wanted to have any part of it. I turned down being on the top-seventy-five voting. I think I was in the coaches' voting. I thought it would come out like it did; too many names left out. Too many current players. English from Denver for sure, led the league in scoring a lot. Bobby Davies should be. Westbrook is an interesting one. Though when I look at it, I guess it's a pretty good list; some debatable people, but a good list.

**SAM:** There was some moaning about Bill Walton.

**PJ:** Landmark guy. He was an important part of how much the game changed around this guy's career. Lillard made it? He's a special player, no doubt. But doesn't it have to do also with winning? Terrific basketball player but really hasn't proved himself.

**SAM:** He was some of the recency bias, I thought. Big current name, but I've seen so many guys like him over the years who became forgotten in time. Sleepy Floyd had 50 in a playoff game. Antawn Jamison had a run of about ten years averaging combined about 20, 25 one season. Ever hear about him?

**PJ:** Bill Fitch told me this guy Derrick Coleman is a man among boys, could have been as good as anyone.

**SAM:** The guy you wanted in '95 for power forward when Horace left instead of Dennis. But Coleman had, I think, three or four years on his deal and Dennis had an expiring, and I know the Bulls are thinking maybe they get a few months out of him and can cut him and not lose much, anyway. Back then no one thinks after the San Antonio debacle Dennis has more than a few months left in the league.

**PJ:** Coleman should have become a Hall of Famer. Like Chris Webber. But a very angry, unhappy kid. Bill is out of there and Willis is GM and Willis wants Kobe in the draft. The agent says he'll go to Europe if they can't make a trade, but Willis knows the kid wants to be in the NBA. They're letting Calipari decide everything, and he wants to win right now and doesn't trust a high school kid, so he picks Kittles. Jerry West had scoped that all out. He was way ahead of all those guys. Coleman is horsing around. Like Embiid. I don't blame Ben Simmons. It's not easy to play with a guy like that. Has a big ego and a temperament that I think it must be tough to play with him. It was like a Kobe/Shaq thing. Ben's saying, I can go in the post and score, I'm talented enough, and then gets blamed for not being a three-point shooter.

**SAM:** You mention Coleman, reminds me of Rasheed Wallace. I still have my T-shirt the NBA printed up during the 2003 playoffs. That was the era of the infamous Jail Blazers, who once got in a fight in the team layup line. Rasheed on a postgame loading dock had threatened referee Tim Donaghy before anyone knew who Donaghy was. Maybe Rasheed knew first. Rasheed should have been a Hall of Fame talent like Coleman. Heard he was the only player Dean Smith asked to go pro as soon as possible. Joe Dumars concocts this great bait and switch where Rasheed goes through Atlanta to the Pistons for nothing and is that legitimate final piece for them. Knocks out you guys in '04, not that you weren't doing it to yourselves with the Kobe/Shaq craziness, but once Karl gets hurt it's over. Huge talent who like Coleman just was distracted and angry a lot.

**PJ:** Alex McKechnie was with us and then went to Toronto and he would tell me, "I have the record for the fewest player games missed.

Nobody is doing the load management. Then Leonard comes." Big hands, does what Michael did with holding the ball with one hand. I once told Jeanie to trade LeBron for Kawhi.

**SAM:** I guess there was nothing to those stories you were some big Lakers adviser.

# Giannis Antetokounmpo

There are plenty of "never seen this coming" stories in the NBA, but the surprise success of Nikola Jokić and Giannis Antetokounmpo perhaps suggests that the league still can't figure out the world three decades after the Dream Team. Greek native Antetokounmpo was a first-round draft pick, but the Bucks were ambivalent at first. They were in your classic small-market malaise going into the 2010s: regular-season finishes between sixth and tenth, a playoff sweep when they finally got in. Management was tempted to cash in the 2013 pick for a veteran to help win a few more games and . . . you know, as Mel Brooks said in *Blazing Saddles*, "We've gotta protect our phony baloney jobs, gentlemen." No, instructed owner Kohl, take someone. Credit John Hammond for getting it amazingly right. Even if the seven-foot, long-armed, elastic-legged Giannis still can't shoot. But those strides! There was other interest at the time, most notably Atlanta with number 17. Hey, take a shot; who's coming to Milwaukee? Talk about a freakishly long stride forward for an eventual league, Finals, and All-Star game MVP, Defensive Player of the Year, Most Improved, multiple and still counting all-league and all-defense first teams, and one of the most creative forces in the game's history.

**PJ:** He's got to be traveling. How is the Eurostep not a travel? You have to pick up the ball on the opposite foot that you normally would, which would be this foot, and then you'd go one-two, right? You've picked it up on the dribble. So it's not your pivot foot yet. The other foot becomes your pivot—at least that's what they say. It's totally illegal. I think San Antonio bargained with the league because Ginóbili was using it.

**SAM:** You've got to give the Bucks credit. Like Denver with second-round pick Jokić. Who saw that coming? It's the art and mystery of scouting. Like Gheorghe Mureşan, remember?

**PJ:** Krause had the offices swept for bugs. Professional spy team. He assumed someone had to tell you.

**SAM:** He was "the sleuth." Pat Williams named him that, slinking around the gyms in an old trench coat, literally hiding behind columns. Drove the other GMs nuts. So when he'd show up on one of those stealth missions, a GM would call me and say, "You know who Krause was scouting?" So he's scoped out Mureşan and is gonna get him in the second round. You didn't really care about the draft then—Tex always said you win with men—but Jerry figured he had a coup with the seven-seven guy. I wrote that he's scouting Mureşan, and when Washington takes him a few picks before you guys, he's pissed. Jerry decides Johnny Bach is my Deep Throat. Of course, there was none—I was traveling with the team for several years and everybody in the NBA talks. Johnny eventually took the fall. It was the most upset I was about the *Jordan Rules* book because my preinterview promise was no one would lose their job or be in trouble with their family. Classy guy, Johnny. He never was the least upset with me. Should be in the Hall of Fame.

**PJ:** Johnny would enlighten me. I told you that story of seeing an offense Del Harris was running in Milwaukee. Johnny takes one look and says that it's Horst Pinholster's old pinwheel offense.

Ever watched European handball? If you see it, you'll go like, "Oh, wow. That's where they got the Eurostep." You can run with the ball, but you have to put another dribble down. Big indoor game in Europe, men's handball. Giannis is terrific. He can't shoot. But it really doesn't matter. How is he in the last round of the playoffs shooting layups with that spin move? He can't shoot threes, he struggles at the free-throw line, but the game they are playing now he can somehow get to the basket.

**SAM:** When the Bulls beat Giannis in the playoffs a few years after Derrick Rose's ACL injury, that was their last great gasp with Rose. Kidd is a really a smart coach. They had been playing Giannis up front since, well, he's seven feet tall. Kidd says, Let's make him a point guard. Maybe only Kidd sees it then.

**PJ:** The Lakers didn't want to lose Kidd. LeBron's people were pushing Jeanie, saying she shouldn't let Kidd go. He had this opportunity with Dallas, but she couldn't fire Frank Vogel. They just won a championship. LeBron's people come and say the Lakers can't afford to lose him. But you can't fire a guy who's just won a championship. Frank's smart. But he also wasn't strong enough for Carmelo. You have to be really strong when you are coaching Carmelo. It takes all types of different people to make a good head coach. Popovich is rigid but has a certain flexibility. He's about getting in touch with his players, a community guy without a doubt. He comes into town the night before a game and says, "Come on down, have a glass of wine." He's rigid and strict with what he's doing. He's like the Bill Belichick of our league. He always talked with his players about getting that cup of love. That you've got to get back with your family and build up that reserve of love again to play on the road. That's been kind of his mantra, having that solid relationship.

**SAM:** I remember when you guys exposed Tony Parker in, I think, '02, and Pop had enough and was all in on getting Kidd as a free agent to replace Parker at some point. Though Jason eventually took the money and ran back to the Nets.

**PJ:** Jason probably saw it with Giannis. Finally, the NBA just basically said, Fuck it, we don't want any post players, we just want guards. Three-point shots and guards. Colangelo is responsible for that. We had always been a league where you win with big guys. Colangelo, who could never bring a big guy to the Suns who worked out, was sitting there saying, "Look what Shaq's doing. That's not an appealing game to watch. Fans don't want to see him backing down Mutombo." That was Larry Brown. Yelling for Mutombo to flop, then Ben Wallace to do the same. They don't want to see that anymore. They just want guards.

# Afterword

**SAM:** You've always believed in and promoted the journey over the result, the foundation of the modern basketball coach's cliché of not skipping steps. That a team would be in the best position for the result if you embrace the journey, and an ancillary benefit: the journey is the reward itself. I feel like it's been that way with this book, the opportunity to appreciate the game and its roots in good company. But as much as you also try to make your career a journey, like any pursuit, your attention has to remain on the road and obstacles ahead. So whether it was Willis walking onto the court for Game 7 or Michael with "the Shot" in Cleveland, Salt Lake, and everywhere else—or Steve Kerr, John Paxson, and Kobe with their "the Shots," or Bird and Magic and Kareem with theirs—there also was the next game and the next plane, the 5:00 a.m. wake-up for that first plane out, and then rushing home to have breakfast with the kids before heading out to practice. And as much as you try, it's still a job. So the exceptional can be overlooked amid the expected. Sometimes I'll make a comparison to the Gettysburg Address—if not for comparable significance—272 words said on a chilly November day, certainly a solemn occasion for the consecration of the Civil War cemetery. Though everyone knew Lincoln was good with a phrase, most there probably were anxious to get back inside for a biscuit and some cider and were wondering why

Abe couldn't just say "eighty-seven years" instead of the four-score thing. And they certainly didn't think two hundred years later we'd still be noting and long remembering those few hundred words offered over about two minutes. That's what I often think when people ask me what it was like seeing the game and its stars so close for so long. You often don't fully appreciate what you witness up close until you step back some, which has been this journey for me. And in a related vein, sort of what your coaching also was about, that playing the right way and being willing to grow and embrace the game is the grist for the journey.

**PJ:** We always used this term of the basketball gods, *playing to the real rules of the game.* Which are hit the open man, cut over for your teammates on defense, see the ball, be alert, know what's going on, watch time on the clock, etc.—be inside the game. And that's kinda what you get with *Golf in the Kingdom*, this crazy half-Irish, half-Scottish guy is just giving the essence of the game, and I think that's kinda about basketball.

**SAM:** I know one of your stealth projects lately was on Zoom teaching a coaching course—University of Wisconsin, I recall—and you used *Golf in the Kingdom*, which also was a loose movie comparison a few years back with Will Smith and Matt Damon, *The Legend of Bagger Vance.*

**PJ:** It was the lead book for the semester I used. It sets the tone for what the class was about. It has a mystical element to it of, if you're going to coach you'll want to have something, intrigue, something you can portray some of your philosophy behind. Or underneath. On some level you really have to love the game. And loving the game is probably not being able to shoot three-point shots so much as it is being in communication with your teammates. Being in kind of sync with, What's the mentality of the moment? What's going on in our group? Where are we at emotionally and physically? And joined at the hip, so to speak, in our process. I've been really fortunate to coach a number of teams and a number of games with those special moments of why you play the game and why you love the game and why you end up being in positions where you can excel.

You hope you have people who have the willingness to have an open mind. One of the variety of things you learn is who's gonna be resistant to this coaching, and you have to either see them bend or come into a viewpoint where they're submitting their own desires to the group or the whole, which is one of the reasons why Kobe and I had this interaction the first two years I coached him where he was wanting to do what he wanted to do and not what was best for the team. I never had that feeling with Michael. He was kind of on the page and other times he felt the team needed him to win and he did what he wanted—or felt he needed—to do. There's that balance between special players and the group. How far do you lean over to accommodate a special player and how much does the talented player incorporate himself into the team? It could be a lot of conflict along the way.

**SAM:** Oh, right, life as basketball and vice versa, and so as we wrap up this journey, hey, what about Nikola Jokić? Too soon to start the top one hundred?

**PJ:** We have never seen a center that can act as the lead player on a team like him. He brings the ball up court after rebounding and finds the open man or takes on the opponent's defense with his own threat of scoring. Denver has had an offense that is a top-scoring offense in the NBA due in large part to this big man. And he is a big man, really big, and often looks like he's struggling to maintain his energy. His nose is red and he is profusely sweating and often gasping for breath, but the next play either after a score or a rebound, there he is orchestrating the offense up the court. His scoring ability largely revolves around his ability to use both hands, and his touch around the basket is remarkable. He has defined the game more than changed the game. There are not many in my memory who have the dexterity and court awareness that might have precluded Jokić's style of play.

**SAM:** What about our late buddy Bill Walton if they'd allowed centers to dribble back then during those few magical seasons in Portland? Bill could shoot, pass, handle, rebound, and finish, sort of a basketball five-tool—which is how you make this list despite maybe just three or four productive seasons, but they were something to see. And reminisce about. Too soon to add Cooper Flagg?

# Acknowledgments

We'd like to especially thank our colleagues, contemporaries, friends, legends, athletes, artists, artistes, and acrobats of the NBA—including mentors like Tex Winter among the basketball guardians of the game—who provided so much grist for this dish of history we're proud to serve. This project began during the pandemic when there wasn't much to do but consider the future and reminisce with friends. And so we found our own center circle and gazed out and across Flathead Lake at the Mission Mountains in fall for a few days here and there with sometimes a cozy lunch at the Somers Cafe. And then watched the fishing boats beat the Pacific sunset chased by the gulls late on winter days in LA after some homemade Jackson soup; oh right, there was some NBA history to discuss and write about, also, amid the reverie. Mostly it just was fun to hang out and again travel that familiar basketball road of our lives with all its joyous detours, digressions, and debates. We hope you enjoyed listening in.

Our thanks to Scott Moyers of Penguin Press, whom Phil has worked with previously and warmly recommended as both teammate and closer. His enthusiasm and support for the project was welcoming and motivating. Thanks to Penguin Press editor Helen Rouner, whose sharp eye and fine pen helped us avoid costly turnovers and ease a pair of Luddites through the technological process. Thanks to photo editor Thea Traff for hyperfocus in the basketball archives. Thanks to Connor Smith for his editing and transcription services and to our families and friends for filling out our sideline triangle.

# Image Credits

# IMAGE CREDITS

# Index

Bold page references indicate main entries.

01 14